D0758841

Praise for *The Power of Communication*

"Helio Fred Garcia coached me a decade ago on the fundamentals of effective communication. I probably wasn't his best student, but I count what I learned from him as one of the most important contributions to my personal growth as an executive. We're fortunate to now have Fred's book *The Power of Communication*, which encapsulates his enormous depth of knowledge and breadth of experience in communication—as a practitioner, as a scholar, and as a teacher. The book contains a wealth of real-life examples of what works and what doesn't in communication, and each chapter provides a recap of best practices and key lessons learned. This book should be on the must-read list of any person who aspires to lead by capturing the hearts and minds of his or her stakeholders."

—Jeffrey Bleustein, Retired Chairman and CEO, Harley-Davidson, Inc.

"*The Power of Communication* is an absolutely terrific book on how to communicate and lead in complex and shifting situations. Helio Fred Garcia has compiled a wealth of compelling examples to illustrate and support a cogent and immensely practical set of principles for leadership communication. The result is a compelling guide for leaders in business and government settings alike."

—Amy C. Edmondson, Novartis Professor of Leadership and Management, Harvard Business School, and author of *Teaming: How Organizations Learn, Innovate, and Compete in the Knowledge Economy*

"Helio Fred Garcia is known as one of the most engaging and effective professors at NYU. Readers of this book will learn why. Only Fred could weave together tales about Abbott and Costello, the Marine Corps, and Cicero into a must-read for anyone who hopes to connect with the American public."

—Louis Capozzi, Chairman, MSL Group (retired), and Adjunct Professor, New York University

"Helio Fred Garcia has had an enormous impact on my career, my practice, and my life since we first met more than 25 years ago when he recruited me to teach at NYU. I have watched him have similar effects on thousands of others. He is the man of eloquence Cicero describes. Fred instructs instinctively. His ability, which is what this book is all about, to look at critically important communication and leadership topics and issues from completely new and important perspectives, in this case the United States Marine Corps *Warfighting* manual, is profoundly interesting and helpful.

"The book is story after story, insight after insight, lesson after lesson, inspiration after inspiration. Just when you think it's impossible to find another important illustration of a crucial communication or leadership principle, Fred gives you another chapter of powerful, sensible, often surprising and charming stories and lessons. Believe me, he is a persuasive orator in person and, as you'll read, on paper.

"Looking to build your powers of communication, to inspire trust and confidence, and to lead effectively? You hold in your hand the key ingredient to a happier, more successful, and influential professional life. Start reading."

—**James E. Lukaszewski**, ABC, APR, Fellow PRSA, President, The Lukaszewski Group Division, Risdall Public Relations

"Professor Garcia's book is great news for decision-makers, leaders, and professionals in the U.S. and any country in the world. He was frequently invited by Tsinghua University to teach in our senior officials' training seminars on crisis communication and was always remembered by our executive students as Professor *Reputation Management*. His class evaluations by the participating state council ministers, senior officials, and corporate leaders were always the best.

"Many thought that American methods of solving crises were not suitable for China, but Fred's lectures rapidly dispelled their skepticism. His vivid examples, drawn from the U.S. Marine Corps as well as corporate experience around the world, made a deep impression on participants, who have since applied their practical and innovative approach to their own work. We truly believe that the book contains some very important global wisdom to save you in crisis in an omni-media age. The pity is that he can visit China only once a year, but that gives us all the more reason to celebrate the publication of this book, a very clear, concise, interesting, and powerful masterpiece."

—**Professor Steven Guanpeng Dong**, Ph.D., Chair and Director, Institute of Public Relations and Strategic Communications, Tsinghua University, Beijing; Vice President, China Public Relations Association; former Shorenstein Fellow on the Press, Politics, and Public Policy, Kennedy School of Government, Harvard University

"Here's what I've come to believe is the indisputable truth with regard to leadership: **If you can't communicate effectively, you will not lead**.

"Fred has written a book that will give anyone who desires to lead people and/or organizations an invaluable tool for success. He provides an organized, rational approach to communicating with any and all stakeholders.

"Fred has taken the Marine Corps' cornerstone publication *Warfighting* and applied the approach and the mentality to professional communication—and it works! I found this book to be a tremendous real-world guide for blueprinting and executing a world-class communication plan—and Ethos.

"This book should be kept on the desk of anyone who leads or anyone who communicates publicly. You will use it often."

—**Lieutenant Colonel Robert Riggle**, USMCR

The Power of Communication

The Power of Communication

Skills to Build Trust, Inspire Loyalty, and Lead Effectively

Helio Fred Garcia

Vice President, Publisher: Tim Moore
Associate Publisher and Director of Marketing: Amy Neidlinger
Executive Editor: Jeanne Glasser Levine
Editorial Assistant: Tamara Hummel
Operations Specialist: Jodi Kemper
Assistant Marketing Manager: Megan Graue
Cover Designer: Chuti Prasertsith
Managing Editor: Kristy Hart
Project Editor: Betsy Harris
Copy Editor: Cheri Clark
Proofreader: Leslie Joseph
Indexer: Erika Millen
Compositor: Nonie Ratcliff
Manufacturing Buyer: Dan Uhrig

© 2012 by Helio Fred Garcia
Published by Pearson Education, Inc.
Upper Saddle River, New Jersey 07458

Neither the United States Marine Corps nor any other component of the Department of Defense has approved, endorsed, or authorized this product.

For information about buying this title in bulk quantities, or for special sales opportunities (which may include electronic versions; custom cover designs; and content particular to your business, training goals, marketing focus, or branding interests), please contact our corporate sales department at corpsales@pearsoned.com or (800) 382-3419.

For government sales inquiries, please contact governmentsales@pearsoned.com.

For questions about sales outside the U.S., please contact international@pearsoned.com.

Company and product names mentioned herein are the trademarks or registered trademarks of their respective owners.

All rights reserved. No part of this book may be reproduced, in any form or by any means, without permission in writing from the publisher.

Printed in the United States of America

Third Printing: September 2014

ISBN-10: 0-13-288884-X
ISBN-13: 978-0-13-288884-4

Pearson Education LTD.
Pearson Education Australia PTY, Limited.
Pearson Education Singapore, Pte. Ltd.
Pearson Education Asia, Ltd.
Pearson Education Canada, Ltd.
Pearson Educación de Mexico, S.A. de C.V.
Pearson Education—Japan
Pearson Education Malaysia, Pte. Ltd.

Library of Congress Cataloging-in-Publication Data

Garcia, Helio Fred.
  The power of communication : skills to build trust, inspire loyalty, and lead effectively / Helio Fred Garcia. -- 1st ed.
    p. cm.
  ISBN 978-0-13-288884-4 (hardcover : alk. paper)
  1. Communication in management. 2. Leadership. 3. Interpersonal communication. I. Title.
  HD30.3.G355 2012
  658.4'5--dc23
                              2012003106

*This book is dedicated to the memory of
my first and best teacher,
Dr. Frederick C. H. Garcia,
Professor of Foreign Languages,
United States Military Academy at West Point
from 1959 to 1984
and
to the men and women of the
United States Marine Corps.
Semper Fi!*

Contents

PART II: STRATEGY AND COMMUNICATION: PLANNING AND EXECUTION

6 Goals, Strategies, and Tactics: Preparing and Planning **123**

PART III: BUILDING SKILLS: GETTING GOOD AT COMMUNICATING WELL

7 Performance: The Physicality of Audience Engagement.....................**159**

Foreword

By Lieutenant Colonel Robert Riggle, USMCR

If I were ever in trouble, publicly, one of my first calls would be to Helio Fred Garcia. I've known Fred for 12 years. I've been a student of his, so to speak, since we first met at the Marine Corps' East Coast Commanders Public Affairs Symposium. I think Fred is an outstanding educator and communicator. "Outstanding" is the highest compliment a Marine can give…just so we're clear.

I've been a Public Affairs Officer and occasionally a Civil Affairs Officer in the Marine Corps and the Marine Corps Reserves for the past 20 years. I've always put a premium on the value and impact of communications. At times, however, it felt like I was in the minority among my fellow Marines. I would often refer to a quote from General Dwight D. Eisenhower that said, "Public opinion wins wars." Still… nothing from those around me.…

In Vietnam, the United States won every major battle we fought and we still lost the war. Why? We lost public support. The same is true for many corporate and/or organizational "wars" as well. Leaders would do well to heed the warning from General Eisenhower.

I spent 9 years on active duty and the last 13 years in the reserves. If you're doing the math and it doesn't add up, it's because I spent my first 2 years in the Marines flying planes. It wasn't my calling. Despite having my pilot's license when I was an undergraduate at Kansas University, I wanted to be an actor, comedian, and writer. Really long story…short, I quit flying and became a Public Affairs Officer. I have no regrets.

During my time in service to the United States, I deployed to Liberia, Albania, Kosovo, and Afghanistan. I also worked at "ground zero" moving rubble by hand, in New York City immediately following the attacks of September 11, 2001.

While stationed in North Carolina as a young 1st Lieutenant, I attended night school and earned my Masters in Public Administration. I am also a graduate of Officer Candidates School, The Basic School, the Warfighting course, Amphibious Warfare School, and Command and Staff College. I've studied and practiced leadership most of my life. Here's what I've come to believe is the indisputable truth with regard to leadership: **If you can't communicate effectively, you will not lead.**

Fred has written a book that will give anyone who desires to lead people and/or organizations an invaluable tool for success. He provides an organized, rational approach to communicating with any and all stakeholders.

Fred has taken the Marine Corps' cornerstone publication *Warfighting* and applied the approach and the mentality to professional communications…and it works! I found this book to be a tremendous real-world guide for blueprinting and executing a world-class communications plan…and Ethos.

I currently work in the entertainment industry. My first big break was as a cast member on *Saturday Night Live.* Following *SNL,* I was a correspondent on *The Daily Show with Jon Stewart* and I've appeared in several feature films. I've found that not much has changed with regard to my thought process when it comes to communicating publicly. However, as a comedian I have a lot more flexibility with regard to my message than I did in the Marines.

For instance…"Poop." There, I just said it. As a comedian I can say that all day and no one bats an eye; in fact, it's often celebrated. As a Marine, I would not say, "Poop." I would say something else.

Fred is going to ask me to remove the previous paragraph, but I won't.

This book should be kept on the desk of anyone who leads or anyone who communicates publicly. You will use it often.

I wish you all luck.

Semper Fidelis,

Lt. Colonel Robert A. Riggle Jr., USMCR

"Fair winds and following seas…"

Acknowledgments

This book is the result of a convergence of circumstances and the contributions and support of a great many people from many walks of life. Thanking and saluting them may take some time, so please bear with me.

This book applies to civilian leadership the strategy and leadership principles of the United States Marine Corps. And there are many to thank both in civilian life and in uniform.

Logos Institute for Crisis Management & Executive Leadership

The book reflects the client practice and intellectual work product of the Logos Institute for Crisis Management & Executive Leadership, and I am both proud of and grateful to the entire Logos team.

The actual book would not have been possible without the dedicated and persistent hard work of two brilliant and tireless Logos Institute analysts, Adam Tiouririne and Katie Garcia. They did the bulk of detailed research on case studies, fact checked, proofread, and otherwise created an infrastructure that made it possible for me to lay out the principles with meaningful and coordinated factual support. Any errors—of fact, interpretation, or judgment—are solely my own.

I also benefited greatly from contributions from Logos Institute senior fellow Oxana Trush and Logos partner Laurel Hart. I also repurposed some prior research from Logos colleagues Elizabeth Jacques and Raleigh Mayer. And I am extremely grateful for the ongoing support and help from my Logos partners Barbara Greene and Anthony Ewing.

Marines

The idea for the book was sparked in conversations I began with Rob Riggle in 2007. We were both teaching in a Marine Corps public affairs symposium in Los Angeles, and during a break I filled him in on what I was up to. Rob at the time was straddling Marine and civilian life: simultaneously a Marine public affairs officer and a cast member on *The Daily Show with Jon Stewart*. As I recount in the Introduction, I had just started teaching *Warfighting* in my NYU classroom, and I showed Rob how I was applying Marine Corps doctrine to civilian leadership communication. Rob was my first champion for making the work available to a wider audience, and we met several times in New York and Los Angeles to imagine how the project might come to pass. I am extremely grateful to Rob for being an early catalyst and supporter of the project, and for his generous remarks in the Foreword.

In 2009 I was again in Los Angeles to work with Marines, and I met with Col. David Lapan, then head of Marine Corps public affairs, who was about to start a new job as head of public affairs for the Secretary of Defense. I shared with him the idea for this book and he asked me to send him a formal proposal. Before he switched jobs, he got the wheels in motion. Maj. Eric Dent managed the approval process for the adaptation rights to *Warfighting*. And the Marine Corps Trademarks Licensing Office gave the green light to use the Marine Corps logo. (Note: Their approval is not an endorsement of this book or of any product or project.) I am grateful for Col. Lapan's and Maj. Dent's support for the project.

There are dozens of Marines whose support over the years made this work possible. I am certain I have inadvertently left some names out, so apologies in advance.

I was first introduced to the Marines in 1991 by an NYU student, Lt. Col. Walt Burzinski. For more than 20 years since, I have taught in the annual East Coast Commanders Public Affairs Symposium in New York. The successive leaders of the New York Mobilization Training Unit-17 have been my primary point of contact. I am particularly grateful to Lt. Col. Stephen Brozak, who was a strong supporter and who introduced me to Marine Corps leadership beyond the New York City unit, including the Director of Public Affairs. Other MTU-17 Marines who have been supportive over the years include Maj. David C. Andersen, Capt. Brian Lippo, Maj. Jennifer Jackson, Lt. Col. Frank Gasper, Lt. Col. David Rosner, Lt. Col. Greg Kelly, Lt. Col. Dan Fernandes, Lt. Col. Joseph J. Wiffler, and Gy. Sgt. Joseph Minucci.

For several years beginning in 2004, I taught in the Brigadier General Select Orientation program in Washington. I am grateful for the help and support of Lt. Col. Francis Piccoli, Capt. Alexandra Davis, and Maj. Steven M. O'Connor.

For several years beginning in 2005, I taught guest lectures at the Marine Corps Command and Staff College. I am grateful for the help and support of Lt. Col. Paul Pond and U.S. Airforce Lt. Col. Justo Herrera.

Since 2005, I have taught in the West Coast Commanders Public Affairs Symposium, managed by the Marines' Motion Picture and Television Liaison Office in Los Angeles. I am particularly grateful for the help and support of Lt. Col. Doug Griffith, Gy. Sgt. Santiago Zapata, Maj. Joseph Marron, Lt. Col. Jason A. Johnston, Capt. Barry Edwards, S.Sgt. Ethan E. Rocke, Maj. Dan Huvane, and Col. Ray Johnson.

In 2010 I spoke in the Marine Corps Officer Candidates School. I am grateful to Lt. Col. Carlton W. Hasle for making it possible and to Capt. Andrew Sylling for coordinating it.

Since 2002, I have benefited mightily from the support of successive directors of Marine Corps Public Affairs. I am grateful to Maj. Gen. (ret.) Andrew B. Davis, Maj. Gen. (ret.) Mary Ann Krusa-Dossin, Lt. Gen. R.E. Milstead, Jr., Col. David Lapan, and Col. Bryan Salas.

New York University

I first assigned *Warfighting* in 2006, the first time the required Communication Strategy course was held in the then-newly-launched MS in Public Relations and Corporate Communication program. I am grateful to the program's Academic Director Professor John Doorley for his encouragement and support of what at the time seemed to be a risky and unorthodox approach. John is also my co-author on the first and second editions of *Reputation Management: The Key to Successful Public Relations and Corporate Communication,* Routledge, 2007 and 2011, respectively. I thank John for all of his support for my teaching and writing over the years.

The strategy course has been taught by other professors, who themselves kept the *Warfighting* content and have encouraged me in my teaching and writing of this book. Particular thanks to professors Claude Singer and Dr. Paul Oestreicher. I am also grateful for the encouragement and support of Professor Bob Noltenmeier and academic advisor Guilaine Blaise.

I joined the NYU faculty in 1998, and for most of that time I have benefited mightily from the friendship, encouragement, and support of Renee Harris, presently the Interim Assistant Dean of the Division of Programs in Business and Chair and Academic Director, of Continuing Education Programs in Marketing, Public Relations, Leadership, and Human Capital Management.

For the past 10 years I have also had the good fortune to teach a crisis management course once per year in NYU's Stern School of Business, where I have also tested and validated many of the concepts in this book. I am particularly grateful to MaryJane Boland, Director, Executive MBA Student Services, for all of her support through the years. And to Janet Vitebsky, Senior Associate Director, and Laura Deffley, Program Coordinator, for all of their help.

The best part of teaching is seeing the change in students as they expand their horizons, enhance their skills, and grow in confidence and capacity. It's why we teach. I want to offer a special thanks to all my NYU students, especially those who found themselves unexpectedly required to read a military doctrinal publication in a civilian strategy course. Their affirmation of the value of the book to their strategic thinking was a big part of my own confidence that the concepts in *Warfighting* deserve a bigger audience.

Wharton/University of Pennsylvania

Many of the concepts of the book have been validated in guest lectures and workshops I have delivered several times a year for the past 10 years in the Wharton Communication Program, University of Pennsylvania.

I am grateful to Lisa Warshaw, Director of the Wharton Communication Program, both for her support over the years and for allowing me to quote her and to profile the Wharton Communication Program in Chapter 7. Most of my work at Wharton has been in collaboration with Senior Associate Directors Carl Maugeri and Margaret Lambires. And recently some of that work has been in collaboration with Operations Director Dr. Lawrence Quartana. Logistics for all the above have been supported by Administrative Coordinator Jarmila Force and Audio Technical Coordinator Victoria Leonard. I am grateful to the entire Wharton Communication Program.

Professional Colleagues

I am grateful to Dr. Amy Zalman of the Strategic Narrative blog for permission to cite her work on the importance of effective public diplomacy. I am grateful to Barry Mike for permission to repurpose his blog posts about his formative experience as a young speechwriter from his Strategic Leadership Communication blog.

For more than 20 years James E. Lukaszewski has been a mentor, colleague, friend, and inspiration. And I have just learned that Jim, who had taught in the Marine Corps East Coast Commanders Public Affairs Symposium since 1986, had initially recommended me to the Symposium the year I started. For many years thereafter we were both involved. I am particularly grateful to Jim for his support and confidence over the years.

My friend and colleague Peter Firestein, president of Global Strategic Communications, invited me to speak at a conference in late 2010. That resulted in my meeting his book publicist Barbara Monteiro, who in turn introduced me to my agent, Leah Nathans Spiro of Riverside Creative Management. I am grateful to Peter, both for his friendship and support and for his catalytic role in making the book possible. And to Barbara Monteiro for connecting me to Leah. And particularly to Leah, who helped me flesh out the idea for the book and who secured my publisher's support.

Corporate Clients

The concepts and case studies in the book have been validated in dozens of professional development and executive education sessions at various corporate clients. Because of nondisclosure agreements, I am not able to name them, even in thanks.

One, a leading financial services firm, initially had me teach a strategy boot camp for its communication strategists in 2007, the first time I applied *Warfighting* to a non-university civilian audience. It worked, and the client has since had me teach the module to more than 400 of its staff. For a global pharmaceutical company I have provided dozens of individual, department-wide, and large group sessions over several years. And I delivered a session for all 500 U.S. employees of a European bank.

I am grateful to all my clients (and you know who you are) for their support and confidence over the years, particularly in their adventurous acceptance of somewhat unorthodox content for a corporate setting.

Family

Finally, I thank the three women in my life: my spouse, Laurel Garcia Colvin, and our two daughters, Katie and Juliana. They endured too-frequent absences and always welcomed me home.

Helio Fred Garcia
New York City
January 2012

About the Author

For more than 30 years **Helio Fred Garcia** has helped leaders build trust, inspire loyalty, and lead effectively. He is a coach, counselor, teacher, writer, and speaker whose clients include some of the largest and best-known companies and organizations in the world.

Fred is President of the crisis management firm Logos Consulting Group and Executive Director of the Logos Institute for Crisis Management & Executive Leadership. He is based in New York and has worked with clients in dozens of countries on six continents.

Fred has been on the New York University faculty since 1988 and has received his school's awards for teaching excellence and for outstanding service. He is an adjunct professor of management in NYU's Stern School of Business Executive MBA program and an adjunct associate professor of management and communication in NYU's Master's in PR/Corporate Communication program. Fred is also on the adjunct faculty of the Starr King School for the Ministry–Graduate Theological Union in Berkeley, where he teaches a seminar on religious leadership for social change. And he is on the leadership faculty of the Center for Security Studies of the Swiss Federal Institute of Technology in Zurich, where he teaches in the Master's in Advanced Studies in Crisis Management and Security Policy. He is a frequent guest lecturer at the Wharton School/University of Pennsylvania, the U.S. Marine Corps Command and Staff College and Officer Candidate School, the Brookings Institution, Tsinghua University in Beijing, and other institutions.

Fred is coauthor (with John Doorley) of *Reputation Management: The Key to Successful Public Relations and Corporate Communication* (second edition 2011; first edition 2007), by Routledge, Taylor & Francis Group. His two-volume book *Crisis Communications* was published by AAAA Publications in 1999. He blogs at www.logosinstitute.net/blog; he tweets at twitter.com/garciahf.

Introduction: Leadership, Discipline, and Effective Communication

Tony Hayward faced the press on a Venice, Louisiana, dock. It was May 30, 2010, and the BP chief executive officer had been living on the coast of the Gulf of Mexico for the past month. On April 20, the Deepwater Horizon oil rig had exploded, killing 11, injuring dozens, and beginning a gusher that in 100 days pumped five million barrels of crude oil into the Gulf waters. The Deepwater Horizon disaster had been the dominant story in the news media—it was All-BP-All-the-Time.

Hayward, clearly beleaguered and sleep-deprived, seemed frustrated with suggestions by the media and others that BP—formerly known as British Petroleum—and its leadership weren't doing enough to stop the flow of oil and protect the Gulf ecosystem. He spoke in front of heavy equipment being readied to be deployed for the cleanup. In a tone of frustration, Hayward tried to show that he cared. He attempted an apology, tried to show that he took the situation seriously: "We're sorry. We're sorry for the massive disruption it's caused their lives. And you know we're—there's no one who wants this thing over more than I do. You know, I'd like my life back."[1]

It didn't work. Hayward's statement had the opposite effect. Instead of showing he cared and that he took Gulf residents' plight seriously, the "I'd like my life back" quote sounded like self-pity. Critics pounced. There were 11 rig workers who would never get their lives back; dozens of injured whose lives would never be the same; thousands on the coast whose lives and livelihoods were disrupted. They wanted their lives back, too.

"I'd like my life back" became a defining moment. It crystallized for the media and for politicians the apparent callowness of BP's leadership. It wasn't the first of Hayward's verbal blunders. The *New York Times* had previously quoted him from an internal meeting: "What the hell did we do to deserve this?"[2] Nor was it the last. But "I'd like my life back" defined Hayward, BP, and the Gulf recovery. The takeaway: Hayward cares only about himself.

"I'd like my life back" also became self-fulfilling. It began Hayward's inexorable decline. Six weeks after the quote he was removed as CEO and given a make-work position; he left the company several months later. In the battle for public opinion—for trust, support, the benefit of the doubt—Hayward lost. It was a failure of leadership on a massive scale. And it began with a failure of communication. And that failure, in turn, was a failure of discipline.

Hayward's blunder is not unique to him. It should be a wake-up call to CEOs and other leaders, to all whose leadership responsibilities require inspiring trust and confidence verbally. Communication has power. But as with any form of power, it needs to be harnessed effectively or it can all too often backfire.

This book applies the Marine Corps' strategy doctrine, as embodied in its *Warfighting* manual, to leadership communication. It seeks to help those who engage audiences for a living—whether in positions of leadership or in communication support functions—to do so at a high level of craft.

Why *Warfighting*?

"The battle for public opinion" is a metaphor. So is "I'd like my life back." Metaphors matter. Metaphors trigger worldviews and set expectations. As the Berkeley cognitive linguist George Lakoff notes, we tend to live our lives in metaphor, but are generally unaware of the metaphors we live by (see Chapter 8, "Content: Word Choice, Framing, and Meaning," for more).[3]

Take, for example, the word "strategy." We may think we know what it means. But it's actually a metaphor. In ancient Greek, the word *strategos* meant a general or the leader of an army. That word derived from two other Greek words: *stratos,* or army, and *agein,* to lead. So *stratos* (army) + *agein* (to lead) = *strategos* (one who leads an army). Note that *stratos,* army, was itself a metaphor. The literal meaning of the word is "organized formation," as in the layers of rock on a cliff wall.

For the longest time, "strategy" or its equivalents in other languages meant only the art of leading an armed force. But in modern times it has become a metaphor for any goal-oriented activity. Business strategy is a metaphor for using the goal-oriented approach of leading an army to lead a company.

War and communication are not the same thing. But many of the goal-oriented principles of leading an effective armed force can be applied to the leadership discipline of public communication.

For example, the 19th-century Prussian military strategist Carl von Clausewitz defined war as, "an act of will directed toward a living entity that reacts."[4] This simple observation is quite profound. War, at its essence, isn't about fighting or killing, at least not for their own sake. Rather, it's about an outcome. A reaction. A change.

So is effective communication. I have long taken the metaphor Clausewitz provides, and have translated it this way:

**Communication is an act of will
directed toward a living entity that reacts.**

Let's parse this definition:

Communication is an act of will...

Effective communication is intentional. It is goal-oriented. It is strategic. Unlike ineffective communication, effective communication isn't impulsive or top-of-mind. It isn't self-indulgent. And communication isn't just about what one says. It's about anything one does or is observed doing. It's about any engagement with a stakeholder, including silence, inaction, and action.

...directed toward a living entity...

Stakeholders aren't passive vessels that simply absorb messages. Rather, they are living, breathing human beings and groups of human beings. They have their own opinions, ideas, hopes, dreams, fears, prejudices, attention spans, and appetites for listening. Most important, it is a mistake to assume that audiences think and behave just as we do. Most don't. Understanding an audience and its preconceptions, and the barriers that might prevent an audience from accepting what one is saying, is a key part of effective communication.

...that reacts.

This is the element most lost on many leaders. The only reason to engage an audience is to change something, to provoke a reaction. Effective communication provokes the desired reaction; ineffective communication doesn't. Ineffective communication isn't noticed, or it confuses, or it causes a different reaction than the one desired. Tony Hayward certainly got his life back, but not in the manner he had hoped.

And whatever the words one uses, we can count on audiences to compare the words to the speaker's own actions as well as to prior words. The words set expectations; the actions fulfill or betray those expectations. Trust arises when expectations are met and is lost when they are not.

So effective communication is hard. It requires discipline. It requires understanding the desired reaction among the groups to which one communicates, which in turn requires knowing all one can about that group. And then it requires saying and doing all that is necessary—and only what is necessary—to provoke that desired reaction. And it also requires understanding the absolutely predictable consequences—both intended and unintended—of words, silence, inaction, and action.

About the Marines

The United States Marine Corps is the nation's mobility force in readiness. The tip of the spear. It's ready to deploy anywhere, any time, on any mission.

The Marine Corps is also a leadership factory. It instills qualities of initiative, teamwork, and dedication to mission. It pushes accountability down to the bottom of the chain of command, even as it holds leaders at the very top of the chain accountable for their subordinates' decisions. Marines follow orders, but not blindly. Commander's intent is an essential part of an order. Understanding a commander's intent is the responsibility of each Marine. And making that intent clear is the responsibility of each commander, of whatever rank.

And at whatever rank, every Marine is a rifleman. Regardless of any Marine's current function, he or she is accomplished in the use of arms. Unlike in other armed services, the expectation is that every Marine, regardless of occupation (lawyer, pilot, public affairs officer, or auto mechanic) is proficient in infantry tactics and the effective use of firearms.

Every Marine is also a spokesman. I was present when the senior Marine public affairs officer—a brigadier general—described to the students of the Marine Corps Command and Staff College the Corps' expectation of any Marine in the presence of the news media: "Make sure each of your Marines knows this: If you're deployed to a war zone and there's a reporter around, we expect you to do three things:

- Engage. Speak with the reporter.
- Tell the truth. Don't lie, but also don't reveal confidential, classified, or sensitive operational information.
- Stay in your lane. If you drive a tank, talk about your tank. If you fly a plane, talk about your plane. Don't talk about anything that isn't your direct responsibility."

This is a courageous policy, and one most employers probably would not adopt. Most organizations try to centralize press communication. But making each Marine a spokesperson is typical of the Marines. They know that the Marines' reputation can be won or lost through the actions of any single Marine. Not just an officer, but a private right out of Parris Island boot camp. So they hold each Marine accountable. But with accountability comes authority.

Communication Is a Leadership Discipline

Whatever else leadership may be, it is experienced publicly. While it may emanate from within, it is a public phenomenon. A leader is judged based on three fundamental public leadership attributes:

- The leader's bearing: how the leader carries himself or herself
- The words the leader uses to engage others
- The manner in which the leader engages others

These are elements of communication. And they apply well beyond the armed services.

And as a leadership discipline, communication benefits from the structures, concepts, and principles of effective leadership in other fields.

The Marines continue to enjoy a reputation as the nation's elite fighting force. It is no surprise to me that they live up to their slogan: The Few. The Proud. They make reputation a priority, both in what they do and in what they say.

The elements that make a good Marine also make a good communicator.

How This Book Came About

I have had the good fortune to provide communication workshops and related services to Marines continuously since 1991, just after the first Gulf War ended. I had published an article that summer in *Public Relations Quarterly* noting that the U.S. military had embraced the principles of Carl von Clausewitz both in its execution of the Gulf War and in its public affairs operations to support the war. Clausewitz, the 19th-century Prussian general, is the author of *On War,* one of the most influential books of Western civilization and the basis of most modern military and business strategy. In my article, I noted that any serious student of strategy or communication should be familiar with the principles of Clausewitz. His most famous principle is that **war is merely the continuation of policy by other means: The goal of the war is not to fight, but to accomplish a political objective.**[5] I argued that professional communicators could learn from him. I translated Clausewitz's principle as follows: **Communication is merely the continuation of business by other means. The goal of communication is not to communicate, but to accomplish some tangible business goal**.

When the *Public Relations Quarterly* article came out, I was in my fourth year teaching public relations strategy and related topics at New York University, and Clausewitz was a big part of my course. Unbeknownst to me, one of my students was a Marine, just back from Iraq, and about to switch jobs: from helicopter pilot to public affairs officer. He had taken my course to get a head start. He asked if he could show my article to his commanding officer. At the same time, my friend Jim Lukaszewski had a scheduling conflict and was unable to teach his usual session at the Marines' annual East Coast Commanders Pubic Affairs Symposium, an annual weeklong introduction to public affairs for all Marines east of the Mississippi who are starting new commands. He recommended me to the commanding officer of the unit that managed the Symposium, who recognized my name from the article. I have taught at that Symposium every year since. For many of those years I taught on a Tuesday and Jim taught on a Thursday. I have also taught at every West Coast Commanders Public Affairs Symposium since 2006. From 2004 to 2009, I taught in the Brigadier General Select Orientation Course in Washington, and for several years I conducted workshops in the Command and Staff College and Officer Candidate School in Quantico, Virginia.

In 2006, I was teaching in Quantico and visited the Marine Corps bookstore. There I found a slim volume called *Warfighting: U.S. Marine Corps Doctrinal Publication No. 1.* It's required reading for every Marine. It lays out an approach to strategy and leadership that informs what all Marines do. Think of it as the Marine Corps Bible. While it isn't as famous as Clausewitz, it has several advantages: It is contemporary, it is assigned reading for every Marine, and it is much easier to read.

Flying home on the shuttle, I couldn't put the book down. Just as I had demonstrated in my article for *Public Relations Quarterly* that changing several words in Clausewitz's *On War* provided a framework for understanding communication, changing just a few words in *Warfighting* led to a much richer and deeper understanding of effective public communication, both for leaders and for those who advise them.

Then I had an idea. I was about to teach a new course on communication strategy in the MS in Public Relations and Corporate Communication program at New York University. I had already decided to assign *Clausewitz on Strategy: Inspiration and Insight from a Master Strategist.* The authors, from the Strategy Institute of the Boston Consulting Group, extract the essence of *On War* and apply it to contemporary business strategy.

I decided to supplement that reading with *Warfighting*, requiring students to read it before the first class. When I sent the syllabus to the department, it raised a few eyebrows. But to his credit, the academic director gave me the green light, and I posted the syllabus online.

In the first class, before discussing the book, I polled the students:

- How many were confused when they saw that the first book in a communication strategy course was a Marine Corps book called *Warfighting?* Nearly every hand went up.
- How many were concerned? Most hands stayed up.
- How many were angry? About a third of the hands stayed up.
- How many are still angry after reading the book? All hands came down.

I found the most counterculture-seeming student who had just put her hand down, and asked, "Why were you angry when you saw the syllabus?" She looked me in the eye and said, "I thought you were going to feed us propaganda, try to get us to like the military, to support the war in Iraq." And now? She smiled, and said, "I love this book. I have given copies to my parents and friends. I want to know why we don't know more about this book."

I've used *Warfighting* continuously ever since. And I've used it beyond my NYU classroom. I've used it in strategy boot camps for the public affairs department of a major insurance company, with the communication staff of a large pharmaceutical company, and even with clergy and not-for-profit executives, sometimes to their initial discomfort. I've urged individual CEOs, CFOs, and other corporate leaders to read it to help them both think strategically and communicate effectively.

In all civilian contexts, my students and clients have enthusiastically embraced *Warfighting*, and the comments have tended to cluster into these three categories:

1. This is one of the single-most-useful insights into how to be strategic in communication that I've ever read.
2. I never knew the Marines were so thoughtful.
3. The lessons of *Warfighting* go well beyond fighting wars or communicating. The book is about how to think strategically. It deserves a broader audience.

I agree. I believe that *Warfighting* is one of the undiscovered gems in strategic thinking, with significant civilian application. This book attempts to do for *Warfighting* what *Clausewitz on Strategy* does for *On War:* extract the essence of a military manual and apply those essential lessons to the nonmilitary, professional practice of public communication as a leadership discipline.

About This Book

This book does three things:

1. It translates core *Warfighting* principles into guidelines for effective leadership communication. These provide an important conceptual framework, and the individual principles serve as guideposts along the journey we will take. But they're merely the starting point.
2. It applies best practices in leadership communication drawn from my 33 years of advising and coaching leaders, and from my 24 years of teaching management and communication in graduate programs in a number of universities. This is the meat of the book—the big takeaway. It could easily exist without the *Warfighting* principles, but I have found in my teaching and coaching that the combination is more powerful than either standing alone.
3. It makes extensive use of case studies and examples, of both effective and ineffective communication by leaders in high-stakes situations.

All three of these strands run through the entire book. Each chapter emphasizes the leadership disciplines particular to that chapter's topic, and closes with two recap sections: The first is the gathering of all the *Warfighting* principles discussed in that chapter. The second is Lessons for Leaders and Communicators, the chapter's key takeaways.

Organizationally, the book is divided into three parts, focused on principles, strategy, and skills.

Part I: "Leadership and Communication: Connecting with Audiences." This takes up about half the book, and is divided into five chapters. The entire part focuses on the foundational principles of effective communication, all of which are grounded in connecting with and influencing audiences.

Chapter 1, "Words Matter," establishes the need to take language seriously as a leadership discipline. It covers the need to adapt language as circumstances change and as audiences, adversaries, and critics react to what a leader is saying and doing. It also focuses on the need to listen and to engage for a purpose: to change the way people think and feel, and what they know and do.

Chapter 2, "Taking Audiences Seriously," is a deep dive into understanding audiences. The leadership discipline here is to think of audiences as living, breathing entities with their own ideas, goals, plans, and desires even to be in relationship with the leader. The key is to recognize that audiences don't think as leaders do, care about what leaders care about, or understand what leaders understand. If we are to move people, we need to meet them where they are, but that means knowing where they are and knowing how to move them.

Chapter 3, "Words Aren't Enough," focuses on how tempting it can be to say all the right things in high-stakes situations. But saying the right thing without delivering on the expectations that communication sets is a recipe for disaster: for loss of trust, loyalty, confidence, and ultimately of competitive position. Trust arises when expectations are met, and the leadership discipline is to align what a leader says with what the leader does.

Chapter 4, "Speed, Focus, and the First Mover Advantage," covers shaping the communication agenda by being the first to define one's situation, motives, and actions. The leadership discipline is to say and do what is necessary to move audiences before critics, adversaries, the media, or social media have a chance to, and then to ensure that all communications, from all sources, are consistent and mutually reinforcing.

Chapter 5, "Initiative, Maneuver, and Disproportionality," focuses on ways to control the communication agenda, and on outsized risk and reward: how relatively minor changes or events can have a significant effect on the outcome. The leadership discipline is to be both disciplined and nimble, to avoid making small mistakes that cause great harm, and to engage stakeholders in such a timely and effective way that we get a higher return on our communication investment than we otherwise would.

Part II: "Strategy and Communication: Planning and Execution." This section has only one chapter, but it's a long one. This part focuses on the need to be intentional, coordinated, and sequenced in planning and implementing communication, especially in high-stakes situations.

Chapter 6, "Goals, Strategies, and Tactics: Preparing and Planning," focuses on the need to think carefully before communicating. It shows how easy it is for leaders to get tied up in the tactics of saying things, rather than being thoughtful about how to win hearts and minds. It also notes that preparing to communicate is often a leading indicator that there are gaps in a leader's thinking. If a leader isn't attentive to those gaps, you can be sure that stakeholders, critics, and adversaries will be. The leadership discipline is to have a clear intent and to organize thinking, decision making, communication planning, and communication implementation in the service of that intent.

Part III: "Building Skills: Getting Good at Communicating Well." This section focuses on the core skills that leaders need to become effective communicators. While not intended as a comprehensive how-to, it focuses on three areas that I have found leaders of all stripes and of all levels of ability need to master: how they carry themselves; how they manage meaning; and how the human brain works. Leaders need mastery of all three to be able to move people and to avoid self-inflicted harm.

Chapter 7, "Performance: The Physicality of Audience Engagement," begins by establishing the leadership discipline of taking seriously the need for continuous honing of communication skills. Even leaders who are good communicators need periodic tuneups or they will be less effective than they could be. The chapter then covers the basic interpersonal and group presentation skills that convey confidence and that engage audiences well.

Chapter 8, "Content: Word Choice, Framing, and Meaning," covers how leaders can shape the frame of reference so that audiences understand what the leader wants them to. The leadership discipline is to take seriously the way that words trigger worldviews, and to understand how framing needs to precede facts. All too often, leaders believe that facts and data are convincing. The chapter explores how facts are convincing only if they make sense within a frame of reference. And there's a first mover advantage: Whoever frames the topic first tends to win.

Chapter 9, "Audiences: Attention, Retention, and How Hearts and Minds Work," is a deep dive into the human brain and what it means for leaders. The leadership discipline is to appreciate that audiences are human and that human nature—literally the way the human brain works—determines what audiences are capable of. The chapter is an overview of current understanding from the fields of neurophysiology, cognitive psychology, and evolutionary biology to provide insights on how leaders can actually connect with audiences and win hearts and minds.

The book closes with two summaries:

Chapter 10, "Putting It All Together: Becoming a Habitually Strategic Communicator," harvests best practices from the previous chapters and organizes them into Nine Principles of Effective Leadership Communication. These can provide a quick reference point for monitoring your own communication leadership skills.

The appendix gathers all the *Warfighting* Principles embedded in the chapters and provides them in a single place, for easy reference.

1

Words Matter

On October 23, 2001, Apple Computer launched a new product that would forever change the world of music. It would eventually also change entertainment, computers, and even Apple itself, which would later drop the word *Computer* from its name. Newly rehired Chief Executive Officer Steve Jobs introduced a new device. It was small. It could link with Apple's Macintosh computer line. And it could play music.

As a computer company, Apple could have highlighted the engineering that went into the new device. Or the unprecedented power of its 5GB of memory. Or it could have focused on the elegance of its design, its ease of use, or even its price. But it didn't. Rather, Steve Jobs spoke a single phrase that captured customers' attention, made them re-imagine what was possible when listening to music. He focused not on the product or the technology. Rather, he simply described what the product meant to the customer:

"iPod. 1,000 songs in your pocket."[1]

It was breathtaking. Up until that moment, most consumers couldn't conceive of carrying 1,000 songs with them—the equivalent of between 90 and 100 CDs. But it captured consumers' imaginations. And their hearts and minds. And because invention is often the mother of necessity, people who had never imagined that they would want that many songs on their person suddenly had to have it.

That simple phrase, a thousand songs in your pocket, changed the way people understood their relation to music. The iPod and Apple would forever change consumer behavior and the entertainment industry. And within ten years, through the iPod's offspring iPhone and iPad, Apple transformed the telecom business too. As Apple said of its iPhone, "This changes everything."[2]

The Power of Communication

Words matter. Words shape worldviews. Words provoke action and reaction, which in turn provoke more words. Getting the words right is critically important. Getting the action right is also critically important. And aligning the words and actions is even more important.

The late Steve Jobs was one of the few business leaders who was able to connect with consumers in powerful ways that had positive impact. He was in a league of his own. Most business leaders are not as good at connecting, at communicating, or at understanding what will get and keep an audience's attention and earn the audience's loyalty, trust, and confidence.

But they can be.

Communication has power, but like any powerful tool, it needs to be used effectively or it can cause self-inflicted harm. Harnessing the power of communication is a fundamental leadership discipline.

This book is about how leaders can inspire, persuade, and earn the confidence of stakeholders through verbal engagement. About how they can build trust, inspire loyalty, and lead effectively.

In 33 years of advising leaders on the actions and communication needed to win, keep, or restore public confidence, I have concluded that many leaders, much of the time, fundamentally misunderstand communication. This misunderstanding has consequences: corporations lose competitive advantage; not-for-profits find it harder to fulfill their mission; religious denominations lose the trust and confidence of their followers; nations diminish their ability to protect citizens and achieve national security goals.

One reason some leaders misunderstand communication is that they think they're already good at it. They've been speaking since before they were one year old; reading since age four or five; writing since soon after that. Unlike just about every other discipline leaders have had to master, they've been communicating their whole lives. It seemed to be no big deal. Just as a fish is unaware of the water it swims in, leaders often are unaware of their own communication abilities. Or lack thereof.

I have found that many leaders suffer career-defining blunders because they don't take communication nearly as seriously as they take most other elements of their jobs. Effective leaders see communication as a critical professional aptitude and work hard at getting it right. This book is for them.

Effective communication isn't about pushing information to an audience. It isn't about facts, or data. It isn't about what sounds good in the moment. It isn't about spin. And it certainly isn't what makes the speaker feel good.

Strategy = Ordered Thinking

Of all the ways I've found to think of effective leadership communication, the most comprehensive approach to being truly strategic is to be found in *Warfighting: United States Marine Corps Doctrinal Publication No. 1.* And that book isn't even about communication. But it also isn't really about war. Rather, it's about clear thinking and effective execution.

Strategy is a process of ordered thinking: of thinking in the right order. Ineffective leadership communication begins with "What do we want to say?" That's both selfish and self-indulgent. And it's unlikely to succeed. And it's in the wrong order: It starts where thinking should ultimately end up. And it skips the essential questions that make sense of the situation, establish goals, identify audiences and attitudes, and prescribe a course of action to influence those attitudes.

A habitually strategic communicator never begins with "What do we want to say?" but rather with a sequence of prior questions.

? Asking Strategic Questions

The habitually strategic communicator always begins by asking questions in a certain sequence:

- What do we have? What is the challenge or opportunity we are hoping to address?

- What do we want? What's our goal? Communication is merely the continuation of business by other means. We shouldn't communicate unless we know what we're trying to accomplish.

- Who matters? What stakeholders matter to us? What do we know about them? What further information do we need to get about them? What are the barriers to their receptivity to us, and how do we overcome those barriers?

- What do we need them to think, feel, know, or do in order to accomplish our goal?

- What do they need to see us do, hear us say, or hear others say about us to think, feel, know, and do what we want them to?

- How do we make that happen?

Warfighting gives us a framework for this kind of ordered thinking. As the preface by Marine Corps Commandant C. C. Krulak states, "Very simply, this publication describes the philosophy which distinguishes the U.S. Marine Corps. The thoughts contained here are not merely guidance for action in combat, but a way of thinking.... [*Warfighting*] contains no specific techniques or procedures for conduct. Rather, it provides broad guidance in the form of concepts and values. It requires judgment in application."[3]

This book is also about a way of thinking. It translates *Warfighting*'s concepts and values into a set of principles for leadership communication. And it adds additional insights on enhancing any leader's capacity to win hearts and minds. As with warfighting, the leadership communication concepts and values described here require judgment in application.

The Nature of Effective Leadership Communication

It's all about interactivity.

From **Warfighting**

War is fundamentally an interactive social process.

*Effective communication is fundamentally an
interactive social process.*

(Note: Neither the United States Marine Corps nor any other component of the Department of Defense has approved, endorsed, or authorized this product.)

Warfighting's first principle points to the interactive nature of war. Leadership communication's first principle is also interactivity.

Effective leadership communication is never one-way. It is always interactive. This was the case long before social networking caused us to think of interactivity as somehow involving technology. Interactivity involves people, either directly or at a distance.

Communication cannot take place in one direction. Sending is not the same as receiving. And receiving doesn't ensure understanding. Effective communication is two-way or multidirectional, and always involves a feedback loop. The core take-away of this entire book is this: Effective communication is an act of will directed toward a living entity that reacts. That reaction is the essential element of effective communication: Was the reaction what we wanted? If not, why not? And how can we provoke the reaction we wanted?

From **Warfighting**

Clausewitz called it a *Zweikampf* (literally, a "two-struggle")
and suggested the image of a pair of wrestlers locked in a hold,
each exerting force and counterforce to try to throw the other.

The metaphor of the wrestlers is a telling one. It suggests that in communication, as in war, each party is trying to exert some force on the other. A continuous feedback loop provides a signal to adapt the engagement in order to accomplish a goal.

That feedback loop needs to be taken seriously.

George Bernard Shaw, the Irish playwright, literary critic, and co-founder of the London School of Economics, once famously said that the biggest challenge of communication is the illusion that it has taken place. Two parties think they're communicating. But they're talking past each other. Each labors under the misapprehension that he has made himself understood. At best there isn't a meeting of the minds; more often there's outright misunderstanding. Sometimes that misunderstanding escalates.

One of the greatest comedy routines ever is "Who's on First" by Bud Abbott and Lou Costello. First performed in 1937 and for decades thereafter, the routine features a baseball team manager (Abbott) and his friend (Costello) having a discussion about the players on the team. Abbott notes that ballplayers have funny nicknames, and proceeds to name the players on the team: Who's on first, What's on second, I Don't Know's on third. The skit opens with this exchange:

Abbott: I say Who's on first, What's on second, I Don't Know's on third.

Costello: Are you the manager?

Abbott: Yes.

Costello: You gonna be the coach too?

Abbott: Yes.

Costello: And you don't know the fellows' names?

Abbott: Well I should.

Costello: Well then who's on first?

Abbott: Yes.

Costello: I mean the fellow's name.

Abbott: Who.

Costello: The guy on first.

Abbott: Who.

Costello: The first baseman.

Abbott: Who.

Costello: The guy playing…

Abbott: Who is on first!

Costello: I'm asking YOU who's on first.

Abbott: That's the man's name.

Costello: That's who's name?

Abbott: Yes.

Costello: Well go ahead and tell me.

Abbott: That's it.

Costello: That's who?

Abbott: Yes.

PAUSE

Costello: Look, you gotta first baseman?

Abbott: Certainly.

Costello: Who's playing first?

Abbott: That's right.

Costello: When you pay off the first baseman every month, who gets the money?

Abbott: Every dollar of it.

Costello: All I'm trying to find out is the fellow's name on first base.

Abbott: Who.

Costello: The guy that gets…

Abbott: That's it.

Costello: Who gets the money…

Abbott: He does, every dollar. Sometimes his wife comes down and collects it.

Costello: Whose wife?

Abbott: Yes.

The routine continues in this vein for six-and-a-half minutes. All the while, Costello fails to understand that the words Who, What, and I Don't Know are names. And Abbott fails to understand that Costello doesn't get the point. As the interaction proceeds, the tempers get hot, voices get raised, and at one point Costello threatens Abbott with violence. Costello says he wants to know who's pitching. Abbott scolds him, with a finger wagging:

> Abbott: Now listen. Who is not pitching.
>
> Costello: I'll break your arm, you say who's on first![4]

I show a video of a 1960s television version of the skit at the beginning of my executive workshops on leadership communication and persuasion skills. In every session I get a powerful response. Executives tell me that they find themselves in similar exchanges all the time. As misunderstanding grows, voices rise, tempers flare, and relations are harmed. I then ask for ways they might change the dynamic. Invariably I get some version of this: "We recognize that we're not communicating, but we blame the other person, and we persist. If only we'd stop, acknowledge that we're not communicating, and find some common ground. But it isn't easy."

 *From* **Warfighting**

War is thus a process of continuous mutual
adaptation, of give and take, of move and countermove.

*Effective communication is thus a process of continuous mutual
adaptation, of give and take, of move and countermove.*

Effective communicators know that they need to adapt. They need to adapt if they recognize that they're not being understood. They need to adapt based on how their audience reacts to the initial engagement; based on what critics or adversaries say; based on changes in the environment in which communication is taking place; as facts become outdated or as new developments require attention.

Adapting to change is not a sign of weakness or of indecision. Rather it is a discipline. But many leaders act like Abbott and Costello. Instead of adapting, they dig in. They persist in speaking the same words in the same way even as the audience becomes alienated, or as the situation changes, as expectations evolve, or as the very meaning of their words becomes moot.

The 19th-century German military strategist Helmuth von Moltke, who followed in Carl von Clausewitz's footsteps as head of the German General Staff, famously said that no plan ever survives its first contact with the enemy.[5] In civilian language, no plan ever survives its initial implementation. Or as boxer Mike Tyson has said, you have a plan up until the moment you're punched in the face.[6]

This wasn't to suggest that you shouldn't plan. Rather, Moltke emphasized that the plan had to be so clear on what the goals are that those in charge could adapt quickly—or to use *Warfighting*'s words, continuously adapt. As an audience, critic, adversary, or ally reacts to an initial engagement, we need to adapt ourselves to continue to make progress toward our goal. As the environment in which we're communicating changes, we need to adapt to take that change into account.

Moltke said:

> No plan of operations extends with certainty beyond the first encounter with the enemy's main strength.... Certainly the commander in chief will keep his great objective in mind, undisturbed by the vicissitudes of events.... Everything depends on penetrating the uncertainty of veiled situations to evaluate the facts, to clarify the unknown, to make decisions rapidly, and then to carry them out with strength and constancy.[7]

If we see effective leadership communication as a process of continuous mutual adaptation, of give and take, of move and countermove, with a goal always in mind, we can maintain control of the communication agenda, even as things change. We avoid the illusion that communication has taken place.

Senator John McCain's Blunder

If we see communication simply as sending messages, we're at risk of seeming out of touch. That's precisely what happened to Senator John McCain in his 2008 campaign against Senator Barack Obama for the presidency of the United States. Senator McCain had included

a line in his stump speech since January of that year: "The fundamentals of the U.S. economy remain strong."[8] The assurance that the
economy's fundamentals were strong was intended to neutralize the
Democrats' criticism of the policies of President George W. Bush.
For most of the campaign the line was uncontroversial. And as Senator McCain got into the rhythm of his campaign, that phrase became
less a matter of discipline than a matter of habit. It simply became his
default.

But on September 15 everything changed. Lehman Brothers went
bankrupt and Merrill Lynch narrowly avoided bankruptcy by agree-
ing to be bought by Bank of America. The stock market crashed; the
debt markets seized up; and the Administration began talking about
some banks being too big to be allowed to fail.

We now know that what followed was the deepest and longest
recession in our lifetime. But on that day all attention was focused on
the calamity that was happening in real time.

 *From* **Warfighting**

Since war is a fluid phenomenon, its conduct requires flexibility of
thought. Success depends in large part on the ability to adapt—to
proactively shape changing events to our advantage as well as to
react quickly to constantly changing conditions.

> *Since communication is a fluid phenomenon, its conduct requires
> flexibility of thought. Success depends in large part on the ability
> to adapt—to proactively shape changing events to our advantage
> as well as to react quickly to constantly changing conditions.*

Senator McCain, on the campaign trail seven weeks before the
election, continued to speak from his stump speech: The fundamentals of the economy remain strong. But all evidence that day suggested that there were serious problems with the economy. Senator
McCain's initial failure to adapt to the new environment gave his
adversary an opening.

Senator Obama, adapting to the changing situation, hit Senator McCain hard: "It's not that I think John McCain doesn't care what's going on in the lives of most Americans. I just think he doesn't know. He doesn't get what's happening between the mountain in Sedona where he lives and the corridors of Washington where he works. Why else would he say that we've made great progress economically under George Bush? Why else would he say, today, of all days—just a few hours ago—that the fundamentals of the economy are still strong? Senator—what economy are you talking about?"[9]

Senator McCain and his campaign continued to stick to their line, even as pundits juxtaposed the two candidates' quotes. Senator McCain seemed out of touch, unaware of what was happening.

His campaign tried to justify Senator McCain's sticking to his prior language—it tried redefining the term "fundamentals of the economy." Before the meaning hadn't been made explicit, but the implication was that "things are going well." Unemployment had been very low; the stock market was high; home ownership had reached record levels. But rather than adapt his message as the situation changed, Senator McCain tried to explain it away. He asserted a very narrow definition of "fundamentals of the economy": the American worker and America's entrepreneurial spirit.

Senator McCain said, "My opponents may disagree, but those fundamentals, the American worker and their innovation, their entre-preneurship, the small business, those are the fundamentals of Amer-ica and I think they're strong."[10] It was too little, too late. But Senator McCain persisted in repeating both his initial statement about funda-mentals being strong and his narrow redefinition of those words. And the more he did, the more he seemed out of touch.

Senator McCain kept losing support throughout the next week. And the news coverage focused both on his failure to understand the major shift in American fortunes and on his failure to adjust his cam-paign rhetoric to fit the new situation.

Then he tried a Hail Mary play—a long shot that he hoped would change the dynamics in his favor. It backfired.

He was scheduled to debate Senator Obama on Friday, Septem-ber 26. Two days before the debate, Senator McCain announced that he was suspending his campaign and asked that the debate be postponed. The reason he cited was the need to get to Washington to help Congress and the White House finalize details of a bailout plan to keep the economy from getting worse.[11]

It was seen as a desperate move. Suspending a campaign was unprecedented, even during previous times of war or much more dire economic emergencies. Stephen Hess, a scholar at the American Enterprise Institute, told *Bloomberg News,* "McCain's move should be judged too clever by half."[12]

David Letterman Jumps In

As part of the suspension of the campaign, Senator McCain announced that he was canceling all interviews immediately, including one scheduled that night on CBS's *The Late Show with David Letterman.*[13] Letterman didn't buy the rationale for the cancellation, saying in his monologue:

> When you call up at the last minute and you cancel the show, ladies and gentlemen, that's starting to smell…. This doesn't smell right. This is not the way a tested hero behaves…. An American hero. Maybe the only actual hero I know. I've met the man; I know the guy. So I'm more than a little disappointed by this behavior. "We're suspending the campaign." Are we suspending it because there's an economic crisis or because the poll numbers are sliding?[14]

Letterman invited a substitute guest to sit in for Senator McCain: Keith Olbermann, then host of MSNBC's *Countdown* and a McCain critic. But before the Olbermann interview got far along, Letterman interrupted it with a breaking development:

> John McCain was nice enough to call me on the phone and say he was racing back to Washington. And our people here were told it's so serious he's getting on a plane immediately and racing back to Washington. And now we've just been told— you have it on the thing?—this is going live. There he is right there. Doesn't seem to be racing to the airport, does he?[15]

Letterman then linked to an in-house CBS video feed that showed Senator McCain beginning a live interview with CBS News anchor Katie Couric. Letterman aired the video while providing an ongoing stream of cynical commentary, including: "Hey John, I've got a question. Do you need a ride to the airport?"[16] He continued to mock Senator McCain while also offering his audience a running commentary on his own emotions:

> Now this stinks. Now you tell me. You know how these things work...I don't want to keep beating this thing but this really is starting to smell now because he says to me on the phone—I took a phone call from John McCain—a lot of senators don't call me—so I said OK, as part of the national good, I understand, and I said good luck, thank you for being attentive to the cause.... And then this. It's like we caught him getting a manicure or something.[17]

As the McCain/Couric interview ended and the Letterman show came back from a commercial, Letterman offered his audience an update:

> We're told now that the Senator has concluded his interview with Katie Couric, and we're told now that he's on [Food Network cooking show host] Rachael Ray's show making veal piccata.[18]

Letterman's public airing of his sense of insult elevated to a national nonpolitical audience Senator McCain's apparent insincerity about why he was suspending his campaign. Critics and pundits interpreted the suspension as a desperate attempt to avoid the debate with Senator Obama.

Senator McCain and his campaign lost sight of the fundamentals of communication as a leadership discipline: the need to continuously mutually adapt. He adapted his language on the economy too slowly, and put himself in the position of seeming unaware of the scope of the significant economic crisis. His ineffective adaptation of language— attempting to justify his original language rather than changing his language—made him seem disingenuous. His campaign suspension was characterized as a panicked move, and the suspension's rationale was obliterated by Letterman's ridicule.

The period of mid-September to late September became a defining moment for the McCain campaign, and caused the campaign to lose much of the positive momentum from the prior two weeks, which saw the nomination of Alaska Governor Sarah Palin to be Senator McCain's running mate. Senator McCain, who is a Naval Academy graduate and decorated combat pilot, should have known better. But his clumsy adaptations caused significant self-inflicted harm.

Both his adversary, Senator Obama, and his critic, David Letterman, adapted fluidly to rapid changes. Both came out ahead.

The Audience Has Its Own Ideas

 From **Warfighting**

It is critical to keep in mind that the enemy is not an inanimate object to be acted upon but an independent and animate force with its own objectives and plans.

> *It is critical to keep in mind that the audience is not an inanimate object to be acted upon but a collection of living, breathing human beings with their own goals, concerns, needs, priorities, attention spans, and levels of desire even to be in a relationship with us.*

An audience is a living, breathing entity. It is a collection of human beings. Collectively, an audience tends to care about certain things in certain ways, and tends not to think at all about the concerns of those trying to influence it. And at any given time any member of any audience can be distracted, inattentive, unconcerned with others' concerns, and focused only on his or her immediate interests.

Influencing an audience requires active engagements that cause the audience to take notice, and to do so in ways we want them to. But this requires knowing what the audience feels, thinks, is capable of, and cares about. And it requires caring about those things too.

Losing Face

In the fall of 2007, the social networking site Facebook introduced a new feature called Beacon. Facebook, then only three years old, was just catching on and changing the way people interacted with each other online. Beacon was intended to let Facebook users share information from its partner shopping sites with their Facebook friends. When a member made a purchase, that purchase would automatically be posted on the user's news feed, for the user's entire network to see.

But some users were concerned about sharing news of their purchases with their entire networks. What about birthday or holiday presents? Recipients would lose the element of surprise. What about rivalry among friends? If a user bought something for one friend, other friends might wonder why they were left out. Users raised concerns about privacy, and especially about the automatic nature of the posting of purchases to the news feeds.

When Facebook launched the service, it didn't appreciate the privacy issues that Beacon triggered. CEO Mark Zuckerberg, then only 23 years old, didn't seem to understand the significance of the users' concerns. He didn't adapt either the service or his communication with users. Instead, when users objected, he encouraged them to try the service anyway.

The design of Beacon put the burden on users to opt-out on a purchase-by-purchase basis, but the opt-out procedure was not readily transparent and was difficult to follow. But if users didn't opt-out, or couldn't figure out how to, Beacon assumed consent and notified the user's friends about the purchase. In addition, Facebook allowed users to opt-out only on a case-by-case basis—there was no universal opt-out. Users asked for an easier-to-find opt-out, and a universal opt-out, so that any given user could choose not to have any purchases made public.

Facebook initially apologized and made some adjustments, but didn't go far enough. In particular, it didn't put in the universal opt-out. Without it critics were still concerned. Instead of responding to users' concerns, Mr. Zuckerberg continued to tell them that when they tried Beacon they'd be convinced, and he put the burden back on them.

Users and critics pushed back more forcefully, and a number of partner sites walked away from Beacon. Facebook members even created anti-Facebook Facebook pages.

On December 5, after months of alienating customers, Facebook finally added a universal opt-out function. Mr. Zuckerberg wrote on his blog, "We've made a lot of mistakes building this feature, but we've made even more with how we've handled them. We simply did a bad job with this release, and I apologize for it."[19]

Mr. Zuckerberg had failed to respond in a timely way to the legitimate concerns Facebook users had, and was far too slow to adapt his and Facebook's message and tone, and finally its policies. Once he did, things calmed down. It wasn't the last time Facebook had a tin ear about privacy concerns, but it was the first that made national headlines.

In late 2011, in a blog announcing Facebook's agreement with the U.S. Federal Trade Commission on new privacy standards, Mr. Zuckerberg referred to the 2007 Beacon controversy as a "high-profile mistake" that overshadowed much of the good work that Facebook had done.[20]

The Struggle to Win Hearts and Minds

If we are to move people, we need to meet them where they are—physically, emotionally, intellectually, spiritually, ideologically. The bigger the gulf between "us and them," the less likely effective communication will take place.

Consider, for example, the U.S. government's communication in the aftermath of the 2001 attacks on the World Trade Center and Pentagon. The Bush Administration concluded that it needed to win the hearts and minds of Muslim communities around the world. The

Administration hoped that building support of Muslim communities would make extremist attacks on the U.S. less likely, and that the U.S. would have more flexibility projecting power to parts of the world whose population is predominantly Muslim.

In 2002 the State Department's Office of Public Diplomacy developed an advertising campaign called the Shared Values Initiative to reach communities in predominantly Muslim countries. It bought more than $5 million of advertising on television networks during the Muslim holiday period of Ramadan. The campaign, hoping to dispel myths about the treatment of Muslims in the United States, showed Muslims living happily in America. Individual Muslims spoke into the camera or while the camera showed them at their jobs—a firefighter, a teacher, the owner of a bakery. They gave first-hand testimony about their positive experiences of living in America—of being Americans and also of being Muslim.

But the campaign misfired. It did not meet Muslim communities where they were. Rather it spoke past them.

A 2008 analysis of the Shared Values Initiative by Dr. Amy Zalman, published by the EastWest Institute, showed that the campaign was doomed from the start by a misunderstanding of the audiences to which it was directed. Dr. Zalman is a national security consultant based in Washington, D.C., whose practice focuses on strategic communication and public diplomacy.

Dr. Zalman's EastWest Institute paper begins by noting that, "good communicators reveal, in speech and action, that they understand the motivations and aspirations of their audiences—and it is via this understanding that they gain their sympathies."[21]

Dr. Zalman says, "A review of U.S. official rhetoric shows an all too persistent absence of this understanding, an oversight which in turn can fan rather than dampen extremist sentiment."[22] She notes that in its communication with Muslim communities around the world, the U.S. government didn't bridge a gulf, but made it wider.

Effective public diplomacy, according to Dr. Zalman, "begins with deep attention to how others think about themselves and their communities. Recent U.S. discourse is characterized by a lack of attention to precisely these issues. It has produced faulty assumptions that have alienated global audiences and clouded debate on violent extremism."[23]

The Shared Values Initiative was based on an assumption, given voice by President George W. Bush, that the terrorists hate America because of our freedoms. The entire campaign was built around this assumption.

Says Dr. Zalman:

> This first official U.S. communication campaign emerged from the view that al-Qaeda hated, above all, Americans' freedom of religious practice. The advertising campaign...sought to differentiate the United States from autocratic states such as Afghanistan under the Taliban, and to reveal the virtues of a U.S. war against terrorism, and *for* religious freedom of practice. Most countries perceived the advertisements as propaganda and refused to air them, but even if they had, Shared Values would have been irrelevant diversion. As poll after poll of Muslim populations has revealed, no mainstream populations contest either the value of civil liberties in the United States or the value of freedom of worship and they do not need convincing of their virtues.[24]

While it didn't do affirmative harm, the Shared Values Initiative consumed significant resources, attention, and time. Worse, it gave policymakers and the U.S. public the false impression that the U.S. was making inroads in perceptions among Muslim communities around the world. Greater than the financial and other costs, though, was the opportunity cost. While Shared Values was underway, we were not effectively winning hearts and minds. And then we invaded Iraq.

The Shared Values Initiative was merely the first major attempt to win hearts and minds. It was not the last. Says Dr. Zalman: "Eager to 'tell our story,' regardless of whether anyone is listening, U.S. communicators have plunged into an ongoing search for the right word to describe actions, actors, groups, and belief systems. These efforts have met with failure."[25]

Connecting with Audiences   .

Communication isn't about telling our story. That's undisciplined, self-indulgent, and often illusory. The power of communication is getting audiences to listen—and to care.

Dr. Zalman conducted a detailed review of U.S. rhetoric that showed a persistent failure to demonstrate understanding of the audiences to whom the U.S. was purportedly communicating.

For example, for years the U.S. government, at the highest levels, used the word "jihadist" to describe our enemies. But in March of 2008 the State Department advised: "In Arabic, jihad means 'striving in the path of God' and is used in many contexts beyond warfare. Calling our enemies jihadis and their movement a global jihad unintentionally legitimizes their actions."[26] Our government's use of language transformed murderers into martyrs. And by the time we stopped, the U.S. government had been using that vocabulary for six years.

In 2009 Admiral Michael G. Mullen, then the newly appointed Chairman of the Joint Chiefs of Staff, addressed the failure of recent efforts to win hearts and minds in Muslim communities. He embraced the *Warfighting* principle of treating the audience as a living entity with its own ideas and plans. Admiral Mullen at the time was the nation's senior-most military officer and by law the principal military advisor to the President, the National Security Council, and the Secretary of Defense. He wrote an article in the National Defense University's journal *Joint Force Quarterly,* titled "Strategic Communications: Getting Back to Basics." In it, he acknowledged that previous attempts were more focused on how we feel and less about the needs, interests, or concerns of the audience.

Admiral Mullen writes:

> There has been a certain arrogance to our "strat comm" efforts. We've come to believe that messages are something we can launch downrange like a rocket, something we can fire for effect. They are not. Good communication runs both ways. It's not about telling our story. We must also be better listeners.[27]

Admiral Mullen implicitly affirms Dr. Zalman's insights about the U.S.'s failure to understand the Muslim audience for much of our public diplomacy efforts. He writes:

> The Muslim community is a subtle world we don't fully—and don't always attempt to—understand. Only through a shared appreciation of the people's culture, needs, and hopes for the future can we hope ourselves to supplant the extremist narrative. We cannot capture hearts and minds. We must engage them; we must listen to them, one heart and one mind at a time—over time.[28]

Dr. Zalman notes that part of our credibility gap with the Muslim world arose from inconsistency between our words and our actions:

> Speakers will be judged by their deeds and policies as well as by their rhetoric. Communications must be crafted in which actions, policies, and rhetoric are mutually reinforcing activities.... Speakers who appear to say one thing while doing another will not be viewed as credible. Speakers whose actions, policies, and words embody a coherent intention have a greater chance of being viewed as credible.[29]

Admiral Mullen goes even further:

> We hurt ourselves more when our words don't align with our actions. Our enemies regularly monitor the news to discern coalition and American intent as weighed against the efforts of our forces. When they find a 'say-do' gap—such as Abu Ghraib—they drive a truck right through it. So should we, quite frankly. We must be vigilant about holding ourselves accountable to higher standards of conduct and closing any gaps, real or perceived, between what we say about ourselves and what we do to back it up.[30]

Admiral Mullen also notes that many failures attributed to communication actually reflect deeper problems:

> I would argue that most strategic communication problems are not communication problems at all. They are policy and execution problems. Each time we fail to live up to our values

or don't follow up on a promise, we look more and more like the arrogant Americans the enemy claims we are.[31]

Recap: Best Practices from This Chapter

From Warfighting

Effective communication is fundamentally an interactive social process. It is thus a process of continuous mutual adaptation, of give and take, of move and countermove.

Since communication is a fluid phenomenon, its conduct requires flexibility of thought. Success depends in large part on the ability to adapt—to proactively shape changing events to our advantage as well as to react quickly to constantly changing conditions.

It is critical to keep in mind that the audience is not an inanimate object to be acted upon but a collection of living, breathing human beings with their own goals, concerns, needs, priorities, attention spans, and levels of desire even to be in a relationship with us.

Lessons for Leaders and Communicators

The only reason to communicate is to change something—to provoke a reaction.

Communication is an act of will directed toward a living entity that reacts. An effective communicator never starts with "What do we say?" or "How do we tell our story?" but rather focuses on the goal:

- What is the goal: How will things be different when communication has taken place?

- Who is the audience: What does the audience care about now; what do we want the audience to care about when we're done; what prevents the audience from caring about it?
- How should we engage the audience so that it does care?
- What does the audience need to see us do, hear us say, or hear others say about us in order to care about what we want it to care about?
- How do we make that happen?

The "1,000 songs in your pocket" slogan is clearly the result of just such a process that Steve Jobs and Apple engaged in to launch the iPod.

Because any engagement provokes a reaction, and because the environment in which we communicate is constantly changing, we need to be able to adapt our engagement:

- Adaptation requires keeping our focus on the goal, and modifying our behavior, our message, and our form of engagement so that we make continuous progress toward our goal.
- Rigidly adhering to language ("Who's on first"; "the fundamentals of our economy remain strong"; "Try it; you'll like it"; "jihad") even as we see we're losing the support of our audience because of our word choice is a recipe for losing trust and confidence.

Taking audiences seriously is hard. It requires us to avoid saying what makes us feel good ("What the hell did we do to deserve this?"; "I'd like my life back") and to speak only in ways that cause the audience to respond the way we want it to.

But this means listening.

We can't move an audience with us if we don't meet the audience where it is.

And we need to walk our talk. As Admiral Mullen says, "Each time we fail to live up to our values or don't follow up on a promise, we look more and more like the arrogant Americans the enemy claims we are."[32]

Communication sets expectations; actions deliver on or shatter those expectations.

2

Taking Audiences Seriously

For Barry Mike it was a defining moment. He was a youngish chief speechwriter for the world's second-largest computer company, Digital Equipment Corporation (DEC). Only IBM was bigger. It was 1992, the era of mainframe computers, and hardware companies were on top of the world. For the moment.

But a rising force in the computer business was a software company run by a dynamic young leader. Microsoft was beginning to flex its muscles, and key to its success would be persuading those who ran computer networks in big companies and governments to prefer Microsoft's operating system and computer applications over more corporate-focused rivals'. It wasn't an easy sell. Most companies' centralized computer systems and data centers ran software other than Microsoft's. Microsoft was big in personal computers, which were just beginning to break out as a consumer market segment. But big companies weren't installing Microsoft software beyond PCs. The perception at the time was that Microsoft may be good at PCs, but it wasn't ready for mainframe prime time.

That year Microsoft and DEC were working together, and the Microsoft CEO was scheduled to be the featured speaker at DEC-World, a one-company trade show that gathered thousands of senior corporate and government officials from around the world. The "Evening with Bill Gates" was a special attraction for DEC's 1,000 top customers. And Mr. Mike was accountable for it.

From a corporate perspective it was supposed to be a win-win for each company. DEC would provide Mr. Gates with the imprimatur of a respected midrange computer hardware manufacturer. And Mr. Gates would provide DEC with a younger, hipper cachet. The focus would be on how the two companies were great partners: He adult enough to be trusted with data centers; DEC hip enough to consider when buying PCs. Mr. Gates had begun to be seen as a celebrity, both within and beyond the world of technology. Part of the win for DEC was simply getting him to speak at the event; part of the appeal for the audience was the ability to see a celebrity in action, and to go away with some sense that they got the inside scoop directly from him.

In the run-up to DECWorld, Mr. Mike met with Microsoft's media relations representative to script the event. After much back and forth, Mr. Mike and the Microsoft rep, described by Mr. Mike as very smart, very focused, and uncompromising, reached an agreement on what Mr. Gates would say. They developed a clear outline that featured information about Microsoft's software, DEC's hardware, and how the two worked well together.

Just before the event, the CEOs and communicators met to review Mr. Gates's remarks. Around the table were Bill Gates, DEC's founder and CEO Ken Olsen—who was revered by the world of technology, including by Mr. Gates—and the two companies' communicators. Mr. Mike walked Mr. Gates through his presentation: the audience, the messages, and the key talking points. Mr. Mike explained the substance of the presentation—the rationale for it, the logic within it, and the reasons both companies' communicators thought the message was right.

Mr. Gates listened respectfully, then paused for a long time. Then he looked up and said, "No."

The others were dumbfounded. No? They had negotiated a deal. And now Mr. Gates said no?

Mr. Gates said simply, "I don't want to say that. I want to talk about something else."

Mr. Mike inquired, "What?"

Mr. Gates said simply, "My house."[1] He didn't mean "house" as a metaphor for company. He meant his own house. He had just completed building a custom, 66,000-square-foot home. It boasted a beyond-state-of-the-art technology infrastructure. It featured a world-class collection of digitized art, including masterpieces for which he had the exclusive digital rights.

Although this was DEC's event, and Mr. Olsen was theoretically the senior-most executive at the table, the group demurred. Mr. Gates would talk about his house. Not about Microsoft. Not about Microsoft's operating system. And certainly not about DEC. It was a big disappointment for the DEC team.

For the next 45 minutes Mr. Gates regaled his audience with tales of his house. He was relaxed, boyish, charming. He was utterly likeable. And his talk featured no discussion of business or computer technology (besides the gee-whiz devices and digital art in his home) or, especially, of DEC.[2]

But, according to Mr. Mike's blog, *Strategic Leadership Communication,* the audience got a very strong message: Microsoft can and should be your corporate partner, whether you go with DEC or not.[3]

According to Mr. Mike, Mr. Gates connected with his audience in ways that the two companies' speechwriting teams could not have imagined. He was simultaneously operating on two levels: While seemingly talking about his house, he was really delivering an identity message about why the audience would want to do business with him.[4]

What Bill Gates Said/What the Audience Heard

When Bill Gates said, "I am building a 66,000-square-foot house," the audience heard, "I'm very rich and very successful. An awful lot of customers must think I'm doing something right!"[5]

When Bill Gates said, "with a sophisticated information technology infrastructure," the audience heard, "I understand how all the elements of technology fit together as well as anyone, including DEC. You can trust me as a corporate technology partner."[6]

And when Bill Gates said, "populated by digital reproductions of great masterpieces," the audience heard, "Olsen may be a pioneer, but I'm a visionary. The world is going digital, even art. And it's all software, where I excel. If you want to be part of the future, work with me."[7]

From Warfighting

It is essential that we understand the enemy on his own terms. We should not assume that every enemy thinks as we do, fights as we do, or has the same values or objectives.

> *It is essential that we understand the audience on its own terms. We should not assume that every audience thinks as we do, decides as we do, or has the same values, goals, or concerns as we do.*

What Barry Mike realized in DECWorld's "Evening with Bill Gates" is that audiences don't care about what companies care about. And that an effective leader knows how to connect with an audience on the things the audience cares about.

Bill Gates knew that an audience of technologists wouldn't necessarily perceive Microsoft's product features or prices as superior to its rivals', even with DEC's backing. And that night they wouldn't even care about product features. They were there for an "Evening with Bill Gates"—to be in his presence—not for a product demonstration. Mr. Gates knew that he needed the audience to do more than just want to hear him speak: He needed the audience to want to do business with him. And he knew that what would turn them on was not the attributes of an operating system, but the consequence of his vision. He needed to get them excited about what the future held, for them and for a world where technology is ubiquitous.

Mr. Mike and his boss, DEC CEO Ken Olsen, and even Mr. Gates's own staff, had approached the evening from the wrong direction: What do we want to say about our companies and products? Mr. Gates approached it from a different perspective: What will it take for the audience to want to do business with me? How can I make a connection with this audience?

It worked. Mr. Gates turned his audience on. He came across as the cool kid that everyone would want to partner with.

He was able to signal that he was ready for corporate prime time, but in a way that seemed totally innocuous. He was able to neutralize the concerns of the audience without showing disrespect to DEC.

In his blog Mr. Mike says that communication comes across on three basic levels: content (what you have to say), identity (how you come across saying it) and relationship (how you relate to those with whom you communicate). Audiences pick up on all three.[8]

Knowingly or not, Mr. Mike and Mr. Gates were channeling Aristotle. The Greek philosopher advised that to engage an audience a speaker must master three things:

1. *Logos:* reasoning, logical argument, empirical evidence, rational explanation, and facts;

2. *Ethos:* an element of personal character, identity, or personal attributes; the characteristic spirit and prevalent tone or sentiment of a person, people, or community;

3. *Pathos:* emotion, passion, and especially triggering an emotional reaction from and connection with the audience.

DEC and the speechwriters had focused exclusively on Logos, on facts and logical exposition of product attributes. Bill Gates chose to lead with Ethos over Logos. There was still argument, but only enough to support the Ethos represented by his story about his home. But the result was Pathos: an emotional connection with the audience.

DEC, in the person of technologist Ken Olsen, had long believed that the best technology would win out. Mr. Gates understood that technology, by itself, didn't sell anything. He needed to make his audience feel that he and Microsoft could be trusted in their data centers. And he knew that getting the audience excited about the potential of software—not what it is but what it makes possible—was the way to do it.

Mr. Gates connected with the audience. He finished his talk to healthy applause. Mr. Olsen got up from his seat and began walking to the stage to thank Mr. Gates. But then Mr. Gates offered to take questions. Mr. Olsen, already at the stage stairs, sat on the stairs in order to give Mr. Gates the stage. A *Boston Globe* photographer captured the moment. The next morning the *Globe* ran a story with the picture. It showed the elder statesman Mr. Olsen sitting at the feet of the up-and-coming Mr. Gates. It told a story in metaphor, signaling a change in the business: the ascendancy of software over hardware.[9]

As the decade of the '90s unfolded, Microsoft went on to fame, fortune, and controversy. Digital Equipment Company, slow to adapt to the changing market, saw its fortunes decline, and eventually was snapped up by Compaq Computer, now part of HP.

Effective leaders begin with stakeholder perspectives always in mind. Then they use all three of Aristotle's attributes—Logos, Ethos, Pathos—simultaneously to both connect with and move their audience.

Companies often dismiss the significance of Ethos and Pathos. They stay stuck in Logos, to their and their stakeholders' ultimate disappointment. Consider the wildly successful video rental service Netflix, and how it failed to consider either Ethos or Pathos in a communication with stakeholders that ultimately cost it dearly.

Netflix Misfires—Twice

On July 12, 2011, Netflix customers received a curious e-mail.

Netflix had become a leader in the home video rental business by leapfrogging rivals such as Blockbuster and offering an easy-to-use service with easy-to-understand pricing. At the time of the announcement, Netflix offered a flat monthly fee for unlimited television and movie viewing in two different formats. Customers could receive DVDs one at a time by mail, and also watch unlimited streaming videos online, for a flat monthly fee of $9.99. Customers who wanted only streaming videos could pay only $7.99. Most customers opted for the bundled service, $9.99 for unlimited streaming videos and one-at-a-time DVDs.

But on July 12, customers' inboxes contained a note from Netflix. The same note also appeared on the company's blog. It began with the name of someone most customers didn't know: "Jessie Becker here to share two significant changes at Netflix with you."[10] Ms. Becker was Netflix's VP of marketing.

Her note began by announcing the establishment of two new DVD-only plans, a one-at-a-time plan for $7.99 per month, and a two-at-a-time plan for $11.99.[11] She emphasized that these were the lowest prices ever for unlimited DVDs. So far, so good.

The next paragraph, however, left people initially confused:

> Second, we are separating unlimited DVDs by mail and unlimited streaming into separate plans to better reflect the costs of each and to give our members a choice: a streaming only plan, a DVD only plan or the option to subscribe to both. With this change, we will no longer offer a plan that includes both unlimited streaming and DVDs by mail.[12]

That somewhat dense paragraph wasn't particularly easy to follow. What did it mean to no longer offer a plan that includes both unlimited streaming and DVD by mail? Were they canceling something, or simply not taking new customers? It wasn't clear. The next paragraph, where one would expect an explanation, was about price. And it made people angry:

> So for instance, our current $9.99 a month membership for unlimited streaming and unlimited DVDs will be split into 2 distinct plans:
>
> Plan 1: Unlimited Streaming (no DVDs) for $7.99 a month.
>
> Plan 2: Unlimited DVDs, 1 out at-a-time (no streaming), for $7.99 a month.
>
> The price for getting both of these plans will be $15.98 a month ($7.99 + $7.99). For new members, these changes are effective immediately; for existing members, the new pricing will start for charges on or after September 1, 2011."[13]

In other words, customers had to choose: Give up DVDs, or give up streaming, or pay $15.98 a month for bundled service that previously cost only $9.99. A price increase of 60 percent. But that increase wasn't made explicit in the e-mail. Customers had to do the math themselves. And it came with an added inconvenience: Instead of a single bundled plan, customers would need to maintain two separate plans. Without any discount for having both.

But the longest section of the note was the explanation. And it wasn't satisfying. It spoke about the company's operations, the company's concerns about the viability of the DVD business, and an internal company reorganization:

> Why the changes?
>
> Last November when we launched our $7.99 unlimited streaming plan, DVDs by mail was treated as a $2 add on to our unlimited streaming plan. At the time, we didn't anticipate offering DVD only plans. Since then we have realized that there is still a very large continuing demand for DVDs both from our existing members as well as non-members. Given the long life we think DVDs by mail will have, treating DVDs as a $2 add on to our unlimited streaming plan neither makes great financial sense nor satisfies people who just want DVDs. Creating an unlimited DVDs by mail plan (no streaming) at our lowest price ever, $7.99, does make sense and will ensure a long life for our DVDs by mail offering. Reflecting our confidence that DVDs by mail is a long-term business for us, we are also establishing a separate and distinct management team solely focused on DVDs by mail, led by Andy Rendich, our Chief Service and Operations Officer and an 11 year veteran of Netflix.
>
> Now we offer a choice: Unlimited Streaming for $7.99 a month, Unlimited DVDs for $7.99 a month, or both for $15.98 a month ($7.99 + $7.99). We think $7.99 is a terrific value for our unlimited streaming plan and $7.99 a terrific value for our unlimited DVD plan. We hope one, or both, of these plans makes sense for our members and their entertainment needs.[14]

What was remarkable about that explanation is that it was all framed from the perspective of the company. Not about customers, or about customer desires, behavior, or preferences. Nothing about customer convenience, ensuring quality service, or broadening the selection. It was all about the internal operations of Netflix and its view of the viability of the DVD business.

It was as if the company didn't care about its customers' likely reaction. There was no acknowledgment of any inconvenience to customers, or even of an all-in price increase. It was an exercise in corporate-speak, not in human connection. And instead of closing with an expression of gratitude for the customer's loyalty, the note simply said,

> As always, our members can easily choose to change or cancel their unlimited streaming plan, unlimited DVD plan, or both by visiting Your Account.[15]

Many chose to cancel. Presented with an apparent take-it-or-leave-it choice, it was easy for customers, especially those who had a negative emotional reaction, to simply click on the link and cancel.

Within hours the blogosphere and Twitter were flooded with customer complaints. The company's own blog saw more than 12,000 comments. Most were very negative. Some were angry, as exemplified in this comment by Aimée Reinhart Avery:

> You've managed to pretty much piss off all your customers, including me! Is this your real plan? If so you're doing a good job. I've decided to become even more friendly with my local Redbox [a competitor that offers DVDs in kiosks at supermarkets]. It may not deliver to my mailbox, but since I have to go to the grocery store to get the popcorn, I'll go ahead and get my movies there too![16]

Some spoke about competitors offering better deals, such as this comment by Craig Harkins:

> Hey Netflix—You just raised my prices 60%.
>
> I'll be giving you some time to fix this before September 1st, but if nothing changes, I will be canceling everything and finding someone else like Amazon to pay. Most of the titles I want to see are only on DVD, so paying that much for streaming, plus that much more for DVD (with no price break for

being a loyal customer and combining the two plans) isn't attractive to me as a consumer.

You have competitors, they are ramping up their offerings, expect to lose a lot of your base soon. (How much are you paying per gross add and net add now? Do you have a big increase in the marketing budget planned to try to acquire enough customers to make up for the churn you'll see from this pricing move?)[17]

And some were in the form of a breakup letter, such as this from Greg Heitzmann:

Dear Netflix,

To say the least, I am shocked and appalled at your recent behavior. It seems like yesterday we were the best of friends. You informed me with your poignant documentaries; I always laughed at your corny B horror flicks. For four years you've been the gracious receptacle of my hard earned money, but alas, your current actions have forced me to reevaluate our relationship. Your nominal price increase, while unexpected, does not deter my loyalty. However, your mouthpiece Jessie Becker's presentation of this upcharge—as an added choice for my own benefit—insults my intelligence and reveals the breadth of your arrogance. Had I been treated like an adult and informed of these changes in a straightforward, honest manner, perhaps we could rekindle our spark. Unfortunately, this course of action is no longer available; your condescending and manipulative tone has irreparably ruined our relationship.

Sincerely,

Your ex-customer[18]

The news media was quick to seize upon the story, with ample coverage of customers' angry reaction. The stock market also reacted. While the stock rose a bit immediately after the announcement, to just about $300 per share, within two months—as investors began to recognize the financial impact of customer defections—the stock had fallen by a third, to $200.

All the while, Netflix was silent, as customers continued to abandon the company in the run-up to the September 1 price increase.

Netflix fell into a trap many companies and leaders often find hard to avoid: It communicated at its stakeholders, not with them. Its leaders saw the world through the perspective of their own operations, and simply conveyed their business decision to stakeholders using their own frame of reference. But that frame of reference almost never succeeds in winning stakeholders' hearts and minds, especially when there's a potentially negative impact on them.

The gifted crisis manager James E. Lukaszewski, in a gem of a book called *Influencing Public Attitudes,* notes that audiences typically don't care about a company's operations. They don't have sympathy for the business challenges or logistical issues a company may face. They care only about the impact on them. Lukaszewski says that audiences don't care because they can't care. Audiences don't know—and don't want or need to know—about a company's internal operations in order to be customers. To get an audience to care, a company and its leaders need to begin with the audience's concerns and then link those concerns to what the company is doing.[19]

For leaders who live and breathe the company's operations, this common-sense observation is hard to grasp. Audiences have their own ideas, their own concerns, their own frames of reference. And if we want to maintain their trust and confidence, we need to start by taking those ideas, concerns, and frames of reference seriously. We can't move them if we don't meet them where they are. But that means knowing where they are, knowing how to meet them there, and then meeting them. But the first step is even caring about where they are.

Netflix didn't meet its customers where they were. Rather, it asked its customers to meet the company where it was. It framed its communication with customers in the voice of the marketing vice president, who spoke about the changes in the service Netflix would provide, and the new pricing, without acknowledging the inconvenience—or even the increased all-in price—to the customers. It was all Logos, no Ethos or Pathos.

In the process, Netflix failed to anticipate the emotional reaction its customers had—both to the price increase and to the manner in which it was conveyed. And Netflix seemed to be blindsided by the anger.

Second Stumble

Netflix was silent for the next two months. Then, on September 18 Netflix customers received an even more curious e-mail, this time from Netflix CEO Reed Hastings. His note was also posted on the company's blog, along with a video version. Mr. Hastings began by acknowledging Netflix's missteps in the July announcement:

> I messed up. I owe you an explanation.
>
> It is clear from the feedback over the past two months that many members felt we lacked respect and humility in the way we announced the separation of DVD and streaming and the price changes. That was certainly not our intent, and I offer my sincere apology.[20]

It was a good beginning. It came from the top of the company. It acknowledged that Netflix was listening to customer feedback. It noted that customers were angry with the company. It started with both Ethos (I messed up) and Pathos (members felt we lacked respect and humility). And his apology seemed (so far) to be sincere.

Then he went on to give an explanation, first about the nature of the July announcement. He noted the need to adapt quickly to a changing market, and made reference to two companies that had been pioneers but had not been able to adapt. One, Borders, had gone out of business earlier that year. His point seemed to be that to continue to survive, Netflix needed to evolve beyond its initial business model. He didn't say it outright, but that was a reasonable interpretation of his explanation:

> Let me explain what we are doing.
>
> For the past five years, my greatest fear at Netflix has been that we wouldn't make the leap from success in DVDs to success in streaming. Most companies that are great at something— like AOL dialup or Borders bookstores—do not become great at new things people want (streaming for us). So we moved quickly into streaming, but I should have personally given you a full explanation of why we are splitting the services and thereby increasing prices. It wouldn't have changed the price increase, but it would have been the right thing to do.[21]

Mr. Hastings noted that the price increase would have been necessary in any event. And he acknowledged his failure to give an appropriate explanation of the reasons. His e-mail continued:

> So here is what we are doing and why.
>
> Many members love our DVD service, as I do, because nearly
> every movie ever made is published on DVD. DVD is a great
> option for those who want the huge and comprehensive selec-
> tion of movies.
>
> I also love our streaming service because it is integrated into
> my TV, and I can watch anytime I want. The benefits of our
> streaming service are really quite different from the benefits
> of DVD by mail. We need to focus on rapid improvement as
> streaming technology and the market evolves, without main-
> taining compatibility with our DVD by mail service.
>
> So we realized that streaming and DVD by mail are really
> becoming two different businesses, with very different cost
> structures, that need to be marketed differently, and we need
> to let each grow and operate independently.[22]

The key new insight in his explanation is the recognition that the
dynamics of the two forms of video delivery—physical DVDs by mail,
and streaming video via the Internet—were diverging into separate
businesses.

But as in the July announcement, the explanation was all about the
company. He didn't explain what he meant by the "need to focus on
rapid improvement as streaming technology and the market evolves,
without maintaining compatibility with our DVD by mail service."
He may have meant the desire to provide faster downloads, greater
selection, greater product variety, or any manner of things customers
might care about. But it seemed to be just more corporate-speak.

But the next three paragraphs went well beyond explaining the
July decision. Rather, they offered a stunning new piece of information. The company would split in two:

> It's hard to write this after over 10 years of mailing DVDs
> with pride, but we think it is necessary: In a few weeks, we
> will rename our DVD by mail service to "Qwikster." We

chose the name Qwikster because it refers to quick delivery. We will keep the name "Netflix" for streaming.

Qwikster will be the same website and DVD service that everyone is used to. It is just a new name, and DVD members will go to qwikster.com to access their DVD queues and choose movies. One improvement we will make at launch is to add a video games upgrade option, similar to our upgrade option for Blu-ray, for those who want to rent Wii, PS3 and Xbox 360 games. Members have been asking for video games for many years, but now that DVD by mail has its own team, we are finally getting it done. Other improvements will follow. A negative of the renaming and separation is that the Qwikster.com and Netflix.com websites will not be integrated.

There are no pricing changes (we're done with that!). If you subscribe to both services you will have two entries on your credit card statement, one for Qwikster and one for Netflix. The total will be the same as your current charges. We will let you know in a few weeks when the Qwikster.com website is up and ready.[23]

Unstated in that explanation "Qwikster.com and Netflix.com websites will not be integrated" was a new wrinkle for those customers who still wanted to maintain both DVD and streaming video service: Not only would they be paying more than previously, but now they would need to log into two separate Web sites and maintain two separate accounts. And the stated reason seemed to be merely the difference in name of the two different delivery options. Customers weighing the inconvenience against the stated reason—the new name—didn't understand how the trade-off benefited them.

Mr. Hastings closed by reaching out to his customers:

I want to acknowledge and thank you for sticking with us, and to apologize again to those members, both current and former, who felt we treated them thoughtlessly.

Both the Qwikster and Netflix teams will work hard to regain your trust. We know it will not be overnight. Actions speak louder than words. But words help people to understand actions.

Respectfully yours,

-Reed Hastings, Co-Founder and CEO, Netflix.[24]

Rather than resolve customer concerns, Mr. Hastings's letter only made matters worse. Although he had apologized for treating customers thoughtlessly in the July announcement, many customers thought this letter was even more thoughtless, and they had an even worse reaction. As in July, this e-mail was framed from the company's perspective: the split between DVDs and streaming were described in language about the company's business model. It didn't acknowledge the impact of the two separate services on customers. Customers were not amused. But Netflix seemed surprised by their reaction.

 From **Warfighting**

We must try to see ourselves through our enemy's eyes in order to anticipate what he will try to do so that we can counteract him.

We must try to see ourselves through our audience's eyes in order to anticipate what the audience will do so that we may adapt our engagement to secure the desired outcome.

The media covered the current wave of customer anger and revisited the initial July backlash, including the fact that hundreds of thousands of customers had canceled their membership.

The next day *Investor's Business Daily* newspaper covered both Netflix customers' anger and its investors' puzzlement. The story, by reporter Patrick Seitz, headlined "Netflix Tries Damage Control; Qwikster Doesn't Help," began, "Netflix on Monday apologized for angering customers over a recent price increase, then turned around and angered them once more by splitting its DVD and streaming video business."[25]

Several days later *New York Times* technology columnist David Pogue captured the mood of his fellow Netflix customers. Mr. Pogue recounted how ten years earlier he had written a column praising Netflix, but how the company's recent stumbles had caused him to reconsider. Writing about his initial praise, he said:

The best part is the conclusion of that column, where I called Netflix "a shining example of a dot-com that's still in business because it's an indisputable consumer win, not just a greed play."

O.K., I stand corrected.[26]

Mr. Pogue then cataloged his and other Netflix customers' disappointment:

In July, Netflix enraged its 25 million customers by abruptly jacking up the price of its DVD plus streaming-movies plan by 60 percent—from $10 a month to $16.

When I wrote about the turnabout, I noted that the most frustrating part was the incomprehensible explanation that Netflix provided…

In any case, Netflix subscribers were furious. In a matter of weeks, one million of them canceled their memberships.

So a few days ago, Reed Hastings, Netflix's chief executive, sent Netflix members an e-mail message that got off to a good start. Mine read:

"Dear David, I messed up. I owe you an explanation.

"It is clear from the feedback over the past two months that many members felt we lacked respect and humility in the way we announced the separation of DVD and streaming and the price changes. That was certainly not our intent, and I offer my sincere apology. Let me explain what we are doing."

Ah. O.K., good. We've seen this movie before. Corporation bumbles, apologizes, makes things right. Business schools take note. Life goes on.

But this time, Mr. Hastings did not follow the formula. He only pretended to.[27]

Mr. Pogue then highlighted the customer service consequences of splitting the DVD service into Qwikster and the streaming service into Netflix: the need to visit two separate Web sites, maintain two accounts, pay two separate credit card bills; view separate movie catalogs; deal with two different order lists—in other words, lots of inconvenience for the customer, all the while costing more.[28]

Mr. Pogue closed his column by criticizing Netflix's leadership:

I confess: I'm utterly baffled.

At why Netflix, long hailed for its masterfully gracious customer focus, has suddenly become tone-deaf to the effects of its clumsy elephant-in-a-china-shop maneuvers.

At the reasons behind all of these shenanigans. Yes, of course, fewer people use DVDs, but come on, they haven't all fallen off a cliff simultaneously.

At why Mr. Hastings thinks it helps to say "I messed up" without actually making things right. That's one of the hollowest apologies I've ever heard. It's lip service. It's like the politician who says, "I'm sorry you feel that way." You're not sorry—in fact, you're still insisting that you're right.

In the end, though, what makes me unhappiest is how calculated all of this feels....

Yes, Mr. Hastings, you did mess up. Twice.[29]

Netflix's stock fell on the news. It had been at $300 just after the July announcement; it was at $233 on September 1. By October 1 it had fallen to $113. In other words, Netflix stock had lost nearly two-thirds of its market value since the July announcement.

Yet Another Stumble?

Then on October 10, just three weeks after announcing the split, a chastened Reed Hastings sent an e-mail to customers (also posted on the company blog). It was not expansive; it offered little explanation or apology. But in it Mr. Hastings reversed course. The very brief e-mail began:

It is clear that for many of our members two websites would make things more difficult, so we are going to keep Netflix as one place to go for streaming and DVDs.

This means no change: one website, one account, one password...in other words, no Qwikster.

While the July price change was necessary, we are now done with price changes.[30]

There was then a single paragraph about increases in the offerings of several movie and TV production studios.[31] Mr. Hastings closed with this:

We value our members, and we are committed to making Netflix the best place to get movies & TV shows.

Thank you.

-Reed[32]

The move was welcomed by some customers, such as Lori Burelle, who posted a comment about Mr. Hastings's post:

Finally, someone at Netflix listened to reason and to the customers. I was telling my mom yesterday that I was going to cancel after a 6 year relationship. Now it looks like I will be staying, at least for now.[33]

But for some customers, such as Alison Green, it was too late:

Was customer discontent with the prospect of 2 separate sites really a surprise? It seems like it could have been easily anticipated by anyone who understands how people use the service. Kind of disconcerting that the company didn't figure this out BEFORE making the initial announcement (and before I canceled my DVD subscription in disgust, something I will not reverse at this point).[34]

But there was also anger at Mr. Hastings, such as from Geoffrey Sperl, who canceled his membership in favor of a much more expensive alternative:

Sorry, Reed...you've already screwed yourself in my eyes (the account was cancelled on Friday and I've already re-subscribed to cable) and I'm echoing what the others said: It's time for you to go. You're no [Apple, Inc. CEO] Steve Jobs, and this sort of flip-flopping is bad for your customers, your employees, and your stockholders.[35]

Balaji Krishnapuram was among many who posted an explicit call for Mr. Hastings to go:

It's time to fire Reed Hastings. Here's a great way to destroy a company:

1. Infuriate customers by nearly doubling prices at one shot.

2. Make sure that significant numbers leave. If they still did not leave because of the price hike, well, kick them out by giving them even less value for the same $ (e.g., they have to maintain separate lists of movies in their queue).

3. Watch the share price drop like a rock.

4. Reverse the decision with a major PR fiasco that broadcasts the total lack of leadership.[36]

The stock would continue its slide, and close at $78 in late October, and under $70 in late November, from $300 just after the July 12 announcement. In other words, a loss of market value of nearly 75 percent. And the defection of more than a million customers. And some meaningful resentment and mistrust among many remaining customers.

Restraining the Imperious Executive

Netflix's self-inflicted harm came from failure to take stakeholder concerns seriously. In the tone and content they seemed not to care about customers' reactions, not even to have anticipated the anger. The communications—directed to millions of customers—seemed to have been dashed off on the spot, without consideration of alternative ways to engage customers, to write from the point of view of customers.

Leaders are particularly prone to seeing the world from the perspective of their own organization, and to fail to consider—or to dismiss as irrelevant—the concerns of stakeholders. This is an occupational hazard that needs to be acknowledged and managed. *The Wall Street Journal*'s "Business World" columnist Holman Jenkins gave such advice to his readers, when he admonished:

> Organizations need defenses against their charismatic leaders. Otherwise such individuals can too readily bully or seduce others into supporting their vainglorious illusions.[37]

I've taught this principle to students and clients since it was first articulated by Mr. Jenkins in 1998. Among the vainglorious illusions leaders often harbor—whether they're CEOs or religious leaders or politicians—is that they don't need to take stakeholder concerns seriously. But they do. At least if they want to establish long-term trust and confidence. And sometimes if they even want to keep their jobs.

Consider Robert Nardelli's experience at Home Depot. If Netflix's customers thought the CEO didn't care, Home Depot's investors thought the CEO was outright hostile towards them.

In the 1990s Bob Nardelli was a superstar of corporate leadership, one of the top contenders to succeed Jack Welch at General Electric. Mr. Welch once called him, "the best operational executive I've ever met."[38] When Mr. Welch announced his pending retirement in 2000, he identified three potential successors: Mr. Nardelli, then head of GE Power Systems; Jim McNerney, head of GE Aircraft; and Jeff Immelt, head of GE Healthcare.[39]

Mr. Immelt got the job, and remains GE CEO to this day. Jim McNerney left to run Minnesota-based 3M and now is CEO of Boeing, Inc.

Minutes after Mr. Nardelli was told he wouldn't get the top GE job, he got a phone call from a GE director who was also chairman of Home Depot. Ken Langone had bankrolled Home Depot's rise to second place, behind Wal-Mart, in American retail. He is sometimes credited as a co-founder. In 1978 he organized the financing for Bernard Marcus and Arthur Blank, the actual co-founders, to start the company. Mr. Langone knew that Mr. Nardelli had just lost out on the top GE position. He told him,

> You probably could not feel worse right now. But you've just been hit in the ass with a golden horseshoe. And I've got the horseshoe.[40]

By early December 2000, Bob Nardelli was chief executive officer of Home Depot. He inherited a company with a freewheeling, customer-focused culture. Store managers enjoyed great freedom with little oversight. It was sometimes referred to as a "cowboy" culture.

Mr. Nardelli launched three initiatives that each put great stress on the company, its culture, and, ultimately, its investors: centralization, cost containment, and diversification.

He centralized operations and disempowered store managers. For example, he collapsed nine regional purchasing departments into one unit, based in the company's Atlanta headquarters. He placed a human resources manager, selected in Atlanta, in each store. He reduced the number of employee evaluation forms across the company from 157 to 2. In other words, he moved the company from a place with significant autonomy and replaced it with a command-and-control culture. The changes caused resistance among the workforce. At the company's 2003 annual shareholder meeting some workers were on hand to cheer him on, but the tensions in the workplace never fully resolved themselves.

Mr. Nardelli undertook significant cost-containment initiatives. He replaced full-time tradesmen (plumbers, carpenters, etc.) walking the floor of Home Depot stores with part-time salespeople. He introduced self-checkout lanes. He abandoned Home Depot's very popular no-receipt, no-time-limit, cash refund policy. And he introduced Six Sigma, the dominant management discipline at GE.

The effect on customers was pronounced. Co-founders Bernie Marcus and Arthur Blank had walked the floor of Home Depot stores preaching that employees should "make love to the customers." Under Mr. Nardelli's cost cutting, the love was nowhere to be found. Customer service complaints skyrocketed as the quality of salespeople's advice and service declined. Rivals, such as the newer and often more tidy Lowe's, attracted customers who left Home Depot.

Employees also bristled under increasing pressure and decreasing autonomy. The introduction of Six Sigma plus the arrival at corporate headquarters of former GE executives into Mr. Nardelli's inner circle led some employees to call the company "Home GEpot."

But it was Mr. Nardelli's diversification strategy that proved most controversial. He sought to expand Home Depot's market by expanding both its customer base and its product offerings. Home Depot entered the market for large home appliances such as stoves, refrigerators, and washing machines. It developed service businesses, such as home installation and repair, a shift from the do-it-yourself model to a we-do-it-for-you model. But most significantly, he expanded into the business of contractor services, providing large-volume materials for construction sites, marketing not to the do-it-yourself home market but to the professional builder market.

The three initiatives led to some success. By 2006 revenues had nearly doubled, and profit margins rose significantly. But the stock didn't keep pace. In fact, it underperformed the Standard & Poor's index. From the time Mr. Nardelli took office to the time of the 2006 annual meeting, Home Depot stock had fallen by 6 percent. That of arch rival Lowe's had risen by 173 percent.

Analysts expressed concern about Home Depot wandering away from its core business into areas it didn't know well. They were also concerned about Mr. Nardelli's compensation. Even as the stock remained flat for the period of his tenure, he received outsized compensation. In early 2006 the *New York Times* calculated his compensation over the previous five years as more than $245 million.[41] Investors' grumbling got louder as the 2006 annual meeting approached.

Typically, companies' annual meetings follow a ritual. The board of directors usually is in town for a board meeting, and all or most of the board members stick around for the meeting. There's usually a company overview by the CEO, followed by questions from shareholders. And shareholders are asked to vote on major matters of governance, such as the election of directors, the appointment of auditors, or various corporate policies. But the 2006 Home Depot meeting would be different.

The meeting was scheduled for May 25, 2006. Investors were already in a foul mood. In February Home Depot had slipped to last place in customer satisfaction among major American retail stores, according to the annual University of Michigan Consumer Satisfaction Index.[42]

A week before the meeting the company announced that it would no longer disclose same-store sales, a crucial metric of revenue growth for retail establishments.[43] It is one of the first pieces of data investors look for to determine the health of a retail company. Home Depot argued that its diversification made same-store sales reporting less relevant than it used to be. Analysts objected. Some called the move "curious," "strange," "irresponsible," and even "highly suspect." They wondered whether the company was trying to cover up or paper over fundamental weaknesses in their retail stores. Others argued that Mr. Nardelli was converting Home Depot from a customer-focused retailer into a diversified, low-margin, business-to-business company similar to what Mr. Nardelli had left at General Electric.

Two days before the meeting, the *New York Times* profiled Mr. Nardelli's compensation. It also predicted a showdown at the Wilmington, Delaware, annual meeting.[44] Investor groups, angry about the CEO's compensation and the poor stock performance, wanted to vote on the board's compensation committee report. They also urged that shareholders withhold their votes for two nominated directors, as a protest over Mr. Nardelli's pay. They planned a rally outside the meeting hall. Institutional Shareholder Services, which advises large investors, told the *Times* that there was a disconnect between Mr. Nardelli's compensation and investors. In a report to its clients two weeks before the meeting, ISS had said,

> ...poor compensation design, a lucrative employment agreement, and arguably egregious compensation practices call into question the fitness of the company's Compensation Committee members to serve as directors.[45]

Emotions were running high. Attendees arriving at the hotel and conference center in Wilmington were greeted by the spectacle of picketers dressed in chicken suits, chanting, "Hey Bob, why are you chicken, while your stock price takes a lickin'?"

This annual meeting was different from most others. To start, except for executives, there were no board members in attendance. This was virtually unprecedented. Charles Elson, a corporate governance expert at the University of Delaware, told the *New York Times*, "Your one obligation as a director is to show up at the annual meeting. The fact that the directors didn't show up is disgusting."[46]

Investors had more disgust ahead of them.

Mr. Nardelli convened the meeting promptly at 10 AM. Rather than the traditional year-in-review corporate overview, Mr. Nardelli began the meeting by moving straight to the election of directors. He announced that questions would be limited to one minute per person. The time limit was reinforced by two large digital countdown timers on the stage. This was also extremely rare.

The first questioner expressed concerns about possible conflicts of interest on the board. He asked, "What steps will the board take to address these conflicts?" Mr. Nardelli dismissed the question. "This is not the forum in which to address these comments," he told the shareholder.[47]

A shareholder asked a question about the nominated directors. "If the candidates are up for election, can we be introduced to them?" Mr. Nardelli said, "They are not in attendance today." The shareholder responded, "I think it is absolutely outrageous that the board is not here. The board is too chicken to face the shareholders." As he spoke, the timer hit zero and his microphone was shut off.[48]

After ten minutes, the question period ended and the meeting turned to the consideration of shareholder proposals. Proponents were given three minutes to explain their motions. The first proposal was that shareholders be allowed an advisory vote on executive pay. The shareholder bringing the motion outlined the reasons. Mr. Nardelli said only, "The board recommends you reject this proposal."[49]

The meeting continued in a similar vein.

One shareholder stood to discuss his proposal that the roles of CEO and chairman be split, but took the occasion to criticize Mr. Nardelli's handling of the meeting. "I love Home Depot. I came here wanting to buy more stock. But I'm totally offended by the way you are conducting this meeting. Are we even going to have an opportunity to ask questions?" Mr. Nardelli declined to answer. The shareholder said, "If this is the way you are conducting this meeting, I can see why GE didn't pick you." Mr. Nardelli said simply, "The board recommends you reject this proposal."[50]

After all eight proposals had been made, Mr. Nardelli called for a vote, and declared the outcome before all ballots were counted and without telling shareholders what the vote totals were or how the shareholder proposals did.

The meeting was adjourned at 10:37 AM. There had been no substantive interaction between the company's management and investors and no introduction of directors (who had been absent). Only procedural, formalistic interaction that was widely seen to be rude, or worse.

New York Times business columnist Joe Nocera, a seasoned annual meeting observer, had been at the meeting. He summarized the shareholders' reactions:

> Afterward, the words on people's mouths are "appalling," "disgraceful" and "arrogant." I would add one more: contemptuous. I'm sure there are plenty of boards and chief executives who have contempt for their shareholders, but most of them are at least smart enough to keep it to themselves. On Thursday morning, in Wilmington, Del., Mr. Nardelli and the Home Depot board let the world know exactly how it feels about the people for whom they are supposed to work.

> One more thing: late yesterday, Home Depot issued a statement that said in part, "While we understand that the approach we took to the annual meeting was a departure from past practice, it should in no way be construed as either a lack of respect for our shareholders or a lessening of our commitment to high standards of corporate governance and transparency."

> Apparently, Mr. Nardelli and the Home Depot board think their shareholders are stupid, too.[51]

The meeting set Home Depot shareholders on a path directly opposed to Mr. Nardelli's continued tenure as CEO. Patrick McGurn, executive vice president of Institutional Shareholder Services, said, "You didn't hear anything close to the level of anger being discussed about Home Depot before the meeting that you did afterward."[52]

A week after the meeting, Mr. Nardelli promised that annual meetings would revert to their prior format. In a statement he declared:

> Consistent with the way we run our company—in which we listen, learn and lead—we will return to our traditional format for next year's annual shareholders meeting, which will

include a business overview, the presentation of proposals, an opportunity for shareholder questions and with the board of directors in attendance.[53]

That still left the issue of compensation. Later in June the board's compensation committee asked Mr. Nardelli to reconsider his pay. Mr. Nardelli offered to relinquish a few perquisites of his job—such as personal use of Home Depot's fleet of six private jets. But he refused to budge on his direct compensation, including his $3 million annual "guaranteed bonus."[54]

Shareholder Relational Investors made an aggressive proposal to the Home Depot board to consider "strategic alternatives"—generally understood to mean selling the company or breaking up the parts and selling them off.

Throughout the rest of the year, the board and Mr. Nardelli went back and forth over compensation. By early January 2007, the relationship was no longer tenable, and Mr. Nardelli agreed to leave the company. But the price of his departure was a severance package of $210 million. For his six years at Home Depot, Mr. Nardelli made nearly half a billion dollars. U.S. House of Representatives Financial Services Committee chairman Barney Frank (D-MA) said that Mr. Nardelli's package was proof that executive compensation was "out of control."[55] Other commentators called the golden parachute "disgusting," "outrageous," and "highway robbery."

Mr. Nardelli was succeeded by his vice chairman and executive vice president, Frank Blake. He too was a GE veteran, but his style was dramatically different from Mr. Nardelli's. He was a consensus builder who listened to the concerns of others. And his compensation was dramatically lower than Mr. Nardelli's. Investment analyst Stephanie Hoff, at the brokerage firm Edward Jones, said that there was only one difference that mattered: "Blake is not Nardelli."[56]

Every year the consulting firm Booz Allen Hamilton (now known as Booz & Company) publishes a study on CEO succession. That year the Booz study concluded:

Bob Nardelli's dismissal from Home Depot was driven by his failure to hear and respond to investors' concerns—very much the actions of an imperial CEO. These concerns included the erosion of the company's competitive position against its chief rival…and his strategy of expanding into a lower-margin, non-retail business, as well as his refusal to answer shareholder questions.[57]

Taking stakeholders seriously is not easy. But failure to do so is a critical failure of leadership.

Bill Gates, at DECWorld, focused completely on the perspective of his audience in rejecting the advice of the host company on what to say. He knew that he needed to connect with them. And they reacted positively.

Netflix, in its initial communication, and in its two CEO communications, seemed completely indifferent to the points of view of its customers. Customers reacted negatively to each of the three communications. And the company suffered significantly, if in no other way than in losing two-thirds of its market value in three months.

Home Depot's board and CEO didn't merely seem indifferent to shareholders. They seemed outright hostile. The CEO was not merely disrespectful of shareholders and their legitimate concerns and expectations. He seemed to be in conflict with them, and behaved and spoke in a manner certain to insult. His 2006 annual meeting was not only a defining moment for him, but a defining moment in shareholders' flexing their muscles. And he was out of a job soon thereafter (insulting even as he left, with an oversized severance package).

Orienting on the Audience

Taking stakeholders seriously requires respecting the point of view of those whom we would engage. It requires curiosity about what matters to them, about what it takes to win them over and to keep their trust and confidence.

From Warfighting

Maneuver warfare attacks the enemy "system."
We should try to "get inside" the enemy's thought processes and
see the enemy as he sees himself so that we can set him up for
defeat.

> *Effective communication focuses on the audience's worldview.*
> *We should try to "get inside" the audience's thought processes*
> *and see the audience as it sees itself.*

Audience Engagement Checklist

Effective leaders connect with audiences by understanding what matters to them, and by speaking in ways that resonate with them.

Bill Gates did so intuitively.

It's also possible to do so intentionally. Here's a simple checklist with three sets of questions for leaders to understand an audience.

Audience Checklist

Over the years, I have used the following checklist with clients and students to help them assess their own level of understanding and readiness to engage stakeholders. Coupled with strategic communication planning (see Chapter 6, "Goals, Strategies, and Tactics: Preparing and Planning"), understanding the audience is critical for leaders to inspire trust and confidence. For any given stakeholder group, a leader should seek to understand three basic things, by asking three basic categories of questions:

1. What do we know about the group?

   An inventory of current knowledge

2. How does the group work?

   Grounding to predict behavior

3. How does the group relate to us?

   The link between audiences and outcomes

Mastering these three categories of consideration is a good starting point to communicate effectively.

1. **The group**

   Which stakeholder group(s) matter(s)?

   What do we know about the group's values, experiences, and level of sophistication?

   What don't we know that we should?

2. **The group's behavior**

   What are the group's hopes, aspirations, and desires?

   What are the group's worries, concerns, and fears?

   How does the group (or its individual members) make decisions?

3. **The group's relationship to us**

   What does the group currently do, think, feel, or know in relation to us?

   What changes in the group's actions, thoughts, feelings, or knowledge would benefit our goals?

   What are the opportunities and barriers for those changes to take place?

Effective leaders consider these questions, whether formally or informally. Bill Gates clearly did when he rejected the proposed remarks developed by DEC and his own staff, and formulated his own speech. It was a smart move. The audience reacted as Mr. Gates hoped it would: with enthusiasm about partnering with him and Microsoft.

Netflix seemed not to have considered the questions at all, and instead spoke only from the point of view of its own. It seemed indifferent to the predictable concerns of its customers, and unprepared for the audience's negative emotional reaction.

And Home Depot seemed to have not considered the questions and seemed to go out of its way to provoke an angry reaction.

Recap: Best Practices from This Chapter

 From Warfighting

It is essential that we understand the audience on its own terms. We should not assume that every audience thinks as we do, decides as we do, or has the same values, goals, or concerns as we do.

We must try to see ourselves through our audience's eyes in order to anticipate what the audience will do so that we may adapt our engagement to secure the desired outcome.

Effective communication focuses on the audience's worldview. We should try to "get inside" the audience's thought processes and see the audience as it sees itself.

Lessons for Leaders and Communicators

Taking audiences seriously is hard work. It requires intentionality, empathy, and sometimes courage. It is a leadership discipline.

Many leaders, much of the time, tend to see the world from the point of view of their own operations, and are unaware of any other way to see the world. They suffer from the curse of knowledge—where they know so much about their topic that they can't conceive of people not knowing what they're talking about. But audiences don't see the world in the same way as organizations do. They don't care about internal operations, and don't need to in order to be in relation with a company or its leaders. But they do care about how the organization can affect them, positively or negatively.

The leadership discipline of taking audiences seriously is to frame all interaction in ways that resonate with an audience. It requires Logos—facts, reasoning, argument, and data. But it also requires Ethos—some element of personal character or experience that connects the speaker to the audience. And it requires Pathos—initially as passion on the part of the speaker, but fundamentally the triggering of an emotional reaction with the audience. Done well, the Pathos can be positive: enthusiasm, support, trust, confidence. Done poorly, the Pathos can be negative: anger, mistrust, a feeling of betrayal, leading ultimately to disengagement of the audience from the leader.

3

Words Aren't Enough

In late August 2005, the communities along the Gulf of Mexico coast braced themselves for the big one: a hurricane of potentially devastating destructive power. Hurricane Katrina had passed through the Caribbean and touched the tip of Key West. Now it had stalled in the warm waters of the Gulf, picking up energy and gathering strength.

On Saturday, August 27, as the storm hovered, Louisiana Governor Kathleen Blanco asked President George W. Bush to declare her state a disaster area, and forwarded to the federal government formal requests for assistance and supplies.[1]

At 5:30 AM Sunday, August 28, the U.S. Federal Emergency Management Agency (FEMA) issued a National Situation Report. It noted that Hurricane Katrina was likely to turn north into Louisiana. The report said:

> Katrina could be especially devastating if it strikes New Orleans because the city sits below sea level and is dependent on levees and pumps to keep the water out. A direct hit could wind up submerging the city in several feet of water. Making matters worse, at least 100,000 people in the city lack the transportation to get out of town.[2]

That morning New Orleans Mayor Ray Nagin ordered citizens to evacuate the city.[3] It was the first time in the city's history that a mandatory evacuation order was given, and neither the residents nor the city quite knew how to do it. The city had buses available, but many bus drivers evacuated themselves, abandoning their buses. Residents were left to their own devices. Many, especially the poor, sick, and elderly, did not have the means or ability to leave. Others stayed behind to take care of those who couldn't leave. Despite the evacuation order, there were still about 100,000 people in New Orleans on Sunday night. About 25,000 moved to higher ground such as the Superdome stadium, where enough food to feed 15,000 for three days had been prepositioned. But many remained in low-lying areas.

That day President Bush went on television to reassure the citizens of New Orleans and the surrounding areas. He said, "We will do everything in our power to help the people and the communities affected by the storm."[4] FEMA Director Michael Brown also reassured the public: "FEMA is not going to hesitate at all in this storm. We're going to move fast, we're going to move quick, we're going to do whatever it takes to help disaster victims."[5]

These were the right things to say. But simply saying them was not enough. Regrettably, both FEMA and the larger U.S. government, having set those expectations, spent the next week dramatically underdelivering on them. As the horror that New Orleans experienced unfolded over the next few days, the government's lack of effective action, and the disconnect between the rhetoric and the work, became a defining moment for the President and his Administration.

Walk the Talk

 *From* **Warfighting**

It is important to recognize that many political problems cannot be solved by military means. Some can, but rarely as anticipated. War tends to take its own course as it unfolds.

> *It is important to recognize that many business problems cannot be solved by communication means. Some can, but rarely as anticipated. Communication tends to take its own course as it unfolds.*

Carl von Clausewitz influenced generations of uniformed and civilian military leaders through his Principle of the Objective: "War is the continuation of policy by other means. The political end is the goal, and war is the means of accomplishing it, and means can never be considered in isolation from their purposes."[6]

Means can never be considered in isolation from their purposes. In my teaching and consulting I pound that idea into my students' and clients' ways of thinking. The confusion of ends and means has potentially catastrophic consequences, whether in war or in government or in business.

And as *Warfighting* notes, war isn't the solution to every political problem. It may be the continuation of policy by other means, but it is not the sole means by which policy outcomes can be attained.

I translate Clausewitz's Principle of the Objective as follows: Communication is the continuation of business by other means. The business objective (or in the case of government or not-for-profit, the organizational objective) is the overriding goal, and communication is merely one of the means of achieving it. And means can never be considered in isolation from their purposes. Just as war is not the sole means by which policy outcomes can be met, communication is not the sole means by which business or organizational outcomes can be achieved.

In the case of New Orleans, the organizational objectives were articulated by the President and the FEMA director: Help the people and communities affected by the storm. At the very basic level this consists of saving lives. It also includes getting people to safety, providing them with emergency relief in the form of food, shelter, and medical care. And over the longer term, helping them rebuild and recover.

Much of my work is in the world of crisis. Of things going wrong. One of the key principles of crisis management is that every crisis is a business problem before it's a communication problem. And you can't communicate your way out of a business problem.

But all too often, especially in a crisis, leaders assume that saying the right thing is enough. It isn't.

Communication is merely one of the ways to fulfill a business or organizational goal. But it is one of many means. By itself it is rarely sufficient to accomplish most organizational goals. Rather, I tend to think of communication as what the military calls a force multiplier: It helps you do more, better, faster than you otherwise would be able to do. Effective communication can help accomplish any particular purpose better, and faster, and with fewer resources. But however effective, it must be paired with action that is consistent with what is said. This was the singular failure of the U.S. government in the aftermath of the flooding of New Orleans.

Hurricane Katrina, New Orleans, and the U.S. Government

In Hurricane Katrina the U.S. government initially said all the right things. And the President, FEMA director, and Homeland Security secretary continued to say reassuring things in the early days of the disaster. Had they delivered on the expectations they themselves set, it would have been a positive defining moment. But in the end it seemed to be all talk, without action to back it up.

Recall also the principles from Chapter 1, "Words Matter": Communication should be framed in order to provoke a particular reaction, and continuing communication should adapt based on that reaction. We saw neither of these principles taken seriously in the federal government's response to Hurricane Katrina. Rather, as the situation got worse and worse, and as the government began to be blamed for not taking the steps it had promised to take, government leaders continued to offer increasingly hollow reassurances.

Overnight, Sunday to Monday: Katrina Strikes

In the overnight hours of Sunday into Monday, August 29, New Orleans residents' fears came true. At 6:10 AM Hurricane Katrina made landfall, with winds of 130 miles per hour. The eye passed nearly directly over New Orleans and created a massive storm surge on Lake Pontchartrain, a form of tidal wave that wiped out lakeside communities outside of New Orleans. (I was in New Orleans two weeks later as part of a corporate recovery effort. I saw boats on the rooftops of houses and in the high branches of trees—testament to the size and power of the storm surge.)

Inside the city, the levees that kept New Orleans dry were breached, and about 80 percent of New Orleans flooded. That morning a FEMA staff member on a U.S. Coast Guard helicopter took a photograph of the city under water, with large portions of the levee on the Industrial Canal missing. The photograph, which was not initially made public, showed submerged homes with only the roofs visible above the water.

Monday: New Orleans Under Water

On Monday morning, August 29, Day One of the flood, the national media had yet to arrive in New Orleans. Most of the coverage was of helicopter flyovers, of evacuees, and of government officials assuring the public that all that could be done was being done.

On Monday evening the Assistant Secretary for Public Affairs at FEMA's parent government department, the Department of Homeland Security (DHS), sent a note to his boss, DHS Chief of Staff John Woods. The e-mail, from a Blackberry handheld device, was headed "FYI from FEMA." It advised that the head of public affairs at FEMA had called to report on the current situation. The e-mail noted, "[She] said the first (unconfirmed) reports they are getting from aerial surveys in New Orleans are far more severe than media reports are currently reflecting. Finding extensive flooding and more stranded people than they had thought—also a number of fires."[7]

So situational awareness at FEMA and its parent department was high: Both had an explicit understanding of the severity of the damage inside New Orleans. But throughout the first 24 hours there was little visible FEMA or other government mobilization inside the city. The National Guard barracks in New Orleans had flooded, and the guardsmen there, who would have been expected to help with rescues, spent the first 24 hours of the flood trying to rescue themselves. Mayor Nagin later said that for the first few days after the flood there were at most only 250 National Guard troops in New Orleans.[8]

During a Monday press conference with state and local officials, FEMA Director Brown gave little indication that the response was less than sufficient. Rather, he boasted that things were going well: "What I've seen here is a team that is very tightknit, working very closely together, being very professional, and in my humble opinion making the right calls."[9] It didn't ring true. The news media juxtaposed his statements with the apparent absence of help for those who were still desperately in need. Five weeks later, on the Public Broadcasting Service documentary program *Frontline*, Mr. Brown admitted that he had lied in that Monday press conference, ostensibly to avoid panic. In the *Frontline* interview Mr. Brown defended his lie by disparaging the state and local officials whom he had praised during the press conference. He told *Frontline*, "I'm not going to go on television and publicly say that I think that the mayor and the governor are not doing their job, that they don't have a sense of urgency. I'm not going to do that publicly."[10]

That evening President Bush declared the states of Louisiana and Mississippi national disaster areas.[11] Theoretically, that declaration set the stage for greater federal presence.

Tuesday: The Reality Sets In

By Tuesday the national news media had arrived in force and was broadcasting 24/7 from New Orleans, some correspondents waist-deep in murky water. And one of the recurring themes was the absence of a visible federal presence. The U.S. Coast Guard was continuing to evacuate victims stranded on rooftops, but the Coast Guard alone didn't have enough helicopters or other resources to do all that was necessary. The media showed dozens of bodies floating in the water. They would continue showing progressively more-bloated bodies in the water for days to come.

Inside the flooded city there was no electricity, no safe drinking water, and very little law and order. Spontaneous fights broke out over scarce resources. Commentators began juxtaposing what they saw with the two statements from before the flood: President Bush's assurance that the government would do everything in its power, and

Director Brown's assurance that FEMA would move swiftly to help those affected. There was scant evidence of either.

Wednesday: The Situation Is Dire; Government Seems Not to Get It

By Wednesday, August 31, Day Three of the flood, the situation on the ground had deteriorated. There was still very little government presence. Many people were still stranded without food, water, medicine, or other help. The news media showed scenes of people in desperation: A young man holding a baby: "How's a three-month-old infant supposed to survive out here with no milk, no water?" A distraught woman: "I don't want to die like this."[12]

President Bush had been on vacation in his Crawford, Texas, home when the hurricane hit. He continued his pre-Katrina schedule, including a Monday–Tuesday trip to the West Coast for a fundraiser and to give speeches on Medicare. Wednesday he left Crawford for Washington, but directed Air Force One to fly over New Orleans for him to get a firsthand look. But rather than landing in New Orleans, the plane circled above the city at 5,000 feet. People on the ground, including the news media, could recognize the distinctive profile of the President's Boeing 747, with United States of America painted on the side. Television cameras focused alternately on people transfixed by the sight, and on the profile of the plane as it slowly looped around the city. Then they watched the plane fly away. It was a metaphor for abandonment, and was reported that way.

In Washington the President spoke to the media and offered reassurance: "The National Guard has nearly 11,000 guardsmen on state active duty to assist governors and local officials with security and disaster response efforts."[13] That may have been a true statement. But the implication was that the 11,000 were in New Orleans. In fact, much of the Louisiana National Guard at the time was in Iraq, along with much of its equipment. New Orleans Mayor Ray Nagin later told *Frontline*, "The National Guard was not on the ground."[14] The President also said, "FEMA is moving supplies and equipment into the hardest-hit areas."[15] New Orleans was considered among the hardest-hit areas, but the news media reported that there was no evidence of FEMA moving supplies and equipment to people who needed it.

From Warfighting

We should base our decisions on awareness *rather than on mechanical* habit. *Rather, we must act on a keen appreciation for the essential factors that make each situation unique instead of from a conditioned response.*

The more the President tried to reassure, the more the media focused on the inconsistency between his statements and the reality they were seeing in New Orleans.

On Wednesday the media covered not only the lack of a FEMA presence on the ground, but also how FEMA prevented or stalled potential aid from other sources. CNN later reported incidents in which FEMA in fact hindered efforts to provide aid for those in need in New Orleans. For example, a 14-car caravan arranged by the sheriff of Loudoun County, Virginia, carrying supplies of water and food, was not allowed into the city. FEMA stopped tractor-trailers carrying water to the supply staging area in Alexandria, Louisiana, because they did not have the necessary paperwork. CNN also reported that during the weekend before the flood, Mayor Nagin had made a call for firefighters to help with rescue operations. But as firefighters from across the country arrived to help victims, they were first sent to Atlanta for a daylong training program in community relations and sexual harassment. When they arrived in New Orleans, the volunteer firefighters were permitted only to give out flyers with the FEMA telephone numbers, but were forbidden from engaging in rescue operations. The media reported not only the resentment felt by the first responders, but also how FEMA's policies hurt those people who were begging for aid in New Orleans.[16]

That day Homeland Security Secretary Michael Chertoff held a press conference in which he said, "We are extremely pleased with the response of every element of the federal government, all of our federal partners, have made to this terrible tragedy."[17] That got people's attention. How could he be extremely pleased with what by all accounts was an inadequate and disorganized response? Perhaps he was mistaken about the nature of the response. Worse, perhaps he knew the response was inadequate, but chose to lie about it, as his FEMA director had. But another alternative began to creep into the news coverage. Commentators contrasted the weak Katrina response to other catastrophes, and noted that the primary difference seemed to be the demographics of the people involved: The residents of New Orleans, especially those trapped in the flood, were overwhelmingly black and poor. Could it be that Secretary Chertoff was telling the truth when he said that he was extremely pleased with the federal response? By Wednesday commentators, New Orleans residents, and prominent African-American politicians and leaders had already begun to give voice to this interpretation. But as the next few days unfolded, it became more and more a prevalent view in mainstream news coverage.

Thursday: Things Fall Apart

On Thursday, September 1, the disconnect between what the government said and what it was perceived to be doing came to a head. President Bush, back in the White House, conducted a television interview in which he justified the government's apparent inability to deal with the flood: "I don't think anybody anticipated the breach of the levees."[18] In fact, a breach in the levees had been expected for years by many experts and government agencies, most recently by FEMA on Sunday morning.

New Orleans Mayor Ray Nagin spoke on a local radio station and expressed deep frustration, both with the lack of federal response and with the rosy picture federal officials were offering the public. He scolded the federal government: "I don't want to see anyone do any more goddammed press conferences. Put a moratorium on press conferences. Don't tell me forty thousand people are coming here. They're not here!"[19]

Over the previous few days the news media had reported that thousands of people had taken refuge in the New Orleans convention center since Monday. But by Thursday there was still little government presence there: no food, water, medicine, or FEMA staff. FEMA Director Brown did a series of television interviews in which he admitted that FEMA had been unaware of the people at the convention center.

Brian Williams on NBC asked, "Where is the aid? It's the question people keep asking us on camera." Mr. Brown replied, "Brian, it's an absolutely fair question. And I've got to tell you, from the bottom of my heart, how sad I feel for those people. The federal government just learned about those people today."[20] An incredulous Paula Zahn on ABC asked, "Sir, you're not telling me you just learned that the people at the convention center didn't have food and water until today, are you? You had no idea they were completely cut off?" Mr. Brown answered, "Paula, the federal government didn't know about the convention center people until today."[21] Soledad O'Brien on CNN told Mr. Brown, "I don't understand how FEMA cannot have this information." He replied, "Soledad, I learned about it listening to the news reports."[22] A clearly frustrated Ted Koppel on ABC's *Nightline* asked, "Don't you guys watch television, don't you listen to the radio? Our reporters have been reporting about it for more than just today." Mr. Brown responded, without explanation, "We learned about it factually today, that that's what existed."[23] As a result of the saturation coverage, by evening Mr. Brown was a laughingstock, held up by late-night comedians as an emblem of incompetence.

That day, the President's former communications director, then serving as Counselor to the President, urged him to watch a DVD of recent news coverage—apparently the first time the President had seen what the media was reporting.

Friday: The President Steps Up But Misfires

On Friday morning, Day Five, President Bush flew to the Gulf. But when the President landed, things went sour. First, he spoke what became a defining sound bite of his presidency. President Bush met with relief officials in the presence of the news media. Addressing FEMA Director Brown by his nickname, the President smiled and said, "Brownie, you're doing a heck of a job."[24] This was unexpected. The media juxtaposed the President's praise against Mr. Brown's day-before performances where he seemed clueless about the people who had taken shelter in the convention center.

The President then compounded that misstep with another one: He expressed sympathy for Mississippi Senator Trent Lott, who had lost his house in the storm.[25] Three years earlier Senator Lott had resigned as Senate Majority Leader after being embroiled in a racially charged scandal. At the 100th birthday party of North Carolina Senator and former segregationist presidential candidate Strom Thurmond, Senator Lott committed a gaffe that propelled him into a two-week media feeding frenzy. His initial comments were widely interpreted as endorsing Senator Thurmond's racial segregation policies when he ran for President in 1948. His ineffective attempts to explain how he didn't intend to give that impression backfired. In the process, Senator Lott became a household name and a racially polarizing figure. The President's explicit sympathy for Senator Lott was juxtaposed against his government's apparent inattention to the mostly black residents of New Orleans. The racial interpretation of the government's response—that aid was intentionally withheld because of New Orleans's demographics—reemerged in the news commentary.

That night the interpretation jumped from the news media into popular culture. NBC sponsored a live variety program as a fundraiser to benefit Katrina victims. Dozens of celebrities performed and asked the audience for contributions to a Katrina recovery fund. During the live broadcast, entertainer Kanye West diverged from the prepared script and declared, "George Bush doesn't care about black people."[26]

Mr. West's verbalization of what some politicians and African-American leaders had already been saying added fuel to the fire, and personalized the issue: The question wasn't merely whether the federal response was racially motivated, but whether the President's leadership of the response set the tone.

The White House was clearly shaken by the day's events, and its communication strategy changed.

From Warfighting

We must make our decisions in light of the enemy's anticipated reactions and counteractions.

We must make our decisions in light of the audience's anticipated reactions and counteractions.

Weekend: Blame Game

On Saturday, September 3, Day Six after the flood, the President spoke to the media in front of the White House. Flanked by Defense Secretary Donald Rumsfeld, Joint Chiefs Chairman Richard Meyers, and Homeland Security Secretary Chertoff, the President acknowledged shortfalls in the federal response and committed to direct a more effective response. He said, "Many of our citizens are simply not getting the help they need, especially in New Orleans. And that is unacceptable." After six days of seeming out of touch, the acknowledgment of the inadequate response seemed a heartening development. That day a larger federal presence was seen in New Orleans and President Bush ordered over 7,000 troops and an additional 10,000 National Guardsmen to the disaster area.[27]

Throughout the weekend the media focused on who was responsible for the failed response. The federal government's strategy for dealing with questions about responsibility seemed to take two parts: First, emphasize that now is not the time to cast blame. Second, find someone else to blame.

In fact, President Bush, his father, former President George H. W. Bush, Press Secretary Scott McClellan, and FEMA Director Brown all used the phrase "blame game" in their commentary during the period. President Bush: "One of the things that people want us to do here is to play a blame game." Press Secretary McClellan: "Some just want to engage in the blame game." President George H. W. Bush: "The media has a fascination with the blame game." FEMA Director Brown: "You're not going to suck me into the blame game."[28]

And throughout the weekend the top Administration spokespeople challenged the effectiveness of New Orleans Mayor Ray Nagin and Louisiana Governor Kathleen Blanco, and placed the blame for the inadequate response on them. Homeland Security Secretary Chertoff appeared on NBC's *Meet the Press* and was questioned by host Tim Russert: "If you knew that a Hurricane Three storm was coming, why weren't buses, trains, planes, cruise ships, trucks provided on Friday, Saturday, Sunday to evacuate people before the storm?" Secretary Chertoff gave a response that was, at best disingenuous. He said, "Tim, the way that emergency operations act under the law is—the responsibility, the power, the authority to order an evacuation rests with state and local officials."[29] Even if the statement were true, it was a sharp contrast from President Bush's and FEMA Director Brown's assurances that the federal government would do everything it could to help those affected by the storm. But as *Frontline* pointed out, evacuation is a shared responsibility. The law establishing FEMA spells out: "The functions of the Federal Emergency Management Agency include…conducting emergency operations to save lives and property through positioning emergency equipment and supplies, through evacuating potential victims, through providing food, water, shelter, and medical care to those in need, and through restoring critical public services."[30]

But the strategy worked in the short term. News coverage shifted from Kanye West's accusation to questions about whether the governor and mayor deserved some of the blame for the bungled response.

Monday, September 5: Self-Inflicted Harm

Monday, Day Eight of the flood, was Labor Day. President Bush's mother, former First Lady Barbara Bush, who lived in Houston, Texas, toured the Houston Astrodome, which had become a shelter for thousands of New Orleans residents who had evacuated a week earlier. The arena was filled with people sleeping in cots, separated from loved ones, who had lost their homes and possessions. Mrs. Bush gave a live interview from the stadium with the NPR radio program

Marketplace. She said, "And so many of the people in the arena here were, you know, were underprivileged anyway, so this is working very well for them."[31] The audio went viral on television news. The dynamic changed again, back to questions about racial motivations in the response.

Wednesday: President Bush and Michael Brown as Laughingstocks

By Wednesday, September 7, the Katrina response had moved from tragedy to farce. Comedy Central's fake news anchor Jon Stewart gave voice to pent-up frustration. He opened that evening's edition of *The Daily Show* with this: "We begin with the subject of crisis management. After 9/11 New York Mayor Rudy Giuliani emerged as a calm leader, inspiring people with hope. Hurricane Katrina has introduced us to a new breed of public servant, inspiring people—with different feelings." He continued, "Michael Brown, the Director of the Federal Emergency Management Agency. Brown was nominated to his post by President Bush in 2003, and intends to start the job any day now. Any day now." He concluded, "Brown has earned widespread scorn and derision for his, let's say, retarded mismanagement of Hurricane Katrina, and for comments like these last Thursday." Stewart then played clips of Mr. Brown the prior week admitting that his agency learned about people in the convention center through the news media. Stewart continued, "Still, in a situation where thousands are dying from lack of food, water, and medicine, isn't it really the thought that counts?" He then played the Thursday clip of Mr. Brown speaking with Brian Williams on NBC: "I've got to tell you, in all sincerity, my heart goes out to those people." Stewart nodded soberly, then asked, "Really? Can they drink your heart? Maybe eat it?"[32]

Friday: FEMA Director Brown Is Out

Stewart's blistering critique of FEMA Director Brown sealed his fate. Having gone from "heck of a job" to laughingstock in one week,

Mr. Brown was no longer tenable. Friday morning, 12 days after the flood, Homeland Security Secretary Chertoff held a press conference with Mr. Brown. Secretary Chertoff announced that operational responsibility for the Katrina response was shifting from FEMA to the Coast Guard, and that Coast Guard Vice Admiral Thad Allen would take charge. Mr. Brown had no speaking role in that press conference and was not permitted to answer questions. The media asked whether FEMA Director Brown was being fired or demoted. Secretary Chertoff answered to the contrary. He said that Mr. Brown would return to Washington for an even more important project: to spearhead the government's preparation for the next hurricane, which threatened to hit the Gulf in the next week or so. He said:

> FEMA has responsibility not only to participate in this recovery and response effort. It's got a lot of other responsibilities. We've got tropical storms brewing in the ocean. We could have other kinds of disasters, natural and man-made. And while it's very important to focus an enormous amount of attention and effort to what is going on here, we cannot afford to let our guard down with respect to other things that might happen. Therefore, I want to make sure FEMA continues to be run the way it needs to be; continues to be prepared, to anticipate other challenges and I want to have people who are present here on the ground, Admiral Allen and his deputy, Joe Picciano, able to focus their full attention on what needs to be done to finish the recovery and rebuilding process.[33]

That statement defied belief. The news media didn't buy the story line, and its coverage reflected it.

Aftermath

That weekend *Time* magazine's September 19 issue, published on September 11, hit the newsstands. The cover—of the U.S. edition as well as the editions for Asia and Europe—featured a close-up of an African-American woman's face, hands over her mouth, gasping in horror. The cover caption, juxtaposed over her face: "System

Failure: An investigation into what went so wrong in New Orleans."[34] The magazine included an editorial cartoon that captured the spirit of the time: An African-American man, waist-high in water, holding up a sign. It was an echo of the images the media had published for the prior two weeks, of people pleading for help. On the sign was written these words: "Leadership Please."[35]

On Monday, September 12, two weeks after New Orleans flooded, FEMA Director Brown resigned.

Nearly 2,000 people died after Hurricane Katrina struck. Of those, nearly 1,500 were in New Orleans. Many of those died in the days after the flood; theoretically, they could have been rescued, given medical care, food, and water. Many might have survived. Approximately 770,000 people were displaced and about 300,000 homes were destroyed or made uninhabitable.

The consequences for President Bush were significant. Until Katrina, he had enjoyed a job approval rating above 50 percent. He had won reelection in a tough campaign just 10 months earlier. But after Katrina, his job approval fell below 50 percent and never recovered. It fell first to 42 percent and a month later to 38 percent, and was below 30 percent the following year. More significantly, in the month after Katrina, President Bush suffered his first major legislative defeat. Ironically, it was at the hands of his own base.

President Bush nominated White House Counsel Harriet Miers to a seat on the United States Supreme Court to succeed Justice Sandra Day O'Connor. The President was accustomed to at least his own party endorsing his nominations. But this time the President was weak, and his base found Ms. Miers to be unsuitable. Unable to persuade the Republican leadership to fight for confirmation, a month after nominating Ms. Miers, President Bush withdrew the nomination. It was the first of many defeats in the balance of his term. He finished his presidency with the lowest approval ratings of any President.

Trust, Consequences, and the Say-Do Gap

At the end of Chapter 1, I noted that Admiral Mike Mullen, then Chairman of the Joint Chiefs of Staff, said, "We hurt ourselves...

when our words don't align with our actions. We must be vigilant about holding ourselves accountable to higher standards of conduct and closing any gaps, real or perceived, between what we say about ourselves and what we do to back it up."[36] I also pointed out that Admiral Mullen notes that most purported strategic communication problems are not communication problems at all. They are policy and execution problems.

That was the challenge in Hurricane Katrina.

Again, *Warfighting* gives us a window into how this works.

 *From* Warfighting

We should recognize that war is not an inanimate instrument, but an animate force which may have unintended consequences that may change the political situation.

> *We should recognize that communication is not an inanimate instrument, but an animate force which may have unintended consequences that may change the business situation.*

As the government communicated, it set expectations. The communication changed the environment in which actions and future communication would be judged. One of the tangible consequences of the U.S. government's response to Hurricane Katrina was a decline in trust and confidence—in individual leaders such as FEMA Director Brown and Homeland Security Secretary Chertoff, and especially in President Bush. Trust and confidence are not givens; they need to be earned. They can be easily lost and are hard to recover.

And one of the primary drivers of loss of trust and confidence is the gap between what one says and what one does. Per our translation of *Warfighting*, communication is an animate force that has unintended—but often quite predictable—consequences.

When leaders make promises, either implicit or explicit, they are establishing criteria by which they ask to be judged. "We'll be there for you" was the big promise made in Katrina. The results are not surprising.

And paradoxically, the more government officials at all levels continued to reassure—that the response was going well; that Brownie was doing a heck of a job; that Homeland Security Secretary Chertoff was extremely pleased with every element of the federal response—the more trust fell. Rather than acknowledge the problems and recalibrate the expectations, the government doubled down. And, to invoke Admiral Mullen, these were not communication problems, but rather problems of strategy and execution—made all the more glaring because of the hyperbolic reassurance.

Of all the ways to understand trust, the one I have found most helpful is the description by Frank Navran, president of the Ethics Resource Center in Washington, D.C. Mr. Navran writes, "Trust is the natural consequence of promises fulfilled."[37] I take that description and add a few nuances: Trust is the natural consequence of promises fulfilled, of predictions that come true, and of values lived.

Says Mr. Navran, "Trust results from having one's expectations met, of having no unrealized expectations (what we refer to as disappointments)."[38] Once an expectation is set, the leader must either fulfill the expectation or reset it, or risk disappointment that shatters trust.

Resetting an expectation may cause some short-term pain. But it's preferable to wholesale disappointment. Take a relatively trivial example: You're running late for a meeting. The meeting is the expectation—that you'll arrive at a certain place at a certain time to meet with someone. If you're 20 minutes late, the person waiting for you will be rightly disappointed, and may form a very negative impression. But if before the appointed time you call ahead and say you're running late, you'll get the benefit of the doubt. You will have reset the expectation. The person may still be disappointed, but less so, and for different reasons.

The same applies to big, complex expectations. Ideally, the leader sets an appropriate expectation and avoids saying what merely sounds good but is unlikely to be fulfilled. And when circumstances change, the leader can adapt to those changes and recalibrate the expectations.

But whether with an initial expectation or a recalibrated expectation, if a leader wants to maintain trust, the promises must come true.

It's not enough to say, "We'll be there for you." The leader's organization must actually be there. Predictions need to come true. It's not enough to say that FEMA is moving supplies into the most hard-hit areas. The supplies must arrive. And they must not be stopped at the border for arbitrary or opaque reasons. And it's not enough to profess values: Our top priority is to take care of people affected by the disaster. The leader's organization must actually take care of the people.

And leaders need to be sensitive to self-contradictory statements. In Katrina, as things began to unravel, the federal government urged the media not to seek someone to blame—"don't play the blame game"—even as it was blaming state and local officials for the ineffective response.

FEMA Resets Expectations

Two years after Hurricane Katrina, FEMA responded to wildfires in California by intentionally setting modest expectations about what it could and could not do—no more rhetoric about doing whatever it takes to help victims. FEMA's role was limited to coordinating logistics and having state and local governments do the lion's share of the disaster response. FEMA was widely praised for meeting those much lower expectations. FEMA's Deputy Director, Harvey Johnson, said at the time that the response reflected lessons learned from Katrina:

> I think what you're really seeing here is the benefit of experience, the benefit of good leadership, and the benefit of good partnership, none of which were present in Katrina. So, I think, as a nation, people should sit up and take notice that you have the worst wildfire season in history in California, and look at how well the state and local governments are performing, look at how well we're working together between state and federal partners.[39]

In Hurricane Katrina, the say-do gap defined President Bush and his Administration. It's an admittedly extreme example of an all-too-common leadership failing: of confusing ends and means. Business and organizational problems cannot be solved by communication means alone.

Recap: Best Practices from This Chapter

From Warfighting

> *It is important to recognize that many business problems cannot be solved by communication means. Some can, but rarely as anticipated. Communication tends to take its own course as it unfolds.*

> *We should base our decisions on* awareness *rather than on mechanical* habit.*Rather, we must act on a keen appreciation for the essential factors that make each situation unique instead of from a conditioned response.*

> *We must make our decisions in light of the audience's anticipated reactions and counteractions.*

> *We should recognize that communication is not an inanimate instrument, but an animate force which may have unintended consequences that may change the business situation.*

Lessons for Leaders and Communicators

However tempting, leaders must resist saying what merely sounds good in the moment. Leaders are judged on the fulfillment of expectations. And especially when things go wrong, leaders learn the hard way that they can't talk their way out of a business problem. They certainly can't talk their way out of a problem they behaved their way into. And once they've committed a say-do gap, it's hard even to talk their way out of a problem they talked their way into.

The burden of leadership is to inspire trust and confidence by fulfilling promises, making predictions that come true, and living stated values. Communication sets expectations; actions fulfill or fail to fulfill those expectations. If the leader concludes that he or she will be unable to fulfill expectations, the leader should seek to reset those expectations as early as possible.

4

Speed, Focus, and the First Mover Advantage

It was to be the most important meeting of the year for McDonald's Corporation. More than 12,000 people who ran 30,000 restaurants in 119 countries were assembling in Orlando, Florida, to hear from the chief executive officer about the company's new strategy.

James Cantalupo, 60, had been brought back from retirement to preside over a strategic repositioning of the company. McDonald's, once an icon of American business, had struggled in recent years as customers complained about service and cleanliness, and health activists criticized the company's food and marketing for contributing to the United States' obesity problem.

Mr. Cantalupo took the helm at the end of 2002 and launched a strategy to change the company. He overhauled the menu to include alternatives to fried foods and sugary drinks. He added grilled chicken, salads, and healthier drinks to the McDonald's menu and he discontinued "supersize" portions.

When Mr. Cantalupo took over, the company's stock was just over $15 per share, and it reported its first quarterly loss since it had become a publicly traded company 38 years earlier. But the next quarter, as the new strategy and menu were rolled out, same store sales jumped nearly 5 percent, the largest sales increase in five years. Same-store sales continued to rise for 11 consecutive months. The company ended the year with a fourth-quarter profit of nearly $126 million, compared to a loss of $343 million in the year-earlier quarter. And in the year just before the Orlando meeting, the stock price of McDonald's doubled, closing at just under $30 in the last trading session before the meeting.

By late April 2004, the people who owned and operated McDonald's restaurants were assembling in Orlando for their every-other-year meeting with the company's leadership team. It was to be their first meeting presided over by Mr. Cantalupo, the first since the new strategy was launched. And as the meeting opened on Monday, April 19, they were eager to hear a progress update from Mr. Cantalupo and his team.

But Mr. Cantalupo never took the stage. He had died overnight, apparently of a heart attack. Paramedics were called to Mr. Cantalupo's hotel just after 3 AM. He died in an ambulance en route to the hospital, where he was pronounced dead at 4:53 AM. Sheriff's deputies reported finding heart medication in the hotel room. The medical examiner said that the death was "probably cardiac related."

McDonald's announced Mr. Cantalupo's passing in a press release at 8:07 AM.[1] The financial markets reacted quickly, with analysts warning investors to sell McDonald's stock. They noted that the company's new strategy was still being rolled out, and without a clear successor it was not certain whether the strategy would be continued.

Some pundits on financial television programs noted the irony of Mr. Cantalupo's apparent cause of death—heart attack—and the criticism McDonald's received for promoting unhealthy food.

The risks to McDonald's were significant. The convergence of thousands of the company's most important stakeholders in one place at the very moment the CEO died was an unusual circumstance to begin with. The passing of the architect of the new strategy also put the company at risk of strategic drift. Operators of the restaurants came to the meeting expecting both an update on the strategy so far and clear guidance about the game plan for the rest of the year.

But by the time the New York Stock Exchange opened at 9:30 AM, the McDonald's board of directors had already met. Several directors were already in Orlando for the meeting with restaurant operators. They convened a board meeting, with other directors attending via telephone conference call. By 9:30 that morning they had selected Mr. Cantalupo's successor, Chief Operating Officer Charlie Bell. They announced his appointment as CEO at 10:42 AM.[2]

Mr. Bell took the stage in Orlando, and after an appropriate acknowledgment of his predecessor's passing, delivered the presentation Mr. Cantalupo would have given. The McDonald's strategy was affirmed. The audience responded well. The company went on to have a very successful 2004. And Mr. Cantalupo's menu remains in place today.

From Warfighting

Speed is rapidity of action. It applies to both time and space.
Speed over time is tempo—the consistent ability to operate quickly.
Speed over distance, or space, is the ability to move rapidly.
Both forms are genuine sources of combat power.
In other words, speed is a weapon.

> *Speed is rapidity of action. It applies to both time and space.*
> *Speed over time is tempo—the consistent ability to operate quickly.*
> *Speed over distance, or space, is the ability to move rapidly.*
> *Both forms are genuine sources of competitive advantage.*
> *In other words, speed is a weapon that provides competitive advantage.*

The speed with which McDonald's took action was uncharacteristic of many companies. But that speed allowed it to keep its most important stakeholders—the men and women who run its restaurants—focused on its strategy and committed to making the strategy work.

McDonald's was able to move quickly for a number of reasons, but primarily because of Mr. Cantalupo's wisdom in establishing a succession plan for himself with the board. Although he had expected to serve for several more years, he had already completed his succession process when he died, and his successor had already been provisionally approved by the board. When he died, the board was faced simply with the task of formally ratifying the work it had already done. The board met immediately on hearing the news, and announced the new CEO as promptly as possible after making its decision.

McDonald's received widespread praise for its ability to name and announce a new CEO so quickly. The *Wall Street Journal* said,

The swift decision gave immediate reassurance to employees, franchisees and investors that the fast-food giant has a knowledgeable leader in place who can provide continuity and carry out the company's strategies. It may also shift any spotlight away from McDonald's high-cholesterol, fat-rich foods and prove a savvy public-relations move.[3]

It noted that most companies are unprepared to name a new CEO, and have at best only a plan for an interim leader, what the paper called a "bus-crash envelope"—an envelope to be opened in the event the CEO gets hit by a bus or otherwise dies suddenly.

Jack Welch, retired chief executive officer at General Electric, told the *Wall Street Journal,* "If there's someone capable who can take over permanently, it's best to name that person quickly. But boards who haven't groomed someone for the job yet shouldn't make a call for the sake of making a call."[4] He noted that his own board would have been able to name a successor within an hour if he had been suddenly unable to serve.

The ability of McDonald's to move quickly was also noted by governance experts. Jay Lorsch, a professor at Harvard Business School, told the *Wall Street Journal,* "The speed with which they've moved is exactly what you would expect to happen, but few companies are as prepared as McDonald's appears to have been for this calamity."[5] And Jeffrey Sonnenfeld, an associate dean at Yale University School of Management, told the *Wall Street Journal,* "The worst-case scenario planning of most companies is only a Band-Aid transitional solution, not a strategic solution. McDonald's directors, by immediately naming a battle-tested insider, showed the wisdom of having a succession plan in place."[6]

Six months after Mr. Bell succeeded Mr. Cantalupo, McDonald's again faced a succession challenge. Mr. Bell, seemingly in good health at the time of his appointment, was diagnosed with colorectal cancer two weeks later. By late November Mr. Bell handed the reins to his own successor, James Skinner, a 33-year veteran of the company. Mr. Skinner committed to continue Mr. Bell's and Mr. Cantalupo's strategy. The markets were heartened by that news. *The New York*

Times declared in a headline: "Change at Helm, but a Steady Course at McDonald's."[7]

The McDonald's board recognized the importance of moving quickly to demonstrate steady leadership at the top, especially as the company was transforming its operations. It took the responsible steps to be able to reassure stakeholders in a moment of sudden concern. And it engaged stakeholders promptly: in the case of the Orlando meeting, telling the 12,000 owners and operators the news, and in the case of the second succession announcement, in a matter-of-fact manner when Mr. Bell's decision to step aside was made.

Speed isn't just acting quickly. Impulsive communication—such as BP CEO Tony Hayward's "I want my life back" quote—is counterproductive. Rather, speed is best understood as tempo: the consistent ability to be effective in a timely way. As with McDonald's, it's about more than just talking. It's about acting effectively and engaging stakeholders promptly.

The consistent ability to act and engage stakeholders quickly and effectively creates a competitive advantage in the best of times. But it is in the worst of times that tempo matters most: it can prevent a negative event from becoming a tragedy, or worse. It is precisely in high-stakes situations that stakeholders, critics, and adversaries look for leadership in the form of effective engagement.

The Second Battle of Fallujah

The United States Marines were fighting the Second Battle of Fallujah, a major city in the heart of Iraq's Anbar Province in the so-called Sunni triangle. It was one of the fiercest battles of the war, the fiercest of many recent wars. It was urban warfare at its bloodiest—a block-by-block, house-by-house, room-by-room infantry battle that has been compared to the World War II Battle of Stalingrad.

In the middle of the battle, an incident occurred that had the potential to become a defining atrocity of the Iraq War. It was November 13, 2004, about 18 months after the United States invaded the country, more than a year after a full-bore insurgency arose, and 6 months after evidence of U.S. abuse of prisoners at Abu Ghraib had provoked outrage in Iraq, the region, the U.S., and the rest of the world.

During the battle, a unit of Marines fought insurgents who were using a Sunni mosque as their base of operations. They killed ten of the insurgents and wounded another five. The Marines could not evacuate the prisoners because the battle was raging around them. So they sheltered the prisoners in place, treated their wounds, secured them, and moved on to continue fighting. When another unit of Marines entered the mosque later in the battle, they had a brief skirmish with the five wounded prisoners, further wounding some of them.

Kevin Sites, a freelance journalist on assignment for NBC News, was embedded with that unit of Marines. He was simultaneously serving as a pool cameraman, feeding his video to all other news organizations, a common practice for combat journalists. As the Marines entered the mosque, Sites videotaped a violent encounter between one of the Marines and one of the wounded prisoners, who was lying prone on the floor. The Marine, clearly agitated and cursing, shot and killed the prisoner. It looked like an execution. And it was on tape.

Executing a wounded prisoner, especially one lying prone, on sacred ground, could easily be seen as an atrocity, immediately interpreted as a crime. And as a violation of the Law of Armed Conflict, the Geneva and Hague Conventions, and the Marines' own rules of engagement. And coming on the heels of wall-to-wall coverage of the U.S. military's abuse of prisoners at Abu Ghraib, this also had the potential to create a global media feeding frenzy. And it was sure to be a local outrage, a sign not only of brutality but of disrespect for religion in general, for Islam in particular, and especially for the Sunni branch of Islam.

Speed matters, especially in controversial situations. The longer it takes to fulfill legitimate stakeholder expectations, the harder it is to win, maintain, or restore trust.

The Administration had played defense during the Abu Ghraib controversy six months earlier. And it hadn't worked.

In the Second Battle of Fallujah the Marines chose to play offense.

From Warfighting

The offense contributes *striking power.*
We normally associate offense with initiative:
The most obvious way to seize and maintain the initiative is
to strike first and keep striking.

The offense contributes the first mover advantage.
We normally associate offense with initiative:
The most obvious way to seize and maintain the initiative is
to communicate first and keep communicating.

The first mover advantage applies particularly in crisis situations. Whoever is first to define the crisis, the motives, and the next steps typically wins. And whenever there's a victim, the single biggest predictor of reputational harm is the perception of indifference. Silence—or delay in engaging stakeholders as a crisis unfolds—creates that perception of indifference, inviting critics, stakeholders, and other audiences to paint a leader or institution as uncaring. And anything that smells of coverup is even worse, leading critics to leap beyond indifference to attribute legal or ethical lapse, guilt, or intentionality in causing harm.

But for the first mover advantage to work, speed is essential. Speed isn't just rapidity of action. The leadership discipline isn't just to say things quickly in a given instance. Rather, it's a predisposition to make sound decisions quickly and communicate them effectively. The Marines call it tempo—the consistent ability to operate quickly.

In maintaining public support in a crisis, the consistent ability to operate quickly becomes a distinctive competitive advantage. And for the Marines in the wake of the Fallujah mosque shooting, tempo made the difference. Their predisposition to operate quickly and for seizing the initiative allowed the Marines to manage the aftermath effectively and protect the Marine Corps' reputation and American interests in the region. They also had focus: All elements of the Marine Corps involved in communicating the aftermath of the shooting were well coordinated, consistent, and mutually reinforcing.

The Marines Act on the Fallujah Shooting

The Marine chain of command in Washington learned of the shooting early on November 15, Washington, D.C., time. Within a few hours the Marines made tough decisions, including these:

- They launched an investigation into what happened and why, to be conducted by the Naval Criminal Investigative Service (NCIS), an independent law enforcement agency under control of the Secretary of the Navy.

- They removed the Marine involved in the shooting from the battlefield.

- They made a public announcement in the name of the top Marine, the Commandant of the Marine Corps, announcing the investigation and affirming the Marines' commitment to the Law of Armed Conflict.

- The Marine commander in Fallujah conducted a press conference, both describing the investigation and affirming commitment to the Law of Armed Conflict.

- They returned the videotape of the incident, which had been temporarily confiscated by the Marines in Fallujah, to the cameraman, Kevin Sites. They also provided facilities for the immediate broadcast of the video.

The Commandant's statement read, in part:

[The Marine Corps] is investigating an allegation of the unlawful use of force in the death of an enemy combatant. The purpose of this investigation is to determine whether the Marine acted in self-defense, violated military law, or failed to comply with the Law of Armed Conflict. The Marine has been withdrawn from the battlefield pending the results of the investigation.[8]

Lieutenant General John F. Sattler, commander of the I Marine Expeditionary Force in Fallujah, echoed the Commandant in his discussion with the media:

Let me make it perfectly clear: We follow the Law of Armed Conflict and we hold ourselves accountable to a high standard of accountability. The facts of this case will be thoroughly pursued to make an informed decision and to protect the rights of all persons involved.[9]

These all seem like common-sense steps to take in the immediate aftermath of a suspicious shooting. And they are. They represent foreseeable expectations of reasonable stakeholders.

But a delay taking and communicating those steps could have deprived the Marines of the first mover advantage. The NBC cameraman could have spoken with other reporters; the rumor mill would have begun, and in the course of the rumors spreading, the incident would likely have been exaggerated (especially in the absence of the tape) into something much worse. The news media would likely have reported the exaggerated rumors plus the apparent coverup due to the confiscation of the tape. It could easily have been reported as a massacre, most likely of more than a single prisoner. The tape confiscation could easily have been transformed into having taken the cameraman into custody. The coverage would have been severe, widespread, and sustained.

Crisis managers speak of the Golden Hour of Crisis Response. It's based on a principle first observed in emergency medicine and now accepted in high-stakes communication as well: Incremental delays in fielding an appropriate response have a greater than incremental effect on the outcome. This is the basis of the principle of disproportionality described in Chapter 5, "Initiative, Maneuver, and Disproportionality."

So what was the effect of the Marines' rapid action and communication?

That night there was minimal coverage in the U.S. media. Television networks aired brief segments about the investigation, using a still photograph from the video, but didn't air the video itself. And the content of the stories wasn't the shooting, but the investigation. There was minimal follow-up coverage in the next few days.

In other words, by taking effective action early and communicating what they had done, the Marines made the story a lot less newsworthy. An investigation of a single shooting isn't nearly as interesting as a massacre and coverup.

Six months later the investigation was concluded and the Marine was exonerated. The investigation, based on a review of the tape, forensic evidence, and interviews with witnesses, concluded that the Marine genuinely feared that the prisoner was about to harm him and his fellow Marines, by either detonating a bomb or shooting at the Marines. The Marine's actions were in response to a legitimate threat, and therefore completely consistent with the rules of engagement, U.S. law, and the Law of Armed Conflict. The Marines announced the result of the investigation, but it got very little press coverage—not a surprise, since the event itself got so little coverage in the first place. But the Marines' reputation and U.S. national interests remained intact.

In publicly communicating in the aftermath of the mosque shooting, the Marines showed a capacity to operate quickly: to fulfill the appropriate expectations of stakeholders before the media had defined the shooting. The Marines themselves defined the crisis, their motives, and their actions. They also showed focus, aligning all communication up and down the chain of command.

Contrast the Marines' handling of the Fallujah mosque shooting with the Pentagon's and Administration's handling of the abuse of Iraqi prisoners in Abu Ghraib prison.

Abu Ghraib and Loss of the First Mover Advantage

Abu Ghraib prison had become notorious during Iraqi President Saddam Hussein's reign—known in Baghdad as Saddam's torture chamber. In 2004 it became notorious for other reasons.

The United States had invaded Iraq on March 19, 2003, and by mid-April had taken Baghdad and sent Saddam Hussein into hiding. In May the U.S. appointed Ambassador Paul Bremer as director of the Iraq Coalition Provisional Authority, effectively naming him governor general of Iraq. Ambassador Bremer then set about establishing a working government. In September he proclaimed that Iraq was free of many of the scourges of the Saddam era:

> The Iraqi people are now free. And they do not have to worry about the secret police coming after them in the middle of the night, and they don't have to worry about their husbands and brothers being taken off and shot, or their wives being taken to rape rooms. Those days are over.[10]

It turned out to be wishful thinking.

At about the same time, the U.S. had begun to repopulate Abu Ghraib prison. Some prisoners were suspected terrorists, insurgents, and allies of Saddam Hussein. Some were common criminals. Others were simply swept up in raids, or turned in by their private enemies.

Soon after Ambassador Bremer reassured the Iraqis, members of the 800th Military Police Brigade, guarding prisoners at Abu Ghraib, began taking souvenir photographs of themselves mistreating prisoners, including sexual humiliation and assault. The abuse continued into October, when an inspection by the International Committee of the Red Cross uncovered the abuse, which was then brought to the attention of the United States government.

In early January 2004, a soldier with the 372nd Military Police Company, on duty at Abu Ghraib, reported both the abuse and the existence of photographic evidence to his chain of command. That month the U.S. military began a formal investigation, led by U.S. Army Major General Antonio Taguba. On January 21, CNN reported on the start of the investigation:

> Sources have revealed new details from the Army's criminal investigation into reports of abuse of Iraqi detainees, including the location of the suspected crimes and evidence that is being sought. U.S. soldiers reportedly posed for photographs with partially unclothed Iraqi prisoners, a Pentagon official told CNN on Tuesday.[11]

All the while, President Bush and others in the U.S. government continued to differentiate between U.S. occupation of Iraq and

Saddam Hussein's tenure. On January 12, President Bush had told a group at an international meeting in Mexico, "One thing is for certain [in Iraq]: There won't be any more mass graves and torture rooms and rape rooms."[12] On February 4, President Bush said that Saddam Hussein, since captured by the U.S. military, "now sits in a prison cell, and Iraqi men and women are no longer carried to torture chambers and rape rooms."[13]

As the investigation proceeded, key personnel in command of the prison were suspended, including Brigadier General Janis Karpinski, commander of the 800th Military Police Brigade.

In early March 2004, General Taguba submitted his report.[14] As a result, formal criminal charges were filed against 6 military police personnel, and 17 other soldiers were disciplined.

General Taguba's report included the following conclusions:

That between October and December 23, at Abu Ghraib Detention Facility (BCCF), numerous incidents of sadistic, blatant, and wanton criminal abuses were inflicted on several detainees. This systematic and illegal abuse of detainees was intentionally perpetrated.... These allegations of abuse were substantiated by detailed witness statements and the discovery of extremely graphic photographic evidence.[15]

The photographic evidence consisted of the souvenir photos and videos taken by the prison guards. The report documented numerous instances of intentional abuse, including the following:[16]

- Punching, slapping, kicking, jumping on their naked feet
- Videotaping and photographing naked male and female detainees
- Forcibly arranging detainees in various sexually explicit positions for photographing
- Forcing detainees to remove their clothing and keeping them naked for several days at a time
- Forcing male detainees to wear women's underwear
- Forcing male detainees to masturbate themselves while being photographed and videotaped

- Arranging naked male detainees in a pile and jumping on them
- Positioning a naked detainee on a [Meals Ready to Eat] Box, with a sandbag on his head, and attaching wires to his fingers, toes, and penis to simulate electric torture
- Writing "I am a Rapist" on the leg of a detainee alleged to have forcibly raped a 15-year-old fellow detainee, and then photographing him naked
- Pouring cold water on naked detainees
- Having sex with a female detainee
- Using military working dogs without muzzles to intimidate and frighten detainees, and in at least one case biting and severely injuring a detainee
- Threatening male detainees with rape
- Sodomizing a detainee with a chemical light and perhaps a broomstick

The report was presented by General Taguba through his chain of command. But it was not initially released to the public. On March 19, the one-year anniversary of the U.S. invasion of Iraq, National Security Advisor Condoleezza Rice told CBS's *The Morning Show*, "There are no more rape rooms and torture chambers in Iraq."[17]

The next morning Brigadier General Mark Kimmitt, Deputy Director for Coalition Operations in Iraq, told a press briefing:

> As you know, on 14 January 2004, a criminal investigation was initiated to examine allegations of detainee abuse at the Baghdad confinement facility at Abu Ghraib. Shortly thereafter, the commanding general of Combined Joint Task Force Seven requested a separate administrative investigation into systemic issues such as command policies and internal procedures related to detention operations. That administrative investigation is complete; however, the findings and recommendations have not been approved. As a result of the criminal investigation, six military personnel have been charged with criminal offenses to include conspiracy, dereliction of duty, cruelty and maltreatment, assault, and indecent acts with another.[18]

On April 15, a month after General Taguba submitted his report, President Bush told an audience in Iowa,

Our military is doing incredibly good work. They've been given a hard job. They've been given a tough job, and they're performing brilliantly. See, the transition from torture chambers and rape rooms and mass graves and fear of authority is a tough transition. And they're doing the good work of keeping this country stabilized as a political process unfolds.[19]

Both CBS News and reporter Seymour Hirsch at *The New Yorker* had acquired the photographs of guards abusing prisoners, and the text of the Taguba report, and had begun putting together stories about the Abu Ghraib abuses. CBS was ready to air its program on April 15, but it delayed the broadcast at the request of the Chairman of the Joint Chiefs of Staff, U.S. Air Force General Richard Myers. CBS delayed the broadcast the following week as well, again at General Myers' request. But on April 28, CBS concluded that *The New Yorker* would publish its article with the photographs within a matter of days, and told the Pentagon that it would go ahead with its broadcast, on CBS's *60 Minutes II.*

The morning that CBS was scheduled to air its program, the U.S. military attempted to establish a first mover advantage. It did so in the form of a briefing for the media at the Pentagon:

As you remember, in January it was announced that a criminal investigation was initiated to examine allegations of detainee abuse at the Baghdad confinement facility at Abu Ghraib. The Criminal Investigation Division investigation began when an American soldier reported and turned over evidence of criminal activity to include photographs of detainee abuse. CBS television has acquired these images and may show some of the evidence tonight on *60 Minutes II....* Shortly after the criminal investigation began, Lieutenant General Sanchez, the commanding general, requested a separate administrative investigation into systemic issues such as command policies and internal procedures related to detention operations. That administrative investigation is complete. Lieutenant General Sanchez has also directed a

follow-up investigation of interrogation procedures in detention facilities, and that investigation is ongoing. The coalition
takes all reports of detainee abuse seriously and all allegations
of mistreatment are investigated.[20]

The statement, in both tone and content, was very matter-of-fact,
business as usual. And coming from a relatively low-level spokesman,
it didn't have the desired effect. It did not effectively define the crisis,
the motives, or the actions the U.S. was taking.

That evening, CBS aired its program, including the graphic photographs.[21] It was scathing. And it led to immediate outrage, in the
United States and elsewhere, about the abuse and sexual humiliation
of prisoners by the U.S. The pictures were on the front pages of virtually every newspaper and at the beginning of every news program
in the world. The prisoner abuse at Abu Ghraib became the defining
atrocity in the Iraq War. And it led to immediate outcries for comment, condemnation, and apology from the senior levels of the U.S.
government. But instead there was near silence from the top.

The next morning, U.S. Secretary of Defense Donald Rumsfeld
told Chris Matthews on MSNBC:

> I watched the program, is all I have seen on it. And I watched
> General Kimmitt on that program who is in Iraq and is a pro-
> fessional soldier. And the pain in his face, the expressions that
> he gave of his disappointment and his heartbreak at seeing
> those accusations and allegations that are there. I'm in the
> chain of command. I am not allowed to opine about things
> like that.... Allegations like that will end up in the military
> justice system as they should.[22]

That statement was remarkable. How could the Secretary of
Defense know nothing about Abu Ghraib except what he had watched
on television? The statement expressed little curiosity about what had
happened; no commitment to get to the bottom of it; no discussion of
justice being sought; no affirmation of core values or of steps that had
been taken and were being taken to prevent further abuse. Rather,
it contained a weak assertion that the Secretary of Defense is not
allowed to opine on such topics.

President Bush did not address the American public, but did share his views with Canadian Prime Minister Paul Martin, who was visiting in the White House the following morning. Speaking with reporters about the meeting, the President said, "I shared a deep disgust that those prisoners were treated the way they were treated. Their treatment does not reflect the nature of the American people."[23] But that quote didn't make the newspapers. What he said later did. Responding to the casualties in Iraq that month, President Bush reminisced about the one-year anniversary of his declaring "Mission Accomplished" in Iraq. The President said:

> A year ago, I did give the speech from the carrier, saying that we had achieved an important objective, that we'd accomplished a mission, which was the removal of Saddam Hussein. And as a result, there are no longer torture chambers or rape rooms or mass graves in Iraq.[24]

The reference to torture chambers and rape rooms, less than 48 hours after the pictures of sexual abuse, humiliation, and torture, left many baffled, many others angry.

On Monday, May 4, National Security Advisor Condoleezza Rice went on the Arabic-language network Al Arabiya, and told the Arabic-speaking world:

> I want to assure people in the Arab world, Iraq, around the world, and the American people, that the President is determined to get to the bottom of it, to know who is responsible and to make sure that whoever is responsible is punished for it and held accountable.... we are deeply sorry for what has happened to these people, and what the families must be feeling. It's just not right. And we will get to the bottom of what happened.[25]

The words were right, but they came from the wrong person. A relatively unknown figure outside the United States at that time, Dr. Rice seemed to be a functionary rather than the principal on whose behalf she was speaking. Her apology and her assurance that the President was determined to get to the bottom of the issue left people wondering why the President hadn't said so himself. An apology by a functionary is not the same as an apology by a principal. In this case, because Dr. Rice was not in the chain of command, her comments weren't taken seriously, especially in the Gulf.

The same day, Secretary of Defense Rumsfeld addressed a Pentagon press briefing, and took issue with reporters' calling the Abu Ghraib situation "torture":

> I'm not a lawyer. My impression is that what has been charged thus far is abuse, which I believe technically is different from torture.... I don't know if it is correct to say what you just said, that torture has taken place, or that there's been a conviction for torture. And therefore I'm not going to address the *torture* word.[26]

The White House also announced that President Bush would speak directly to the people of Iraq and of the Arab world in two separate interviews: The first was to be with Alhurra, a U.S.-operated Arabic-language television station based in Iraq and part of the U.S. government; the second was with Al Arabiya. Pundits and commentators assumed that President Bush would apologize to the people of Iraq, and the White House did not dissuade them from that assumption. But in neither interview did he apologize.

He told Alhurra:

> First time I saw or heard about pictures was on TV. However, as you might remember, in early January, General Kimmitt talked about an investigation that would be taking place about accused—alleged improprieties in the prison. So our government has been in the process of investigating.[27]

He told Al Arabiya:

> The practices that took place in that prison are abhorrent and they don't represent America. They represent the actions of a few people....

> In our country, when there's an allegation of abuse...there will be a full investigation.... We have a presumption of innocent until you're guilty in our system.... This is a serious matter. It's a matter that reflects badly on my country.[28]

The lack of an apology, and the statement about the presumption of innocence, caused the opposite reaction than had been hoped. Many in the intended audience—who were unaware of American jurisprudence and the constitutional presumption of innocence—interpreted the statement as an assertion that the prison guards were in fact innocent.

The White House had set an expectation that the President would apologize. It then had to field questions about failing to fulfill those expectations. Press Secretary Scott McClellan faced the media:

Q: "Okay, a simple question. The President had two interviews today the White House set up for Arabic TV networks. In neither did the President apologize. Why was that?"

McClellan: "We've already said that we're sorry for what occurred, and we're deeply sorry to the families and what they must be feeling and going through, as well. The President is sorry for what occurred and the pain that it has caused. It does not represent what America stands for."[29]

Later in the briefing he was asked again:

Q: "If the Arab world had heard him—heard the President personally apologize—it would have gone a long way. Why did he choose not to use those words?"

McClellan: "Well, I just told you, the President is deeply sorry for what occurred, and the pain that it has caused."

Q: "Why didn't he say so himself?"

McClellan: "The President is deeply sorry for it. And he was pleased to sit down and do these interviews and address the questions that were asked of him."

Q: "Why didn't he say so himself?"

McClellan: "I'm saying it for him right now."[30]

A functionary describing the principal's regret is not the same as the principal expressing regret, and a spokesman saying he's apologizing for the principal is not the same as the principal apologizing. One of the burdens of leadership is to say things that are uncomfortable. President Bush seemed unwilling or unable to utter the words to the people of Iraq.

From Warfighting

Also inherent [in maneuver warfare] is the need to *focus* our efforts in order to maximize effects. We must focus efforts not only at the decisive location but also at the decisive moment. We achieve focus through cooperation toward the accomplishment of a common purpose. This applies to all elements of the force, and involves the coordination of ground combat, aviation, and combat support services. The combination of speed and focus adds "punch" or "shock" effect to our actions. It follows that we should strike with the greatest possible combination of speed and focus.

> *Also inherent in effective communication is the need to focus our engagements in order to maximize effect. We achieve focus through consistency of message and tone, delivered in a timely way, across multiple spokespeople and multiple communication channels. The combination of speed and focus provides maximum impact. It follows that we should engage stakeholders with the greatest possible combination of speed and focus.*

The next day President Bush met in the Oval Office with Jordan's King Abdullah. Afterward, the President and the king met with reporters in the Rose Garden, and President Bush said,

> I told him I was sorry for the humiliation suffered by the Iraqi prisoners and the humiliation suffered by their families. I told him I was equally sorry that the—that people would see those pictures, didn't understand the true nature and heart of America.[31]

The President had not apologized on Arabic-language television to the people of Iraq. But he told the King of Jordan, Iraq's neighbor, that he was sorry for the humiliation of the Iraqi prisoners. Telling the king of a neighboring country that he was sorry about what happened in Iraq was not the same as saying he was sorry to the people of Iraq.

That day *New York Times* columnist Thomas Friedman called on the President to fire Defense Secretary Rumsfeld:

This administration needs to undertake a total overhaul of its Iraq policy; otherwise, it is courting a total disaster for us all. That overhaul needs to begin with President Bush firing Secretary of Defense Donald Rumsfeld—today, not tomorrow or next month, today. What happened in Abu Ghraib prison was, at best, a fundamental breakdown in the chain of command under Mr. Rumsfeld's authority, or, at worst, part of a deliberate policy somewhere in the military-intelligence command of sexually humiliating prisoners to soften them up for interrogation, a policy that ran amok.[32]

Finally, the next day Secretary Rumsfeld apologized to the people of Iraq. Ten days after the photographs were made public, the Defense Secretary delivered a statement in front of two congressional committees: first the Senate Armed Services Committee, then the House Armed Services Committee. In those statements he finally gave voice to what should have been said on the very first day:

> So to those Iraqis who were mistreated by the members of the U.S. armed forces, I offer my deepest apology. It was inconsistent with the values of our nation; it was un-American.[33]

The apology was the right thing to say, and coming from the Defense Secretary, speaking on his own behalf, it was seen to be from someone accountable in the chain of command (compared to a third-party expression of apology from the National Security Advisor some days earlier). It came eight days after the Defense Secretary had said that he wasn't supposed to opine on such matters.

If Secretary Rumsfeld had said those words the night the program aired—or better yet, before it aired—the coverage could have played out differently, and the outrage may have been more muted. But by the time he said it, the apology seemed forced, insincere, and contrived.

The contrast between the Marines' handling of the mosque shooting and the Pentagon's and Administration's handling of the Abu Ghraib photographs is stark:

- The Marines played offense: They seized initiative to take the first mover advantage by communicating first, forcefully, and consistently from high in the chain of command. On Abu Ghraib the Pentagon played defense, poorly. It allowed the photographs to air without a senior policymaker shaping the public perception. And senior policymaker silence in the immediate aftermath left the impression that the Administration didn't care or that it condoned the mistreatment of prisoners.

- The Marines' commentary was consistent throughout the chain of command. The Pentagon's and Administration's response on Abu Ghraib lacked focus. It was inconsistent across the chain of command and even among individuals. For example, Secretary Rumsfeld initially said he shouldn't opine, but later apologized. National Security Advisor Rice and White House Spokesman McClellan both spoke about President Bush being sorry for what happened, but President Bush didn't express that regret directly to the Iraqi people, even as he described his regret indirectly to the Prime Minister of Canada and to the King of Jordan. And President Bush and others in the Administration continued to repeat their comments about a post-Saddam Iraq no longer having torture chambers and rape rooms, even while pictures of sexual humiliation and torture were appearing on television and on newspaper front pages.

- The Marines fulfilled the appropriate expectations of both Americans and international observers; the Pentagon and Administration did not.

The first mover advantage applies well beyond matters of life and death or national security. It applies whenever there's a need to manage the interpretation of events.

The First Mover Advantage and Celebrity Scandal

On October 1, 2009, comedian and late-night television host David Letterman looked his studio audience in the eye and matter-of-factly said, "I'm glad you folks are here tonight, and I'm glad you're in such a pleasant mood because I have a little story that I would like to tell you and the home viewers as well. Do you feel like a story?"[34] The audience applauded and cheered, not knowing what the story would involve, but assuming that it would be part of his usual irreverent commentary on the news of the day.

Letterman, host of *The Late Show* on CBS, then spent ten minutes telling a personal anecdote outside the usual scope of his comedy. The key elements of his narrative were these:[35]

- Several weeks earlier he had found a package in his car, with a note saying that the note's author knew and could prove that Letterman had done "terrible things."

- The note's author said that he planned to write a screenplay featuring Letterman and his misbehavior. But he would not write the screenplay if Letterman paid him "some money."

- Letterman called his lawyer, who suggested that they meet with the person to determine what was going on.

- They met, and the person told them that he would produce a very damaging film about Letterman unless he received a "very large sum of money."

- The lawyer contacted the Manhattan District Attorney's office, which concluded that Letterman was being blackmailed. Letterman then cooperated with the District Attorney's investigation.

- Letterman and his lawyer met again with the blackmailer, who confirmed that he knew that he was committing a crime, and raised the stakes: unless he was paid, he'd write not only a damaging screenplay but also a damaging book.

- They arranged a third meeting, at which time Letterman paid the extortionist $2 million, in the form of a personal check.

- That morning Letterman had testified in front of a grand jury. The testimony involved not only the extortion attempt, but also the details of the misbehavior that the extortionist had threatened to expose.

Letterman's narrative continued:

And I had to tell them how I was disturbed by this, I was worried for myself, I was worried for my family, I felt menaced by this. And I had to tell them all of the creepy things that I have done, that were going to be [laughter]. Now why is that funny? That's, I mean.... [laughter/applause] So the idea is that if they believe, in fact, a crime has been committed, then they issue a warrant, and that's exactly what happened. And a little bit after noon today, the guy was arrested.[36]

The audience cheered at the news that the extortionist had been arrested. But they still hadn't heard what the misbehavior in question had been. Letterman finally, more than seven minutes into his story, delivered the news:

Now, of course, we get to, "what was it?" What was all the creepy stuff [laughter] that he was gonna put into the screenplay and the movie? And the creepy stuff was that I have had sex with women who work for me on this show.[37]

The audience let out a quiet gasp. Letterman, looking the TV audience in the eye, continued, "Now. My response to that is, yes I have."[38]

The audience laughed and applauded. He went on: "I have had sex with women who work on this show." The audience applauded more strongly. "And would it be embarrassing if it were made public? Perhaps it would. Perhaps it would." The audience laughed. "Especially for the women." More laughter and applause. He didn't name the women, and said it was up to them to decide whether they would talk about the matter.[39]

Letterman then thanked the District Attorney and described his motive in coming forward:

It's been a very bizarre experience. I feel like I need to protect these people. I need to certainly protect my family. I need to protect myself—hope to protect my job—and the friends, everybody that has been very supportive through this. And I don't plan to say much more about this on this particular topic. So, thank you for letting me bend your ears.[40]

The audience applauded, and Letterman closed by making fun of himself:

Now. I know what you're saying. "I'll be darned, Dave's had sex!" [laughter] That's what the grand jury said also. [laughter] "Really? You've had sex?"[41]

Letterman thanked the audience for listening, and went to commercial.

The news coverage that night and the following days was less on the scandal of Letterman's affairs and more on the extortionist and the women. The extortionist was revealed to be Robert Joe Halderman, a CBS News producer whose girlfriend was one of the women Letterman had been involved with. Halderman was promptly fired by CBS News. After a week of low-intensity coverage about Letterman, the scandal subsided and Letterman kept his job.

Letterman had used the first mover advantage effectively. He took the initiative and kept it. He defined the crisis as an extortion attempt. He defined his motives as self-protection and the protection of his friends and family. He defined his actions as coming clean and getting the extortion behind him: "What you don't want is a guy saying, 'Oh, I know you had sex with women so I would like $2 million or I'm going to make trouble for you.' So that's where we stand right now."

By communicating first and fully, Letterman controlled the agenda. He controlled the narrative, even referring to it as a story. If he hadn't, the likelihood is that the arrest report would have made it into the celebrity gossip world, into the entertainment media, and then into the mainstream media. Reporters would have camped out near the Letterman studios, and CBS executives would have been called on to fire Letterman as well as the extortionist.

Letterman also understood who his key stakeholder group was: the audience of his television program. He didn't release an impersonal statement to the media; he didn't hold a press conference. He made his statement directly to his television audience as part of his show. The audience heard directly from him, in his voice, with his characteristic irreverence, this time directed at himself.

Operationalizing the First Mover Advantage

Leaders all too often allow delicate situations to linger too long. Worried about embarrassment, litigation, or being fired, they become paralyzed with fear and either make poor decisions or no decisions. All the while their stakeholders—including employees, customers, business partners, and investors—are looking to the leaders for a sign that they're in control. And in the silence the vacuum gets filled by critics, adversaries, the media, and others.

So leaders need some mechanism to determine when to communicate: Communicate too late and they lose the trust and confidence of their stakeholders; too soon and they may unleash a set of events beyond their control.

◆ The Four-Question Test

The most effective way to make decisions about when to communicate is to operationalize the first mover advantage by asking four related questions, all of which have to do with stakeholder awareness and expectations:

1. **Will those who matter to us expect us to do or say something now?** If so, we need to act and communicate now.

    In the case of the Marines and Fallujah, those who matter to them could reasonably expect the Marines to take the shooting incident seriously, and an investigation seemed like an appropriate first step.

    Similarly, the government's failure to act in the aftermath of the release of Abu Ghraib photographs left people wondering: Are they not taking this seriously? If the President and Defense Secretary were in fact sorry, why didn't they say so themselves? Did they in fact support or endorse the mistreatment of prisoners?

If David Letterman had not told his audience about both the extortion attempt and his own misbehavior, the audience would likely have been similarly puzzled when they read or heard about it from news sources. And their trust could easily have been strained or lost.

2. **Are others talking about us now, shaping the perception about us, among those who matter to us? Do we have reason to believe they will be soon?** If so, we need to communicate quickly and fully before others define the crisis, our motives, or our actions.

In the case of the Marines at Fallujah, the NBC cameraman would likely tell his colleagues and bosses about the event and the confiscated tape. By communicating first (and by returning the tape to prevent the charge of coverup), the Marines were able to define the story as an investigation into an allegation of an unlawful use of force, not as an execution. And they defined their motive as seeking the facts and truth, and of complying with the law.

In contrast, the government's silence, poor communication, and inconsistent communication in the aftermath of Abu Ghraib, while all the world's media was covering the story, caused trust and public support to fall dramatically.

And David Letterman knew that the arrest of his blackmailer would be newsworthy and would prompt lots of media speculation about what the blackmail was all about. His framing the story in his way—including coming clean about the affairs—allowed him to control the communication agenda.

3. **Will silence be seen as indifference or as an affirmation of guilt?** If so, we need to not be silent, but rather to engage fully to prevent the perception of indifference.

Silence on the Marines' part would certainly have been seen as indifference or as coverup.

Silence in the Abu Ghraib aftermath in fact was so interpreted.

And Letterman's silence would have been interpreted as embarrassment about his own conduct, which would have become the subject of ongoing news coverage.

4. **If we wait, will we lose the ability to control the outcome?** If so, we should not wait.

     McDonald's knew that a convention center full of restaurant operators expected clarity about the future of the company. By naming a new CEO quickly, McDonald's controlled the content, tone, and tenor of its most important meeting of the year.

     The Marines and Letterman effectively contained their outcome and suffered no lasting damage. The Marines' reputation remained intact. Even the Marine who did the shooting was later found to have behaved appropriately.

     Abu Ghraib became a defining event in the U.S. war in Iraq. It provoked a much stronger insurgency than had been experienced to date (in many ways making the Second Battle of Fallujah necessary six months later). And it convinced many in and out of Iraq that the U.S. was not the liberator it claimed to be, but rather an occupying and oppressive power.

If the answer to all of the four questions is no, then the leader should watch and wait, prepare to engage stakeholders, and then engage whenever the answer to any one of them turns from no to yes. But as soon as the answer to any of the four questions is yes, the leader needs to overcome fear, inertia, embarrassment, or anxiety, and engage stakeholders effectively and quickly.

Recap: Best Practices from This Chapter

From Warfighting

*Speed is rapidity of action. It applies to both time and space.
Speed over time is tempo—the consistent ability to operate quickly.
Speed over distance, or space, is the ability to move rapidly.
Both forms are genuine sources of competitive advantage.
In other words, speed is a weapon that provides
competitive advantage.*

*The offense contributes the first mover advantage.
We normally associate offense with initiative:
The most obvious way to seize and maintain the initiative is
to communicate first and keep communicating.*

*Also inherent in effective communication is the need to focus
our engagements in order to maximize effect. We achieve focus
through consistency of message and tone, delivered in a timely way,
across multiple spokespeople and multiple communication channels.
The combination of speed and focus provides maximum impact.
It follows that we should engage stakeholders with the greatest
possible combination of speed and focus.*

Lessons for Leaders and Communicators

In controversial situations leaders need to step up and control the communication agenda, thereby controlling their destinies. The consistent ability to operate quickly in high-stakes situations—to make smart decisions and to engage stakeholders effectively—creates a powerful competitive advantage. This is true in business—per McDonald's—and in nonbusiness settings.

The longer it takes to fulfill appropriate stakeholder expectations, the harder it becomes. Incremental delays in fielding an appropriate response have a greater than incremental effect on the outcome. An apology on Day 1 may be sufficient to prevent expressions of outrage; an apology on Day 10 after uninterrupted expressions of outrage probably won't be sufficient.

The first mover advantage prevents critics and adversaries from framing the situation. Leaders need to define the crisis, their motives, and their actions first, consistently, and persistently. When stakeholders expect their leaders to step up, the leaders need to. Subordinates describing a leader's regret is not the same as the leader expressing regret.

As important as the consistent ability to operate quickly is focus: the ability to concentrate attention on the right thing, and to align multiple communications by multiple parties. The burden of leadership is to seize the initiative when it can do the most good.

5

Initiative, Maneuver, and Disproportionality

On July 22, 2009, President Barack Obama launched his single-most-important legislative initiative: a proposed reform to the United States healthcare system. He knew that healthcare reform would be a tough sell. President Bill Clinton had tried and failed to reform healthcare in his first term.

President Obama wanted to seize the initiative and control the terms of debate. So he launched his campaign using all the magisterial authority of his office: an hour-long, prime-time press conference in the East Room of the White House. He strode confidently down a red carpet, through an oversized doorway that served as a proscenium arch, up to the presidential lectern. An American flag stood stage right; the presidential flag, stage left. It was a portrait of power, the very image of a president in control.

And for the first 50 minutes he was masterful, making his case to the American people about why healthcare needed to be reformed, how he proposed to go about it, and how the Congress should proceed. His proposals were bold and very straightforward: provide every American with access to affordable healthcare; eliminate the exclusion of preexisting conditions in health insurance coverage; provide an alternative to private healthcare plans for those who could not afford them—a so-called "public option." He called on the United States Senate to pass healthcare reform before its August recess—just three weeks away. He parried reporters' questions effectively, constantly bringing the topic back to his core themes.[1]

But in the final moments of the hour-long press conference, the President lost control. Just for a moment. But it was a decisive moment. And in that moment he lost the war. While something called "healthcare reform" eventually passed, it fell well short of his goals: It didn't cover every American, it delayed meaningful elimination of the preexisting condition exclusion for many, and there was no public option.

From Warfighting

Minor actions and random incidents can have disproportionately large—even decisive—effects.

> *In communication, incremental changes or minor events can have a greater-than-incremental impact on outcomes.*

The principle of disproportionality says that not all actions are equivalent, and that there isn't necessarily a one-to-one stimulus-response relationship. The same applies in communication: Not all words are created equal. Different words have different impacts. And because communication is a process of mutual adaptation, of move and countermove, the leader needs to consider the response his or her words are likely to provoke. And to resist the temptation to say anything that triggers a response different from the desired response. Because saying the wrong thing even once can derail an otherwise carefully planned event and hand the initiative to one's opponents.

Race Trumps Healthcare

President Obama inadvertently did just that. He took one final question, from a reporter from his hometown newspaper, whom he knew well and who had covered his political rise since 2004. Lynn Sweet of the *Chicago Sun-Times* asked a question unrelated to healthcare.

Several days earlier, Henry Louis Gates, Jr., a Harvard University professor and producer, writer, and host of several public television series on race relations in America, had returned from an overseas trip and had trouble opening the door to his Cambridge, Massachusetts, home. He struggled with the lock for some time. Eventually, with the help of his taxi driver, a Moroccan immigrant, he got the door open. Then he went inside. An observer saw two black men struggling to get into the home and called the police. The Cambridge police arrived and demanded to see professor Gates's identification, to prove that he actually lived in the house. Professor Gates refused, and the police took him into custody.

Professor Gates is director of the W.E.B. Du Bois Institute for African and African American Research, and is a friend of President Obama. His arrest in his own home provoked widespread accusations of racial profiling—that he was arrested for looking out of place. It generated moderate levels of media coverage, mostly for the irony that the black man arrested for looking out of place was a prominent figure in the study of the African American experience in America.

At President Obama's press conference, Lynn Sweet asked the President to comment on the implications of the arrest: "Recently, Professor Henry Louis Gates, Jr., was arrested at his home in Cambridge. What does that incident say to you, and what does it say about race relations in America?"[2]

It was a perfectly reasonable question. And it would have been perfectly appropriate for the President to decline to talk about it, if for no other reason than that his commenting might compromise an ongoing investigation into whether the Cambridge police had violated professor Gates's rights. President Obama began his response by acknowledging that he and Professor Gates were friends and that he didn't know what had actually happened: "Well, I should say at the outset that Skip Gates is a friend, so I may be a little biased here. I don't know all the facts.... Now, I don't know, not having been there, and not seeing all the facts, what role race played in that."[3] This would have been a sufficient response. Or he could have said something more along the lines of "...and therefore I'll wait until the investigations are concluded before offering an opinion." Such a response would have been seen as an appropriate way to answer the reporter's appropriate question. And it likely would have been forgotten.

But President Obama said something else. He offered an opinion: "But I think it's fair to say, number one, any of us would have been angry; number two, that the Cambridge police acted stupidly in arresting somebody when there was already evidence that they were in their own home; and number three, what I think we know separate and apart from this incident is that there is a long history in this country of African Americans and Latinos being stopped disproportionately—and that's just a fact."[4]

The President took Lynn Sweet's bait and spoke about race in America. And in the process he criticized the Cambridge police. His single phrase—"the Cambridge police acted stupidly"—was repeated endlessly in the ensuing media coverage. The President had inadvertently said something far more interesting than the need to reform healthcare. He put himself in conflict with the Cambridge police. And he lost the first mover advantage in controlling the debate about healthcare. And although a very watered-down version eventually was enacted into law, it was such a watered-down version that it was criticized by both his opponents and his supporters.

In other words, the response to Lynn Sweet's question cost the President his most important legislative initiative.

Seemingly minor incidents can have major consequences. And a relatively minor phrase—"the Cambridge police acted stupidly"—can derail a carefully constructed political process. In politics this is sometimes called "stepping on your message."

The President's goal in his press conference was to prime the political pump—to create momentum, initially through press coverage and then through a concerted legislative campaign, to control the healthcare debate. And to do that by controlling the communication agenda. But he never controlled the agenda, and therefore never got that momentum. His offering of his opinion showed an uncharacteristic lack of discipline. And it caused self-inflicted harm.

That phrase led to a news media feeding frenzy and elevated what had been mostly a local police matter into a national story on race in America, complete with presidential validation. It put the country's most prominent African-American in a personal dispute with local law enforcement. And it crowded out most of the healthcare coverage the President had hoped for.

That small phrase eclipsed the President's healthcare message. While the news media dutifully reported the President's healthcare proposal in the first news cycle, the overwhelming news coverage for more than a week—especially on television—was on the dispute between the President and the Cambridge cops. Instead of 24/7 coverage of healthcare, there was 24/7 coverage of racial profiling.

After three days of all-Cambridge-cops-all-the-time on TV, President Obama admitted that he could have "calibrated those words differently."[5] But his admission didn't change the story.

Eight days after the press conference, with the race story still in full bloom, the President chose a grand gesture that he hoped would finally put the story to rest. He invited the police officer and professor Gates to the White House to "share a beer" and thrash things out. The media dubbed the meeting the White House Beer Summit. That evening the news media stood behind a rope line outside the White House, with cameras trained on a table with four chairs that had been set up in the Rose Garden. Then the President, Vice President Joe Biden, the professor, and the police officer took their seats and drank their beers. The news media noted that the four couldn't even agree on which brand of beer to drink—so each had his own particular brand. Rather than conciliation and reconciliation that would put the story to rest, the Beer Summit kept the focus on race relations and on disagreement. It also provoked another side issue: none of the four beers was made by an American company, something that caused minor protests and further distraction.

The President's and news media's distraction gave the President's opponents an opening, which they exploited. They organized an extensive campaign to turn public opinion against the President's proposal. Pundits and interest groups began calling the plan a "massive government takeover of healthcare" in which bureaucrats would make life-and-death choices about medical treatments. A relatively benign and long-accepted provision to compensate doctors for consulting with patients and their families on end-of-life options was characterized as "death panels," and members of Congress took to the House floor to warn that seniors were at risk.

Initiative and Response

 *From* Warfighting

All actions in war, regardless of the level,
are based upon either taking the *initiative* or reacting in *response* to
the opponent. By taking the initiative, we dictate the terms of conflict
and force the enemy to meet us on our own terms. The initiative
allows us to pursue some positive aim even if only to preempt an
enemy initiative. It is through the initiative that we seek to impose
our will on the enemy.

> *All communications are based upon either*
> *taking the initiative or reacting in response to the audience,*
> *adversaries, or the environment.*
> *By taking the initiative, we dictate the terms of discussion*
> *and the communication agenda. It is through the initiative that*
> *we seek to influence our audience.*

In Chapter 4, "Speed, Focus, and the First Mover Advantage," we
noted that there's a first mover advantage in war and in communication. Whoever controls the communication agenda typically wins. The
communication agenda consists of both the topics for discussion and
the vocabulary for that discussion. In American politics we see this in
the labels various parts of the political spectrum use to name the same
thing: The tax on large estates after someone dies, long called the
estate tax, is labeled a "death tax" by those who oppose it. The abor-
tion debate is typically framed as between those who call themselves
"pro-choice" and those who call themselves "pro-life."

The first mover advantage is a further example of disproportionality. A delay of just a few minutes can allow an adversary, a critic, a
competitor, the media, social media, or others to seize the initiative
and move an audience to think, feel, or·do the opposite of what we
might want it to.

President Obama wanted to control the healthcare debate:
to frame the issues on his terms. He wanted to outmaneuver his

opponents, to shape public opinion and win hearts and minds before they had a chance to respond. That was the whole point of the press conference. And the whole reason he made it such a big event.

From Warfighting

The Marine Corps concept for winning is a warfighting doctrine based on rapid, flexible, and opportunistic maneuver. The essence of maneuver is taking action to generate and exploit some kind of advantage over the enemy as a means for accomplishing our objectives as effectively as possible.

> *Our concept of effective communication is based on rapid, flexible, and opportunistic maneuver. The essence of maneuver is taking action to generate and exploit some competitive advantage to influence audiences so as to accomplish our objectives as effectively as possible.*

But the President stumbled, and his opponents stole the march on him when he took a reporter's question about race and racial profiling. Rather than controlling the agenda—or even being able to address the agenda—the President spent more than a week trying to put out a fire of his own making. Instead of using maneuver to his advantage, he inadvertently handed the opportunity to maneuver to the other side.

The President's opponents seized the initiative for themselves. The United States Senate did not pass healthcare before the August recess. As a body it didn't even consider healthcare. During the recess, in turn, congressional town hall meetings on healthcare reform were subject to organized and orchestrated disruptions. Democratic congressmen found themselves on the receiving end of shouting, interruptions, and other displays of incivility. The media initially reported the disruptions as spontaneous, but soon it became clear that a series of interlocking front groups funded by business interests· had organized the disruptions, complete with how-to kits on how and when to disrupt, and busing protestors from meeting to meeting.

Along the way, the media noted that a potent political force had emerged to oppose both healthcare and the President's larger agenda: the Tea Party movement. Named for the 1773 Boston rebellion against taxes imposed by Britain against the American colonies, the Tea Party had taken tentative steps to protest taxes and President Obama in the spring of 2009, but it found its voice and its organizing power in the August healthcare town hall disruptions and protests.

By early September, the President needed to change the dynamic in his favor. He needed to reclaim the agenda and restore the terms of discussion back to his own vocabulary.

He chose another grand gesture—this time a joint session of Congress. The trappings of the White House East Room would no longer suffice. He needed to address the Congress itself from the podium of the House of Representatives. A giant American flag hung behind him. House Speaker Nancy Pelosi presided over the chamber, Vice President Biden to her right, both sitting just behind and flanking the President.

 *From* **Warfighting**

The flux of war is a product of the continuous interaction
between initiative and response. Actions in war
more or less reflect the constant imperative to seize
and maintain the initiative. The initiative is clearly
the preferred form of action because only through
the initiative can we ultimately impose our will on the enemy.

> *Communication is a product of continuous interaction between initiative and response. Effective communication is more or less the constant imperative to seize and maintain the initiative. The initiative is clearly the preferred form of action because only through the initiative can we ultimately impose our will to influence our audience.*

By using the even greater magisterial authority of a joint session, the President thought he could change the game. He needed to overcome the news media's fascination with conflict, recapture the initiative from the Tea Party, and get the debate back to his actual proposal.

And in his speech to Congress he took a sharper tone than usual when highlighting the many mischaracterizations and misstatements about healthcare. He said,

> Given all the misinformation that has been spread over the past few months, I realize that many Americans have grown nervous about reform. So tonight I want to address some of the key controversies that are still out there. Some of people's concerns have grown out of bogus claims spread by those whose only agenda is to kill reform at any cost. The best example is the claim, made not just by radio and cable talk shows, but by prominent politicians, that we plan to set up panels of bureaucrats with the power to kill off senior citizens. Now such a charge would be laughable if it weren't so cynical and irresponsible. It is a lie, plain and simple.[6]

At that point Democrats in Congress rose in a standing ovation, while Republicans stayed seated, some chatting nervously to their colleagues.

The President continued his litany of mischaracterizations: "There are also those who claim that our reforms would insure illegal immigrants. This too is false. The reforms, the reforms I'm proposing, would not apply to those who are here illegally."[7]

As he spoke, a relatively obscure congressman named Joe Wilson, a Republican from South Carolina, interrupted the President with a shouted outburst: "You lie!"[8] In tone it resembled the disruptions of congressional town hall meetings. But the context was completely different. It was an unprecedented breach of decorum and of House rules, and a remarkable display of incivility toward a President of the United States. A stunned Nancy Pelosi, in the Speaker's chair, focused her eyes on the congressman, a look of horror on her face. Vice President Biden looked down, as if embarrassed. Members of Congress reacted to the outburst with their own: booing Congressman Wilson. The President, taken aback, pointed a finger in the direction of his heckler, and said, "It's not true."[9]

The President continued down his list, but the damage was done. The media coverage the next day and throughout the next week was on Congressman Wilson, who quickly became a household name. Congressman Wilson called the White House that night to apologize for his outburst, but he refused to apologize to House of Representatives colleagues for his breach of House rules. He became the darling of conservative talk radio, and coverage of his outburst dominated the Sunday political talk shows, even as the President's staff appeared on the programs to defend healthcare reform. Congressman Wilson's Web site got so much traffic that it crashed. And he raised millions of dollars for his reelection campaign.

That Sunday, President Obama went on the CBS news magazine *60 Minutes.* He acknowledged that he had lost control of his health-care message. Asked about Congressman Wilson's outburst, the President said:

> Well, see, this is part of what happens. I mean, it becomes a big circus instead of us focusing on healthcare. You know, this is a story that people will run with for a week. In the meantime, we have stopped serious debate about how are we going to make sure that insurance companies who don't treat their customers right are checked. That's the conversation I want to have.[10]

By the President's own admission, his attempt to reclaim the initiative faltered. For the rest of the legislative session the President was playing catch-up.

After his proposals were watered down to overcome Senate filibusters, and other legislative maneuvering, a bill labeled healthcare reform finally passed both houses of Congress and was signed into law on March 23. But it was a very tepid version of what the President had laid out in July. It failed to cover all uninsured, it lacked a public option for those without insurance, and it delayed implementation of many key provisions—including guarantees of insurance despite pre-existing conditions. Just getting something passed was an accomplishment. But what was actually passed was not what the President had in mind when he began the process.

The healthcare debate is an object lesson in leaders' need to control the initiative. Throughout, the President tried big gestures, first to get control, and then to get it back. But it wasn't a big gesture that deprived the President of the momentum to control the agenda in the initial moments of the campaign, but a relatively minor one whose impact was disproportionate to the words spoken. He stepped on his message and said something wildly interesting, thereby losing the critically important first news cycle. And the vacuum was filled by his opponents, who masterfully capitalized on the opening the President provided.

Adventures in Time

Disproportionality applies not only to what one says but also to when one says it. Ideally a leader can exercise the first mover advantage. But sometimes that isn't possible. But even when others begin to define a situation before a leader can, there's still an opportunity to protect one's reputation and regain control of the agenda. It just gets harder and harder to control the agenda as time passes.

In Chapter 4 we mentioned the Golden Hour of Crisis Response, which is part of operationalizing the first mover advantage. The Golden Hour doesn't refer to a particular number of minutes, but rather to the observation that incremental delays in controlling the communication agenda lead to greater-than-incremental harm.

The Golden Hour arose out of emergency medicine. We know that the longer it takes to get competent medical care after a serious accident or heart attack, the slimmer the chances of survival. And that medical procedures that would work in the first few minutes would be woefully inadequate 90 minutes later. That's because the patient's condition is dynamic—it is constantly changing. It isn't enough to address the patient's condition at the moment of injury. Rather, medical professionals know that they need to address the medical condition at the moment of treatment. And the longer it takes to get the treatment, the more robust the response will have to be.

The same applies in the quest to win or keep hearts and minds. The longer it takes to control the communication agenda, the harder it becomes. That's because more and more people are reaching conclusions about the situation, making judgments, and believing and acting on what they hear. What would have been sufficient in the early phases of a situation becoming public would be woefully inadequate hours or days or weeks later.

As illustrated in Figure 5.1, the general principle in applying the golden hour to controlling the communication agenda is the rule of 45 minutes, six hours, three days, two weeks. That's the sequence of disproportionate effects that arise in particular intervals in the cycle of visibility—what used to be called the "news cycle" but with the ubiquity of social media is now far more widespread. This principle suggests that it's possible to defend one's self against negative visibility, but that the longer it takes to organize a sufficiently persuasive response, the harder it becomes.

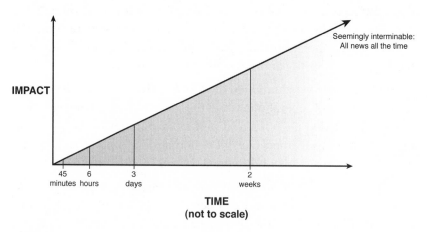

[Illustration by Adam Tiouririne]

Figure 5.1 The Golden Hour of Crisis Response: rule of 45 minutes, six hours, three days, two weeks.

That's why speed is so important—speed defined not as impulse but as the predisposition to make sound decisions quickly and to communicate them effectively.

Of course, the best way to control the communication agenda is through the first mover advantage: Be the first to fully define the issue, your motive, and your actions. We saw this in the Fallujah mosque shooting.

But what if that's not possible? If something happens unexpectedly? Or if others start talking about you before you're ready? Then there's a need to be nimble.

From Warfighting

The defense, on the other hand, contributes *resisting power,* the ability to preserve and protect ourselves. The defense generally has a negative aim: that of resisting the enemy's will.

The defense, on the other hand, contributes resisting power, *the ability to preserve and protect ourselves. The defense generally has a negative aim: to avoid losing the trust and confidence of stakeholders.*

If you can effectively define the agenda within the first 45 minutes of an issue becoming public from some external source, relatively few stakeholders will have heard of the issue from others, and things are likely to settle down with minimal impact.

If you miss the first 45 minutes, given the proliferation of social networking and citizen journalism, the likelihood is that more and more people will hear very quickly about the issue, with critics, adversaries, commentators, and others defining the issue, your motives, and your actions. It is still possible to take control of the communication back, but it will be harder: You'll need to reach more people, and overcome more competition for attention. And some people may have already formed opinions that will be very hard to change. But if it can be done within the first six hours of the issue becoming public, then things should settle down relatively quickly.

This is what happened with McDonald's when its CEO died suddenly, as we saw in Chapter 4. McDonald's lost the first mover advantage when the news media, investment community, and restaurant operators were all speaking about the risks to the company of being leaderless during its most important meeting. But within several hours McDonald's was able to definitively take back control of the agenda with the announcement of a new CEO and with his affirmation that the strategy would remain in place. There was no lasting reputational or other damage to McDonald's even though the company was at risk for several hours.

If it takes more than several hours to define the situation, motives, and actions, then a company and its leaders will be at risk for three days. That's because of the dynamics of daily newspaper publication, television and social media reaction to the newspaper story, and the inevitable second-day newspaper story and subsequent reaction. During this period, even more people are being made aware of the issue by critics, the media, or others. And the company and its leaders are more and more at risk. But if within three days the company and its leaders engage stakeholders effectively, the situation should resolve itself.

We saw this happen in early September 2011. In the back-to-school sales cycle, retailer J. C. Penney offered a back-to-school T-shirt for teenage girls. The shirt was adorned with a saying in whimsical typeface: "I'm too pretty to do homework so my brother has to do it for me." Some customers found the shirt offensive. A young woman saw a Facebook posting about the shirt and decided to do something about it. Lauren Todd launched a petition on the social network site Change.org, which allows individuals to initiate petitions online. Change.org, in turn, promoted the petition through Twitter and to parenting blogs, asking people to post directly onto J. C. Penney's Facebook page. Within a day more than 1,600 people had signed the petition. By the end of the day, J. C. Penney had pulled the shirt from its stores and apologized. It posted on its various sites, "We agree that the 'Too Pretty' T-shirt does not deliver an appropriate message, and we have immediately discontinued its sale."[11] Once stakeholders saw the retailer doing the responsible thing, the controversy abated and the company suffered no meaningful harm to its reputation.

If it takes more than several days for a company or its leaders to define the issue, its motives, and its actions, then the likelihood is that significantly more people will know about the issue, and it will be even harder to resolve the issue. And because of the publication schedule of weekly magazines, weekly newspaper sections, weekly blogs, and television programs, the likelihood is that a controversy will be alive for at least two weeks. We saw that in Chapter 1, "Words Matter," in John McCain's failure to adapt quickly to the changing economy in September 2008. For two full weeks he was playing catch-up, first from his failure to adapt, then from his suspension of his campaign just days before the first debate with Senator Obama.

If it takes more than two weeks to define your issue, motives, and actions, then there's a very good chance of significant damage, sometimes irreparable. We saw that with Tony Hayward and BP: He became untenable as CEO and had to leave the company. And we saw it in President Obama's healthcare reform initiative. Because of an unforced error, he was unable to get or keep control of the communication agenda, and had to settle for a very watered-down healthcare reform law.

Recap: Best Practices from This Chapter

 From **Warfighting**

In communication, incremental changes or minor events can have a greater-than-incremental impact on outcomes.

All communications are based upon either taking the initiative or reacting in response to the audience, adversaries, or the environment.
By taking the initiative, we dictate the terms of discussion and the communication agenda. It is through the initiative that we seek to influence our audience.

Our concept of effective communication is based on rapid, flexible, and opportunistic maneuver. The essence of maneuver is taking action to generate and exploit some competitive advantage to influence audiences so as to accomplish our objectives as effectively as possible.

Communication is a product of continuous interaction between initiative and response. Effective communication is more or less the constant imperative to seize and maintain the initiative. The initiative is clearly the preferred form of action because only through the initiative can we ultimately impose our will to influence our audience.

The defense, on the other hand, contributes resisting power, *the ability to preserve and protect ourselves. The defense generally has a negative aim: to avoid losing the trust and confidence of stakeholders.*

Lessons for Leaders and Communicators

Controlling the communication agenda requires both discipline and nimbleness. Ideally, leaders can take the first mover advantage, a form of maneuver that allows them to influence audiences effectively before the audience has been influenced by other points of view.

But all too often leaders lose discipline, if only for a moment. And in those instances there's a significant risk of losing the advantage, and even of handing the advantage to others. President Obama's uncharacteristic loss of discipline in fielding a question unrelated to healthcare cost him the first mover advantage and may well have cost him meaningful parts of his legislative agenda.

Especially in contested situations, there is a constant interplay between being in control of the communication agenda and having to respond to others who are trying to control it. Because the battle for hearts and minds is often a competitive one, it's critical for leaders to be able to capture, retain, and exploit the initiative.

But even minor blunders can have a major impact. The principle of disproportionality suggests that there isn't a one-to-one relationship of input and outcome. A single slip-up in a high-stakes situation (the Cambridge police acted stupidly; I'd like my life back; Brownie, you're doing a heck of a job) can overshadow even the otherwise most effective communication. And incremental delays in fielding a sufficient response to an issue that becomes public independent of the leader can have a disproportionate and negative effect on the outcome.

This places a premium on speed as it is defined by the Marines— the consistent predisposition to make sound decisions quickly and to communicate them effectively.

6

Goals, Strategies, and Tactics: Preparing and Planning

On August 6, 2010, late on a Friday afternoon, investors in HP (formerly known as Hewlett-Packard) got a surprise. The company announced that Chief Executive Officer Mark Hurd, who was widely credited with turning around the troubled company, was resigning.[1]

That was surprising enough. But the reasons given were both murky and baffling. And it began a year of communication, strategy, and execution missteps that caused confidence and trust in the leadership of the company and its board to plummet.

In its announcement the company said that the general counsel, overseen by the board, had conducted an investigation of an allegation of sexual harassment against Mr. Hurd. Readers of the announcement might have concluded that the next sentence would confirm the allegation. But it didn't. It said that the investigation had concluded that he had *not* violated the company's sexual harassment policy. So why was he leaving? It wasn't clear. The announcement said that the investigation had found "violations of HP's Standards of Business Conduct."[2]

The announcement did not specify anything about either the sexual harassment allegations that prompted the investigation, or the nature of the violations of the code of conduct that apparently led to the resignation. It did quote Mr. Hurd saying:

As the investigation progressed, I realized there were instances in which I did not live up to the standards and principles of trust, respect, and integrity that I have espoused at HP and which have guided me throughout my career. After a number of discussions with members of the board, I will move aside

123

and the board will search for new leadership. This is a painful decision for me to make after five years at HP, but I believe it would be difficult for me to continue as an effective leader at HP and I believe this is the only decision the board and I could make at this time. I want to stress that this in no way reflects on the operating performance or financial integrity of HP.[3]

Investors were confused and alarmed. Shaw Wu, an analyst at Kaufman Brothers, told investors, as quoted by the *Associated Press,* "We are frankly surprised and disappointed as Hurd was a strong leader and helped transform HP into a leading player."[4]

The public announcement gave few details about what had happened and why. But soon after that announcement, an internal e-mail from interim CEO Cathie Lesjak gave a little more information to employees. The e-mail promptly leaked and was part of the initial round of press coverage. Ms. Lesjak told employees that Mr. Hurd had

failed to disclose a close personal relationship he had with [a] contractor that constituted a conflict of interest, failed to maintain accurate expense reports, and misused company assets. Each of these constituted a violation of HP's Standards of Business Conduct, and together they demonstrated a profound lack of judgment that significantly undermined Mark's credibility and his ability to effectively lead HP.[5]

The e-mail didn't give more specifics about the "misuse of company assets." But failing to disclose a close personal relationship with a contractor and filing inaccurate expense reports seemed relatively minor compared to the dismissal. The remedy seemed out of line with the offense.

The company's general counsel briefed reporters by conference call that afternoon and added a bit more detail. He said that Mr. Hurd had a "close, personal relationship" with a female contractor for two years that he had not disclosed to the board. He said that Mr. Hurd's conduct "exhibited a profound lack of judgment" and that HP's board had insisted that he resign.[6] The board's insistence that he resign for failing to disclose a personal relationship with a female contractor also sounded out of proportion. Did he have a relationship before that person became a contractor? Did he develop it while she was a contractor? What kind of relationship, and why would that require disclosure to the board? And saying that the board insisted that Mr. Hurd resign meant that he was essentially fired. He wasn't leaving by his own choice, but by theirs.

So the three different statements provided three different levels of detail:

1. The announcement mentioned an investigation of an allegation of sexual harassment, noted that Mr. Hurd had not violated the company's sexual harassment policy, but found that he had violated the code of conduct. It didn't give details. It quoted Mr. Hurd as saying that he had failed to live up to a standard of trust and integrity. He also said that the issues were unrelated to the operating performance or financial integrity of the company. That suggested some personal failing.

2. The internal e-mail gave a bit more detail: an undisclosed relationship with a contractor, inaccurate expense reports, and misuse of company assets.

3. The press conference call went a bit further: the undisclosed relationship was with a female contractor, and the board had lost confidence in him because of a lapse in judgment, and forced him to resign. Could it be that he had harassed the woman but because she wasn't an employee he technically hadn't violated the company policy?

The three public statements were consistent in not giving any details that would allow stakeholders to understand what had actually happened, how big it was, and what it meant.

On Monday, August 9, the first business day after the announcement, CNBC reported that Mr. Hurd would collect between $34 million and $40 million in severance payments. Other news reports calculated it to be closer to $50 million. Kevin Murphy of the University of Southern California Marshall School of Business told CNBC that he was puzzled by the validity of a severance package if Mr. Hurd was essentially being terminated for an ethical breach. Frank Glassner of the compensation consulting firm Veritas Frank Glassner went further, calling Mr. Hurd's removal and the manner in which it was announced "a huge lapse in thought and judgment by the board."[7] Over the weekend commentator Henry Blodget had asked, "So, on behalf of HP shareholders, we have a question for HP: Why is Mark Hurd getting a $50 million severance payout if he filed bogus expense reports? And why was he allowed to 'resign'? Why wasn't he fired for cause?"[8]

These were all reasonable and appropriate concerns and questions, and easy to anticipate with a little planning. But they were left open for commentators, critics, and competitors to raise. The stated reasons, frankly, didn't make much sense.

Larry Ellison, Chief Executive of Oracle Corporation, told the *New York Times*, "The HP Board just made the worst personnel decision since the idiots on the Apple board fired Steve Jobs many years ago. That decision nearly destroyed Apple and would have if Steve hadn't come back and saved them."[9] Oracle was both a competitor and a partner of HP, depending on the business line.

Business partners were also surprised. "I am shocked. It's always a shock whenever someone of that stature departs suddenly for any reason," said Mont Phelps, CEO of HP partner NWN. Chris Case, CEO of Sequel Data Systems, another HP partner, said, "It's disappointing news because Hurd was always a huge advocate for partners." Future Tech Enterprises CEO Bob Venero said, "Mark had a clear vision of where he was going," and wondered, "Are they going to stay on that line or is whoever they're going to bring in going to change that dynamic? From a partner perspective, that's a scary thought."[10]

HP stock fell more than 9 percent after the initial announcement, losing more than $8 billion in market value. The stock would continue to fall as events played out in somewhat predictable ways and as more and more stakeholders began to question the thoughtfulness, judgment, and ultimately the effectiveness of the board. And as the board gave stakeholders more and more reasons to.

One week after the announcement, the board was sued by investors who alleged "gross mismanagement and waste of corporate assets" related to the severance package and other missteps.[11]

Planning Isn't Looking at a Calendar; It's Looking at a Chessboard

Sir John Harvey-Jones, the British industrialist and later host of the BBC *Troubleshooters* television program, famously said that, "the nicest thing about not planning is that failure comes as a complete surprise."

That seemed to be the case at HP. The initial announcement was so vague, and with so many inconsistencies and gaps, that stakeholders predictably needed far more information to be able to make a judgment about the company: investors about whether to continue to have confidence in the company as an investment; employees to get clarity about what was expected of them; business partners about whether to continue to do business with the company, and on what terms.

HP's board left stakeholders wanting and needing to know much more than what the company, in its three initial communications, told them.

 From **Warfighting**

To influence the action to our advantage, we must project our thoughts forward in time and space. We frequently do this through planning.

> *To influence our stakeholders to our advantage, we must project our thoughts forward in space and time. We frequently do this through planning.*

Projecting thoughts forward is the key to planning. And as we project our thoughts forward, we need also to project our stakeholders' thoughts and likely reaction forward. As we have noted in earlier chapters, all communication is a process of continuous mutual adaptation, of give and take, of move and countermove. And there's a powerful competitive advantage in being the first mover, which HP was in this case. But for the first mover advantage to work, it needs to be implemented well. Like any other powerful tool, used poorly it can cause significant self-inflicted harm, as it did for HP.

And part of getting the first mover advantage right is to anticipate stakeholders' reactions and to adapt the initial communication to neutralize those concerns before they are raised. Here's the rule of thumb for communicating bad news:

- Tell it all.
- Tell it fast.
- Tell 'em what you're doing about it.
- Tell 'em when it's over.
- Get back to work.

"Tell it all" means saying all that is necessary to establish stakeholder understanding, buy-in, acceptance, or at least neutrality. "Tell it fast" means getting all the news out at once, in a single news cycle, and preventing the dripping out of new details over time, each of which creates a new news cycle and causes stakeholders to continue to wonder about the leadership skills of those who are communicating.

Indeed, veteran journalist and chronicler of corporate malfeasance James B. Stewart wrote in *SmartMoney* magazine:

> When will the Hewlett-Packard board learn the most fundamental lesson of corporate governance and public relations? That lesson is simple: Disclose all relevant facts, get ahead of the media, and don't turn a one-day story into a media frenzy.

> In U.S. public companies, the directors are supposed to serve the owners the shareholders [sic] and not management or themselves. Shareholders deserve, and are entitled by law, to material information about the company. Boards should err on the side of transparency. Concealing facts only breeds suspicion, not to mention intense media coverage. That someone might be embarrassed by full disclosure is irrelevant and shouldn't factor in any disclosure decisions.[12]

There are other reasons besides public relations to anticipate stakeholder reactions. The very process of considering likely reactions to proposed communications can reveal failures of planning in the actual business decision making. As Admiral Mullen noted in the first chapter, too often what are labeled failures of communication are really failures of strategy and execution. Communication planning can serve as the canary in the coal mine—as a leading indicator that something is amiss in the business planning process. The need to explain something often calls attention to some inconsistency in decision makers' thought process.

Indeed, commentators told the *New York Times* that the rationale for the termination didn't seem to add up. Shane Greenstein, a business professor at Northwestern University's Kellogg School of Management, said, "There is a missing piece here because it doesn't make sense."[13] Oracle's Larry Ellison went further, suggesting that the board was insincere in giving its reasons for Mr. Hurd's departure:

> What the expense fraud claims do reveal is an H.P. board desperately grasping at straws in trying to publicly explain the unexplainable; how a false sexual harassment claim and some petty expense report errors led to the loss of one of Silicon Valley's best and most respected leaders.[14]

In *SmartMoney* James B. Stewart said,

> When I contacted H-P, a spokesman declined to answer any of my questions and said the company had nothing to add to what it said Friday when it announced Hurd's resignation. He would not say whether, as part of Hurd's agreement to resign, H-P promised not to disclose…any details of what its own investigation uncovered. In my view, that is not good enough. H-P still has plenty of questions to answer, including its justification for paying Hurd an exit package worth more than $35 million even while forcing him to resign. Until it does, it is hard to have any confidence in the judgment of H-P's board and as an investor, I'd avoid the stock.[15]

Planning isn't just determining a sequence of actions and writing a statement based on what you want to say or are minimally required to say. It's about a chessboard, not a calendar. It's about thinking several moves ahead: If we do X, what will they do, and what will we then need to do next? If we do Y, what will they do, and so on. So planning requires understanding the absolutely predictable and appropriate expectations of stakeholders, anticipating and then meeting those expectations. As Mr. Stewart noted in *SmartMoney*, failing to meet stakeholder expectations can cause them to lose trust and confidence.

 *From* **Warfighting**

[Planning] does not mean that we establish a
detailed timetable of events. We have already concluded
that war is inherently disorderly, and we cannot expect to dictate
its terms with any sort of precision. Rather, we attempt to shape
the general conditions of war.... Through shaping,
commanders gain the initiative, preserve momentum,
and control the tempo of operations.

> *Planning does not mean that we establish a*
> *detailed timetable of events. Rather, we attempt to shape*
> *the general conditions under which our communication*
> *will work.... Through shaping, leaders gain the initiative,*
> *preserve momentum, and control the communication agenda.*

The HP board failed to shape the communication agenda. It failed to recognize a paradox of crisis communication: that if you want others to not talk about you, sometimes you need to say more than you may initially want to. Because all effective communication is goal-oriented, intended to change something, an effective leader or leadership team focuses on what it wants stakeholders to know, think, feel, and do, and the ways to get those stakeholders to change so that they will know, think, feel, and do so.

Shaping the communication agenda requires considering more than what we may be minimally required to say, but rather identifying what we optimally should say in order to maintain trust, confidence, and loyalty.

In HP's case, right up until the very moment of its announcement, stakeholders held Mr. Hurd in the highest regard, thinking of him as the white knight who had rescued HP from itself as it was spiraling out of control. He was the hero. And for him to leave so suddenly, something quite egregious must have happened; still, if he had to leave that way, why did he receive severance?

The circumstances all called to mind the very kinds of problems, embedded deep in the governance of HP, that Mr. Hurd had supposedly fixed.

Hurd to the Rescue

Before Mr. Hurd's arrival five years earlier, HP had developed a reputation as a company that couldn't shoot straight. It had gone through serial blunders, of strategy, of execution, and of ethics.

Early in the decade, then-newly-arrived CEO Carly Fiorina pushed through a highly controversial acquisition of Compaq computer, against the strong objections of many investors, including the heirs to the company's founders. The merger proved to be a disaster, and in early 2005 Ms. Fiorina was fired. She was succeeded as board chair by Patricia Dunn, former CEO of Barclays Global Investors, and as CEO by Mark Hurd, former CEO of NCR Corp.

Ms. Dunn had a rocky tenure as board chair. Alarmed that the media was publishing information about private board discussions, in early 2006 Ms. Dunn authorized external security consultants to spy on board members and journalists. Among the techniques the investigators used was "pretexting," pretending to be board members and asking phone companies to send them copies of recent bills. That way they could see whether the directors had contacted the news media. Pretexting is a crime, a form of identity theft. The investigators discovered the leaker, but when Ms. Dunn informed the board of the manner in which the leaker was identified, there was a boardroom rebellion.

Tom Perkins, a member of the board and chair of its nominating and governance committee, resigned in protest. Under U.S. law, when a director resigns from a board because of a disagreement about the company's operations, policies, or practices, the company is required to so disclose. But the company's filing with the Securities and Exchange Commission did not mention the reasons, and its press release about the departure merely thanked him for his service.

When the story about Ms. Dunn's investigation, the boardroom rebellion, and Mr. Perkins' reasons for his resignation became public, there was a loud public outcry and Ms. Dunn was forced to resign. She was indicted by the California Attorney General, but the charges were later dropped.

Mr. Hurd, who was not implicated in the spy scandal, was called to testify in front of a congressional committee. He apologized to the board members, employees, and journalists whose privacy had been violated; confirmed a commitment to integrity; and outlined steps the company was taking to get to the bottom of what had happened and to put structures in place to prevent a recurrence.[16]

The scandal died down, and Mr. Hurd got on with the job of running the company. He was wildly successful, at least in investors' eyes. He reorganized the company into three divisions, making each division head accountable for sales targets. He cut expenses significantly, including through large staff reductions. During his five years in office, revenues grew by a third, net income tripled, and the stock more than doubled.

So after five years at the helm, it was quite startling for investors to hear that Mr. Hurd was leaving under an ethical cloud.

Hurd on the Street

What happened? According to published reports, HP had a marketing program whereby Mr. Hurd would attend big industry conferences. At those conferences the company would invite executives from some of HP's largest customers to relationship-building events it called "Executive Summits." HP contracted with Jodie Fisher to serve as a hostess at the summits, to chat up customer executives to make them feel at home, and at the right moment walk them over to Mr. Hurd to talk business.

Time magazine described Ms. Fisher as "a former actress and reality-television personality."[17] She and Mr. Hurd became friendly as they got to know each other, and they would often dine together while on the road. It was those dinners, apparently, that were characterized inaccurately on Mr. Hurd's expense reports. The total amount in question was under $20,000. Both Ms. Fisher and Mr. Hurd have said publicly that they never had an affair or any sexual relationship. In the ordinary course of business, the program was discontinued and Ms. Fisher's contract was terminated.

On June 29, 2010, Mr. Hurd received a letter from celebrity lawyer Gloria Allred alleging that Mr. Hurd had made improper advances to Ms. Fisher during her tenure as a contractor for the company. The letter was unsealed by the courts in late 2011 but was not available publicly as the events unfolded in 2010. It outlined in dramatic detail vivid accounts of Mr. Hurd's conversations with Ms. Fisher. Ms. Allred said she was "prepared to move forward and seek all available legal remedies" on Ms. Fisher's behalf.[18]

Mr. Hurd forwarded the letter to HP's general counsel, who notified the board. The company retained the law firm Covington & Burling to conduct an internal investigation. That investigation turned up inconsistencies in Mr. Hurd's account of his relationship with Ms. Fisher, and inaccuracies in his expense reports.

According to an account of board deliberations by *Fortune* magazine,

> Whether or not the two had been physically intimate—representatives of both Hurd and Fisher have publicly asserted that the two did not have a sexual relationship—several directors felt that Hurd's story had changed from their initial informal inquiries to his answers to the investigators. Hurd's initial denials of an inappropriate relationship with Fisher had been so vehement that, when it turned out there was evidence of a close relationship—including the fact that Hurd and Fisher dined together out of town on two occasions when Fisher was not working at an HP event—some members of the board simply lost their trust in Hurd.[19]

At that point the question shifted from *whether* Mr. Hurd should go to *when and how.* He suggested a minimal disclosure about the lawsuit, and his resignation several months later, which could be characterized as a retirement. The board rejected that proposal.

The board's lawyers had scheduled a mediation session with Ms. Fisher for the first week in August in which they hoped to get to the bottom of what had happened. But late in the evening of August 4, Mr. Hurd settled Ms. Fisher's lawsuit. The terms were confidential. The board had not been aware that Mr. Hurd was negotiating a settlement, and was surprised to learn about it the morning of August 5. By settling the suit, Mr. Hurd essentially prevented the board's lawyers from hearing from Ms. Fisher directly. So the board would not be able to learn Ms. Fisher's side of the story. It was the last straw. The entire board lost trust in Mr. Hurd, and he had to go. HP announced his resignation the next day.[20]

Measure Twice, Cut Once

Then on September 6, just one month after leaving HP, Mr. Hurd joined Oracle as co-president, essentially becoming CEO Larry Ellison's right-hand man.

HP investors were outraged. How could the former HP CEO get a severance package between $34 million and $50 million and be allowed to join another company—especially one that was HP's competitor in important business lines—just a month later? Although California law makes noncompetition agreements nearly impossible to enforce, investors believed HP should have found some way to ensure that Mr. Hurd would not join the competition.

The next day HP sued Oracle, and asked the court for an injunction preventing Mr. Hurd from starting at his new position. The lawsuit said,

> Hurd's position as a President and a member of the Board of Directors for Oracle puts HP's trade secrets and confidential information in jeopardy. He will be responsible, in whole or in part, for the direction of the company. As a competitor of HP, he will necessarily call upon HP's trade secrets and confidential information in performing his job duties for Oracle.[21]

Investors, for their part, wondered why HP hadn't thought about that before, but saw the lawsuit as an unnecessary distraction. Investment analyst Felix Salmon blasted the HP board in the investment newsletter *Seeking Alpha:*

What on earth is the point of Hewlett-Packard suing Mark Hurd? The mutual mudslinging has been decidedly unedifying to date, and now it's certain to get much worse—and to take place in open court, to boot. With a market capitalization of over $90 billion, suing its former CEO certainly isn't going to move the needle financially. And it's going to take up a large amount of the valuable time not only of HP's executives but of HP's board members too.

I don't know who made the decision to launch this lawsuit, but it looks very much like it was filed in a fit of passion after hearing that Hurd had signed on with Oracle. There's no tactical or strategic rationale for this: it's just petulance, really.

Does HP even *have* a chairman right now? It definitely needs one: a grown-up who can tell these people to put away their silly squabbles and concentrate on actually running their business. This lawsuit might be a distraction for Hurd, but it's going to be much more of a distraction in HP's executive suite. *Basta.* Please.[22]

Oracle shot back with its own criticism of HP's board. In a press release Oracle CEO Larry Ellison said,

> Oracle has long viewed HP as an important partner.... By filing this vindictive lawsuit against Oracle and Mark Hurd, the HP board is acting with utter disregard for that partnership, our joint customers, and their own shareholders and employees. The HP Board is making it virtually impossible for Oracle and HP to continue to cooperate and work together in the IT marketplace.[23]

HP stock fell about 4 percent on the news of the lawsuit. Two weeks later the two companies settled. CNET, the technology newsletter, speculated about the real reason for the lawsuit:

> The terms of the settlement are confidential, according to an HP spokesperson. HP said today that Hurd, now co-president of Oracle, has agreed to "adhere to his obligations to protect HP's confidential information while fulfilling his responsibilities at Oracle." But an SEC filing today gives away the real

resolution: Hurd agreed to return some of the stock he was granted while still employed by HP.[24]

In other words, HP convinced Mr. Hurd to soften the blow of his massive severance package.

The board was busy that month. Just ten days after settling the lawsuit, HP announced a new CEO: Léo Apotheker, who had previously served as CEO of the German software giant SAP. The board also elected Ray Lane as non-executive chairman. Mr. Lane, a venture capitalist, had once been president of Oracle.

Mr. Apotheker was a curious choice. The circumstances of the board hiring him weren't known at the time, but a year later, when rumors swirled of Mr. Apotheker's pending demise, James B. Stewart put the pieces together in the *New York Times,* raising further questions about the leadership ability of the HP board:

> The mystery isn't why Hewlett-Packard is likely to part ways with its chief executive, Léo Apotheker, after just a year in the job. It's why he was hired in the first place. The answer, say many involved in the process, lies squarely with the troubled Hewlett-Packard board.... Interviews with several current and former directors and people close to them involved in the search that resulted in the hiring of Mr. Apotheker reveal a board that, while composed of many accomplished individuals, as a group was rife with animosities, suspicion, distrust, personal ambitions and jockeying for power that rendered it nearly dysfunctional.[25]

From Warfighting

We should try to shape events in a way that allows us several options so that by the time the moment for decisive operations arrives, we have not restricted ourselves to only one course of action.

Mr. Stewart noted that when the four-member search committee nominated three finalists to the full board, the other board members declined to meet with any of the finalists. And when the committee recommended Mr. Apotheker, none of the other directors chose to meet with him. So the new CEO was hired after only one-third of the board had met him. One former board member told Mr. Stewart, "I admit it was highly unusual. But we were exhausted from all the infighting."[26]

There was no particular reason to rush the decision. The board could have waited, either to meet with Mr. Apotheker or to explore additional candidates. But the board, according to Mr. Stewart, decided to go with the best choice of a very unattractive group. The announcement was made on September 30, and noted that the new CEO and new chairman would start on November 1.[27]

Investor reaction was immediately negative. Mr. Apotheker had left SAP after only 7 months as CEO, embroiled in a scandal involving alleged theft of trade secrets and copyright infringements from Oracle. He was virtually unknown in the U.S.

Fortune magazine editor at large Adam Lashinsky pointed to the integrity questions that led to his departure from SAP and noted that Mr. Apotheker didn't have experience in the middle market or in the consumer market, where HP is strong.

> HP's board of directors could have taken the easy way. It could have named a CEO with a proven track record of growth or innovation. Experience that spanned the bulk of HP's revenue base would have been a plus too. It could have promoted someone from within. It might have found a young, up-and-coming executive at a major competitor who was champing at the bit to be a CEO but was blocked by one of the old guys at the top. It could have found someone with a job. It didn't.[28]

Mr. Lashinsky quoted one European investor as saying the appointment was "idiotic"; an American software executive said it was "astonishing." HP stock fell about 4 percent in the two days following the announcement.

This is yet another demonstration of communication being a leading indicator: If they had thought through the likely stakeholder reaction to Mr. Apotheker, the board could have found ways to neutralize the objections in advance, or revisited their own decision-making process.

Mr. Apotheker didn't get off to a good start, and his reign was rocky.

He had been on the job less than a week when the *Wall Street Journal* published a bombshell: a story about Mr. Hurd's final days based on unnamed sources and recounting confidential board discussions, the contents of Ms. Allred's letter, and discussions between the board and Mr. Hurd. Some of the details were genuinely alarming; some were tawdry.

In particular, the story said that Mr. Hurd had told Ms. Fisher that HP was in confidential discussions to buy Electronic Data Systems Corp. (EDS) several weeks before the deal was announced. If true, that put Mr. Hurd at risk of a charge of insider trading. Mr. Hurd denied the allegation, and the board seemed inclined to believe him. But the story said that the main reason the board lost trust was in his account of his relationship with Ms. Fisher:

> In one previously undisclosed example: The CEO had told directors he didn't know Ms. Fisher acted in adult movies, say people briefed on the matter, but investigators hired by H-P learned he had visited Web pages showing her in pornographic scenes.... Another: Mr. Hurd told the board he didn't know Ms. Fisher well; later, in talking to investigators hired by H-P, he said they had a "very close personal relationship."[29]

Stakeholders' reaction to these disclosures was surprisingly positive. Finally, after months of speculation and an intangible feeling that the stated reasons for Mr. Hurd's departure didn't add up, they seemed to understand the reasons the board had lost confidence in Mr. Hurd. The new revelations caused even prior critics to say that terminating Mr. Hurd seemed like the right call. What hadn't made sense in August made sense now, because investors now had a more complete picture.

Commentator Henry Blodget, who had been sharply critical of the board, wrote in *Business Insider,*

After months of being pummeled for firing financially successful CEO Mark Hurd, HP's board has finally done what it should have done at the beginning: Tell the whole story....

They couldn't prove he was lying, but his story shifted enough over the course of the investigation that they no longer believed his denials. And so they canned him.

And under the same circumstances, any competent board would have done the same. Believing that an employee is lying to you, even when you can't prove it, is more than enough grounds for termination. Because this particular employee had a contract that presumably specified that he could only be fired for "cause," the board was presumably (and justifiably) worried that it would not be able to prove the "cause" if the case ever ended up in court. And that explains Hurd's huge severance payment....

The one thing every employee needs to do is maintain the trust and support of the people he or she works for. Mark Hurd failed to do that. And for that he has only himself to blame.[30]

In other words, given what the board knew at the time, terminating Mr. Hurd was a common-sense thing to do. Mr. Blodget did criticize the board for not having communicated better and sooner:

The HP board did blow it here, in several respects. But based on the details in the *WSJ*, the errors appear to have been in how the board negotiated the severance and communicated the reasons for Hurd's termination rather than the termination itself.[31]

Commentator Jay Yarrow, also writing in *Business Insider*, echoed Mr. Blodget and summarized the prevailing sentiment that day:

Finally! We now know the really real reason Mark Hurd was tossed from HP. And it finally makes sense.[32]

Maureen O'Gara wrote on the technology portal SysCon:

> An allegation of disclosing inside information has now been added to the otherwise flimsy story of why the HP board asked for the resignation of its star CEO Mark Hurd in August. It's the first thing that makes any sense in this whole benighted tale.[33]

Those comments immediately raise questions about whether and how the board might have been able to disclose more than it did in its initial announcement. Once stakeholders understood the reasons for the board's loss of trust in the CEO, the dismissal made sense. But none of that was conveyed on August 6. It took a leak of confidential board deliberations, by unnamed sources two months later, to set the record straight.

 *From* **Warfighting**

Planning plays as important a role in the preparation
for war as it does in the conduct of war.

> *Planning plays as important a role in the preparation for communication as it does in the implementation of communication.*

Several months later, HP's board went through a shake-up. HP announced the appointment of five new board members and the departure of four current members at the spring annual meeting. So the board would briefly expand to 17, then shrink to 13. The new directors were widely viewed as bringing adult supervision to a very dysfunctional board. They included Meg Whitman, former eBay CEO who had just run unsuccessfully for governor of California, plus several other seasoned and experienced executives. Among those leaving were board members who had been seen by their colleagues to be particularly contentious.[34]

In late February HP announced disappointing sales forecasts, and the stock fell about 13 percent. Three months later it fell another 8 percent when the company announced is first-quarter results.

By the summer of 2011, Mr. Apotheker was struggling, and was severely criticized for several strategic decisions and the way they were communicated. He pulled the plug on the company's TouchPad—its answer to Apple's iPad—after only about a month on the market, and said the company would exit the business of smartphones and mobile devices. He later had to clarify that the smartphone software business would remain, and would be licensed to other hardware makers. HP confirmed plans to acquire the British software firm Autonomy for nearly $12 billion, in what one investment analyst called a "value destroying deal." But most significantly, he announced the possibility of HP selling or spinning off its personal computer business. The head of the PC division got only 24 hours' notice that such a change was being considered. Big corporate customers were concerned, worrying about the reliability of the supply of HP computers. Dartmouth College Tuck School of Business professor M. Eric Johnson told the *New York Times* that the communication of the new strategy, "was botched in a big, big way.... It came out in dribs and drabs in a very confusing set of announcements."[35]

By late August, just a year after Mr. Hurd left, investors had had enough. Reuters reported that Mr. Apotheker's credibility with investors was plummeting along with its stock price:

> In a resounding rejection of Apotheker's grand vision, shareholders sent HP shares down almost 20 percent on Friday, wiping out $16 billion of value in the worst single-day fall since the Black Monday stock market crash of October 1987.
>
> Since Apotheker joined HP early last November, the company has lost almost 44 percent of its value, and he has lost a significant amount of investor support. "We wonder whether activist investors will—and should—begin to exert pressure on the board," said Toni Sacconaghi, an analyst with Sanford Bernstein. "If HP's results don't improve, the company will ultimately restructure its portfolio and/or replace its leadership."
>
> Pat Becker, Jr., fund manager at Portland, Oregon–based Becker Capital Management Inc., which owns HP shares, noted that Apotheker has continually failed to instill confidence in his conference calls with investors. "Every time he

has gotten on the call, the stock has gone down substantially," Becker said.[36]

Within a month Mr. Apotheker was out. He had received a $4 million signing bonus and a salary of $1.2 million, and would walk away with an additional $25 million in cash and stock as severance. Rumors of Mr. Apotheker's impending departure sent the stock up nearly 7 percent.

On September 22 HP announced that Mr. Apotheker had been fired and would be replaced by board member and former eBay CEO Meg Whitman.[37] A month later Ms. Whitman announced that HP would keep its PC business, and the stock rallied, rising nearly 9 percent.[38]

In the 13 months between Mark Hurd's departure and Meg Whitman's arrival as CEO, HP stock went from just under $46 to just above $23 per share, a loss of nearly half its value, representing $46.72 billion in market capitalization.

 *From* **Warfighting**

Strategy involves establishing goals, assigning forces, providing assets, and imposing conditions on the use of force in the theaters of war. Strategy derived from political and policy objectives must be clearly understood to be the sole authoritative basis for all operations.

> *Strategy involves establishing goals, assigning resources, and imposing conditions on the scope of communication. Strategy derived from business or organizational objectives must be clearly understood to be the sole authoritative basis for all communication.*

At every step in its decision making and communication, from Mr. Hurd's termination to Ms. Whitman's hiring, the HP board seemed to be acting on impulse, communicating without thinking. It didn't seem to be weighing options, considering stakeholder perspectives. By leaving gaping holes in its account of what it was doing and why, it left investors scratching their heads and selling their shares. It allowed negative information to dribble out, prolonging news cycles and diminishing loyalty, trust, and confidence. And the only public communication that gave stakeholders any comfort was unofficial, leaked, and anonymous.

Any corporate board's first responsibilities are to its investors, whose interests it is supposed to protect. By any measure the HP board failed dismally in its leadership duties. Indeed, former HP board member Tom Perkins, who resigned in 2006 in protest of the pretexting scandal, told the *New York Times* in 2011 that HP "has got to be the worst board in the history of business."[39]

In particular, the HP board's frame of reference seemed to be purely tactical: What do we do now? It didn't seem to be goal-oriented, or based on a strategy. If anything, it resembled the arcade game Whac-a-Mole, in which you smack a critter that pops out of a hole, only to have another one pop out somewhere else; you smack that one only to have yet another pop out; and so on. It was purely responsive. The board didn't recognize that its leadership duty is to keep its eye on the horizon, to make choices and to communicate in ways that move the organization in the right direction. In other words, it needs to be strategic.

Understanding Strategy: Thinking Clearly on Three Levels

Strategy is the process of ordered thinking: of thinking in a particular order. Effective leaders never confuse means with ends, goals and strategies with tactics. The key is to have clarity about the situation as it presents itself, the goal one is trying to accomplish, and the means by which one will accomplish it. As Figure 6.1 shows, the strategic, operational, and tactical level have an order of priority. The strategic comes first.

From Warfighting

Activities in war take place at several interrelated levels which form a hierarchy. These levels are the strategic, operational, and tactical.

> *Activities in communication take place at several interrelated levels which form a hierarchy. These levels are the strategic, operational, and tactical.*

Figure 6.1 Hierarchy of war/communication.

From Warfighting

The highest level is the *strategic* level. Activities at the strategic level focus directly on policy objectives. We distinguish between national strategy, which coordinates and focuses all elements of national power to attain the policy objectives, and military strategy, which is the application of military force to secure the policy objectives. Military strategy thus is subordinate to national strategy. Military strategy can be thought of as the art of winning wars and securing peace.

*The highest level is the strategic level.
Activities at the strategic level focus directly on
achieving objectives. We distinguish between business
or organizational strategy, which coordinates and focuses all
elements of a company's or organization's resources to
attain its objectives, and communication strategy, which is
the application of stakeholder engagement to secure the
business or organizational objectives. Communication strategy thus
is subordinate to business or organizational strategy.
Communication strategy can be thought of as the art
of winning in the marketplace and securing trust and confidence.*

Communication cannot be crafted in a vacuum. All communication tactics (the specific engagements with stakeholders) need to be directly supportive of communication goals (the outcomes we want to achieve). Communication goals, in turn, need to support business goals. Any communication goals or tactics conceived or executed in the absence of clearly defined business goals are likely to be ineffective. The business goals describe changes or outcomes in the business environment or in a company's competitive position: build market share, attain fair stock market valuation, enhance employee productivity, secure regulatory approval of a new product, and the like. The communication goals describe changes in stakeholder attitudes, feelings, understanding, knowledge, or behavior. Each needs to be clearly articulated, with communication goals subordinate to, and supportive of, the business goals. There will be other ways to achieve the business goals, but communication should make the attainment of those goals faster and easier. Table 6.1 shows how business and communication goals align.

Table 6.1 Aligning Business and Communication Goals

Stakeholder	Business Goal	Communication Goal
Customers	Build market share	Enhance demand for our products
		Enhance customer preference for our product over our competitors'
Investors	Attain fair valuation of our stock	Increase investor confidence in the management team
		Enhance investor understanding of a new business strategy

Table 6.1 Aligning Business and Communication Goals

Stakeholder	Business Goal	Communication Goal
Employees	Improve productivity	Improve employee morale
Regulators	Approve new product	Ensure regulator understanding of both benefits and risks of the new product

As a goal-oriented activity, all communication must be directly supportive of a goal. That communication goal, in turn, needs to have a clear line of sight to a business goal: If we accomplish the communication goal, we will be more likely—all else being equal—to achieve the business goal faster and more efficiently.

Warfighting gives us a way not only to understand goals, but to understand the organization of resources to effectively plan communication.

The Strategic Level

From **Warfighting**

[The strategic level] focuses directly on achieving policy objectives: Winning wars.

> *The strategic level focuses directly on achieving business objectives: Winning the marketplace.*

Planning at the strategic level begins with desired outcomes. What do we need our stakeholders to think, feel, know, and do if we are to change the business environment or our competitive position? The more clarity we have about each of these questions, the more likely we are to be able to plan effectively.

The Operational Level

From **Warfighting**

[The operational level is] the link between strategy and tactics. The science of winning campaigns. Deciding when, where, and under what conditions to engage an enemy.

> *The operational level is the link between the strategic level and tactics. The science of winning campaigns. Deciding when, where; and under what conditions to engage an audience.*

The operational level is where the actual planning of stakeholder engagement takes place. Once we know (from the strategic level) what we want the change in our stakeholders to be, we can then determine the best manner, time, message, and messenger to engage stakeholders. The operational level is where we make choices. Of what to say, of when to say it, and of how to say it. It is at the operational level that we anticipate stakeholder reaction by inventorying their current level of awareness; their concerns, fears, and hopes; and their likelihood to care about our content. It is at this level that we can project alternative ways of engaging, alternative content, and alternative messengers to anticipate reactions and choose the more likely effective path.

It is precisely at the operational level that many leaders and leadership teams fall short. By failing to anticipate and adapt, they end up speaking in ways that may make them feel better but that aren't necessarily going to move stakeholders the way we need them to be moved.

The Tactical Level

From Warfighting

[The tactical level] focuses on winning engagements.

The tactical level focuses on engaging audiences.

The tactical level is where communication actually takes place. Tactics are the ways we talk to people, what we actually say to them, the contact we actually make. The tactical level is where we have the press release, the speech, the employee e-mail, the press conference.

Most leaders default to the tactical as a first resort. HP's board certainly seemed to. But the tactical must be in the service of the operational, which in turn is in the service of the strategic. Rather than default to the tactical, effective leaders get to the tactical by considering the other levels first. Table 6.2 illustrates the ways the strategic, operational, and tactical relate in communication planning.

Table 6.2 The Three Levels of War/Communication

	War, from *Warfighting*	Effective Leadership Communication
STRATEGIC	Focuses directly on achieving policy goals: on winning wars	*Focuses directly on achieving business or organizational goals: on winning in the marketplace*
	National strategy: coordinating all the instruments of policy to achieve policy goals	*Business strategy: coordinating all business functions to achieve business goals*
	Military strategy: the art of winning wars and securing peace	*Communication strategy: the art of securing, maintaining, or restoring trust and confidence*
OPERATIONAL	The link between the strategic and the tactical levels	*The link between the strategic and the tactical levels*
	The science of winning campaigns	*The science of winning campaigns*
	Deciding when, where, and under what conditions to engage an enemy	*Deciding when, where, and under what conditions to engage an audience*
TACTICAL	Individual engagements with an enemy	*Individual engagements with an audience*

To communicate effectively, we need to understand what we are trying to achieve.

From Warfighting

The first requirement is to establish what we want to accomplish, when, and how. Without a clearly defined concept of intent, the necessary unity of effort is inconceivable.

> *The first requirement is to establish what we want to accomplish, when, and how. Without a clearly defined concept of intent, the necessary unity of effort is inconceivable.*

Unity of effort is alignment of all communication tactics and messages. Consider, for example, the initial inconsistencies in HP's first-day communications. Three different public statements gave three slightly different accounts of the reasons for Mr. Hurd's departure. But none of them was sufficient to satisfy stakeholders that it was the right move on the part of the company.

Think also of the focus discussed in Chapter 4, "Speed, Focus, and the First Mover Advantage." All Marine Corps communication in the aftermath of the Fallujah mosque shooting was well-coordinated, consistent, and in line with stakeholders' reasonable expectations of what a responsible organization would do when confronted with such a situation. The U.S. military's response in the aftermath of the abuse of prisoners at Abu Ghraib was not. That response also seemed purely tactical, unfocused, and uncoordinated, and it failed to meet the appropriate expectations of stakeholders.

Unity of effort in the service of clearly defined goals, with an operational framework that makes smart choices about what to say, when, how, and to whom, is the key to effective leadership communication.

Template for Planning: For Being Strategic in Leadership Communication

The three levels from *Warfighting*—the strategic, the operational, and the tactical—lead to a framework for effective communication planning.

? Asking Strategic Questions

In Chapter 1, "Words Matter," we noted that a habitually strategic communicator never begins with "what do we want to say" but rather with a sequence of prior questions:

- What do we have? What is the challenge or opportunity we are hoping to address?

- What do we want? What's our goal? Communication is merely the continuation of business by other means. We shouldn't communicate unless we know what we're trying to accomplish.

- Who matters? What stakeholders matter to us? What do we know about them? What further information do we need to get about them? What are the barriers to their receptivity to us, and how do we overcome those barriers?

- What do we need them to think, feel, know, or do in order to accomplish our goal?

- What do they need to see us do, hear us say, or hear others say about us to think, feel, know, and do what we want them to?

- How do we make that happen?

Here's a planning template that can help leaders be strategic in preparing and planning for communication. It's the template I use with my clients and students to help them think through communication with the goal in mind.

◎ Communication Planning

The communication planning process has two parts: the Analysis and the Communication Plan.

1. The **Analysis** assesses the situation and its potential impact on the organization's operations and reputation.

2. The **Communication Plan** describes the steps the organization should take to communicate strategically about the opportunity.

It is important to follow the sequence of steps in developing the plan. Otherwise, your communication tactics may be ineffective.

1. Analysis
What Do We Have?

Situation
A detailed description of the issue or event; the reason to communicate.

Magnitude
The estimated impact of the situation on the organization's operations and reputation.

Likelihood
The estimated likelihood of various scenarios, if there are multiple possibilities.

Affected stakeholder groups
The stakeholders affected by the situation:

- Which stakeholder groups matter?

- What do we know about each group's values, experiences, and level of sophistication?

- What are each group's hopes, aspirations, and desires?

- What are each group's worries, concerns, and fears?

- How does each group (or its individual members) make decisions?

- What does each group currently do, think, feel, or know in relation to us?

- What are the opportunities and barriers for changes in each group's actions, thoughts, feelings, and knowledge?

Note: Recall that Chapter 2, "Taking Audiences Seriously," contained a similar approach, the Audience Checklist, for understanding the people and groups who matter to us.

Additional information required

What don't we know that we should in order to plan effectively?

Where and from whom can we get that?

2. *Communication Plan*
What Do We Want, and How Do We Get It?

STRATEGIC   Desired outcomes for the organization and for communication.

Organizational Objectives

The desired outcomes: What are the desired changes in our business environment or competitive position?

Communication Objectives

The desired outcomes: What are the desired changes in the emotions, attitudes, knowledge, or behavior of stakeholders that contribute to organizational objectives? What do we need our audiences to think, feel, know, and do when we engage them?

OPERATIONAL   Ways to organize communication: Where, when, and how to engage audiences so that they think, feel, know, and do what we want them to.

Audiences

Specific groups to whom communication will be directed.

Messages

What do our audiences need to hear us say in order to think, feel, know, and do what we want them to?

Specific engagements with audiences, each delivering at least one message, in fulfillment of at least one strategy, to achieve at least one objective.

Tactics

Each specific engagement (e.g., press release, speech, e-mail, blog post, conference call).

Implementation

The creation of documents necessary to implement tactics, considering available human, logistical, and budgetary resources; deployment of resources.

Recap: Best Practices from This Chapter

From Warfighting

To influence our stakeholders to our advantage, we must project our thoughts forward in space and time. We frequently do this through planning.

Planning does not mean that we establish a detailed timetable of events. Rather, we attempt to shape the general conditions under which our communication will work.... Through shaping, leaders gain the initiative, preserve momentum, and control the communication agenda.

We should try to shape events in a way that allows us several options so that by the time the moment for decisive operations arrives, we have not restricted ourselves to only one course of action.

Planning plays as important a role in the preparation for communication as it does in the implementation of communication.

Strategy involves establishing goals, assigning resources, and imposing conditions on the scope of communication. Strategy derived from business or organizational objectives must be clearly understood to be the sole authoritative basis for all communication.

Activities in communication take place at several interrelated levels which form a hierarchy. These levels are the strategic, operational, and tactical.

The highest level is the strategic level. Activities at the strategic level focus directly on achieving objectives. We distinguish between business or organizational strategy, which coordinates and focuses all elements of a company's or organization's resources to attain its objectives, and communication strategy, which is the application of stakeholder engagement to secure the business or organizational objectives. Communication strategy thus is subordinate to business or organizational strategy. Communication strategy can be thought of as the art of winning in the marketplace and securing trust and confidence.

The strategic level focuses directly on achieving business objectives: Winning the marketplace.

The operational level is the link between the strategic level and tactics. The science of winning campaigns. Deciding when, where, and under what conditions to engage an audience.

The tactical level focuses on engaging audiences.

The first requirement is establish what we want to accomplish, when, and how. Without a clearly defined concept of intent, the necessary unity of effort is inconceivable.

Refer back to Table 6.2 for a recap of the three levels of war/ communication.

Lessons for Leaders and Communicators

Planning isn't scheduling events on a calendar, but rather working on a chessboard to anticipate stakeholder reactions several moves ahead. As in the rule from carpentry—measure twice, cut once—we need to be so well prepared at the moment of execution that we get the communication right the first time.

The key to planning is projecting thoughts forward: our own thoughts and our stakeholders' thoughts. Because all communication is a process of continuous mutual adaptation, we need to consider our stakeholders' reaction before we communicate with them. The first mover advantage can work only if we say what is sufficient to neutralize their concerns before they arise. The rule of thumb in communicating bad news includes the following:

- Tell it all—say all that is necessary to establish stakeholder understanding, buy-in, or neutrality.
- Tell it fast—bundle the bad news into a single news cycle, and avoid dripping out new details over time, which creates a new news cycle and causes stakeholders to question the leadership skills of those communicating.
- Tell 'em what you're doing about it.
- Tel 'em when it's over.
- Get back to work.

Planning communication is important for reasons beyond public relations. It can also provide clarity in decision making. The very process of considering likely reactions to proposed communications can reveal failures of planning in the actual business decision making. In other words, communication planning serves as a leading indicator that something is amiss, and the need to explain something often calls attention to some inconsistency in a leader's thought process.

Strategy is the process of ordered thinking—of thinking in a particular order. Effective leaders never confuse means with ends, tactics with goals and strategies. The key is to have clarity about the situation as it presents itself, the goal one is trying to accomplish, and the means by which one will accomplish them.

All communication tactics (the specific engagements with stakeholders) need to be directly supportive of communication goals (the outcomes we want to achieve). Communication goals, in turn, need to support business goals. Any communication goals or tactics conceived or executed in the absence of clearly defined business goals are likely to be ineffective. The business goals describe changes or outcomes in the business environment or in a company's competitive position: build market share, attain fair stock market valuation, enhance employee productivity, secure regulatory approval of a new product, and the like. The communication goals describe changes in stakeholder attitudes, feelings, understanding, knowledge, or behavior. Each needs to be clearly articulated, with communication goals subordinate to, and supportive of, the business goals. There will be other ways to achieve the business goals, but communication should make the attainment of those goals faster and easier.

Planning at the strategic level begins with clarity about the situation and the desired outcomes. What do we need our stakeholders to think, feel, know, and do if we are to change the business environment or our competitive position? The more clarity we have about each of these questions, the more likely we are to be able to plan effectively.

The operational level is where the actual planning of stakeholder engagement takes place. Once we know (from the strategic level) what we want the change in our stakeholders to be, we can then determine the best manner, time, message, and messenger to enage stakeholders. The operational level is where we make choices. Of what to say, or when to say it, and of how to say it. It is at the operational level that we anticipate stakeholder reaction by inventorying their current level of awareness; their concerns, fears, and hopes; and their likelihood to care about our content. It is at this level that we can project alternative ways of engaging, alternative content, and alternative messengers to anticipate reactions and choose the more likely effective path.

It is precisely at the operational level that many leaders and leadership teams fall short. By failing to anticipate and adapt, they end up speaking in ways that may make them feel better but that aren't necessariliy going to move stakeholders the way we need them to be moved.

The tactical level is where communication actually takes place. Tactics are the things we actually say to people, the contact we actually make. The tactical level is where we have the press release, the speech, the employee e-mail, the press conference.

Most leaders default to the tactical as a first resort. HP's board certainly seemed to. But the tactical must be in the service of the operational, which in turn is in the service of the strategic. Rather than defaulting to the tactical, effective leaders get to the tactical by conisdering the other levels first.

Unity of effort in the service of clearly defined goals, with an operational framework that makes smart choices about what to say, when, how, and to whom, is the key to effective leadership communication.

7

Performance: The Physicality of Audience Engagement

Lisa Warshaw was starting on her fourth career. It was the year 2000, and Ms. Warshaw had just been named Director of the Wharton Communication Program. That program was supposed to prepare MBA students at the Wharton School of the University of Pennsylvania to be effective communicators in business settings.

Ms. Warshaw had spent the previous 11 years teaching part-time in that program while she and her husband raised four sons. She had started her first career in statistics at the International Monetary Fund. She then earned an MBA from the Harvard Business School, and worked as an operations manager and investment banker. During that time she observed that the most successful senior managers tended also to be the most compelling communicators. Other senior managers, at least as smart and hardworking, were not quite as successful. Says Ms. Warshaw, "I also found that the brightest people weren't necessarily the best communicators. When it came to inspiring trust and confidence, intelligence and technical skills weren't enough."[1]

Ms. Warshaw's observations were validated by her conversations with recruiters and Wharton alumni. Recruiters told her that one of the challenges in placing senior executives is that the higher positions require the ability to inspire and persuade. But most MBAs didn't learn that skill in business school. They either had it all along or acquired it some other way in their careers. If Wharton, long regarded as one of the top business schools in the world, were truly to train the top business leaders, it had to teach more than the quantitative skills; it would also teach how to inspire and persuade.

With that insight in hand, she overhauled the Wharton Communication Program. With a grant from the marketing powerhouse Omnicom Group, she focused the program on what executives would have to do in the workplace: Get on their feet and engage audiences. The students would still learn theory, but class time would be devoted to students speaking. Says Ms. Warshaw,

> I just didn't see a shortcut to having students speak and giving them lots of feedback—from each other, the teaching assistants, and from the teachers. Students learn the theory and prepare outside of class; our goal for the classroom is for students to speak 90 percent of the time. Communication has been required in Wharton's curriculum for over 30 years. I inherited a course with a strong skill-based component and have worked with terrific colleagues to build on that foundation.[2]

From Warfighting

Training programs must reflect practical, challenging, and progressive goals beginning with individual and small-unit skills.

> *Training programs must reflect practical, challenging, and progressive goals beginning with individual interpersonal communication skills and small-group dynamics.*

Every first-year Wharton MBA goes through the communication course as part of the school's core curriculum. Starting in 2000, Ms. Warshaw changed the course to include second-year teaching assistants in the classroom and to focus exclusively on persuasion. Classes were kept small: eight to nine students on average. Teachers were not traditional academics, but rather business veterans who were both excellent communicators and passionate teachers. Their backgrounds were often in quantitative fields like engineering, closer to the backgrounds of their students. They would be supplemented by guest speakers from a range of disciplines. (I have been a guest speaker in the program each semester since 2000.)

Each student would have to stand and deliver—a short speech, a business plan, a strategy—verbally, in front of a group, at least five times per course. The teacher would assume the persona of a skeptical senior decision maker. Says Ms. Warshaw,

> The more senior you are in a company, the more skeptical the audience becomes—whether it's a boss or an executive committee or a board of directors. We have the teacher assume the role of skeptical audience member. We want students to focus on persuasive speaking as if they're in a challenging business setting.[3]

Ms. Warshaw says that a key to success is that students learn by doing, and by watching themselves on video:

> Content is what's most important in public speaking. But people tend to worry about the issues we call "delivery"—how they look and sound. In our courses, students are completely exposed, standing in front of the class without a lectern. But they learn. It's one thing to tell them how they did, but we show them by reviewing the video of their speech. The key to students' learning about delivery is to show them the dozen minor things they do that weaken their presence. Then they're motivated to change. They learn from watching their classmates, we help them change, and they improve.[4]

The Wharton Communication Program caught on. Over the next 10 years the basic communication course became the only required MBA course for which students consistently asked for more sessions. Alumni, out in the world of business, reported that they were able to harness their skills in both business and personal settings. And the program grew to include advanced electives and more robust content. Beginning in 2012, it will expand even more—students will present ten times per course, rather than five.

When Ms. Warshaw began in 2000, the program had about ten full- and part-time teachers and no teaching assistants. Starting in 2012, it will have 30 teachers, both full- and part-time, 70 teaching assistants, and another 40 writing coaches to help students master the written word. It will serve about 1,000 entering first-year MBA and Executive MBA students.

What Wharton figured out is that effective leaders need to be good at the nonquantitative interpersonal skills. At Wharton and other enlightened business and professional schools, aspiring leaders have the opportunity to learn those skills. Most leaders have to learn them a different way.

From Warfighting

Marine Corps doctrine demands professional competence among its leaders. As military professionals charged with the defense of the nation, Marine leaders must be true experts in the conduct of war.

> *One of the burdens of leadership is professional competence.*
> *As professionals charged with inspiring trust and confidence,*
> *leaders must be true experts in the persuasive art.*

Commitment to Self-Development

The 2011 film *The King's Speech* tells the true story of George VI, who surprisingly and reluctantly became monarch of the United Kingdom in 1936 when his brother abdicated the throne less than a year after their father's death. Early in the film, his father, George V, coaches the young prince on the burdens of leadership. He speaks about the need to connect with the people via the relatively new social media technology of radio—what was then called "the wireless":

> This devilish device will change everything.... In the past all a king had to do was look respectable in uniform and not fall off his horse. Now we must invade people's homes and ingratiate ourselves with them. This family has been reduced to the lowest and basest of all creatures. We've become actors![5]

The rest of the film focuses on the relationship between the king, who has a debilitating stutter, and his speech coach, and on the king's progress as he masters the leadership burden of connecting with his subjects.

Just as the emerging technologies in the 1930s created new expectations for leaders, the present environment of social media, of instantaneous communication where audiences have multiple sources of information available to them at any time, creates new burdens. Stakeholders expect leaders to be good at connecting with them.

In more than 30 years, I have coached more than 250 chief executive officers and thousands of executives and other high-profile people in complex fields, including doctors, lawyers, financial executives, and military officers. These leaders were in sectors as diverse as pharmaceuticals, heavy manufacturing, energy, biotechnology, computer software, financial services, law firms, advertising agencies, religious denominations, universities, and not-for-profit advocacy groups.

What they all had in common was a need to win hearts and minds. And a sense that they weren't quite up to the task. Yet. They didn't have the same obstacles as George VI, but they all needed to get better at this core leadership skill.

 From **Warfighting**

The purpose of all training is to develop forces that can win in combat. Training is the key to combat effectiveness and therefore is the main effort of a peacetime military. However, training should not stop with the commencement of war; training must continue during war to adapt to the lessons of combat.

The purpose of all communication training is to develop the capacity to build trust, inspire loyalty, and lead effectively. However, training should not stop when that trust and loyalty has been won; training must continue throughout a leader's tenure in office, to adapt to changing circumstances and needs.

In many cases the skills that get leaders to the top of their organizations are not sufficient to do the work at that level. The higher one goes in a company, not-for-profit, or government agency, the more success is measured in winning hearts and minds rather than in the mastery of some technical skill—from medicine, law, finance, education, engineering, and the like. It isn't that their core disciplines don't matter—they do. But they're table stakes. They're what's minimally necessary to get the job. But they're not enough.

Rather, leaders need to be good at interpersonal verbal engagement—one-on-one and large group, in person and at a distance. I have found a high correlation between leaders seeing part of their work as continually developing their communication skills and their overall success.

I have one client—who is now the CEO and chairman of one of the largest companies in the world—whom I first worked with 13 years ago, when he was head of the company's research and development subsidiary. He's a PhD in one of the sciences, and he saw developing his communication skills as an essential part of managing his own career. We met at least once a year for a half day or full day just to hone his skills—plus in between to prepare for particular high-stakes events. Over the years he became president of the U.S. subsidiary, then chief operating officer of the corporation, then president, and then CEO. He eventually added chairman to his title. All the while, he would do an annual tuneup of his skills. I don't suggest that he'd be CEO if he wasn't also a good manager and brilliant scientist. But his own investment in his communication aptitude is part of his success.

Another client is the chief financial officer of a large financial institution. When he became CFO he was very strong at the numbers. But with the new position came the need to stand in front of large groups of employees and investors and to inspire confidence. He had never needed to do that before. And it was a bit scary. But he made getting good at it a priority. It took a lot of work. I meet with him every few months—sometimes just to build skills, more often just before a big event such as an investment conference or a quarterly earnings call. And he has risen to the occasion. He got better at it, and more confident about it, because he saw it as an investment in his career. Not as a duty to slog through, but as a way to build and maintain a core leadership competence.

The Marines show us a model for this. Every Marine is a rifleman, regardless of his or her primary occupational specialty. Whether a lawyer, an auto mechanic, or a pilot, every Marine must be skilled in the use of firearms and in infantry tactics. That means they need to invest in those skills—to stay in top physical condition; to periodically practice their shooting skills; to stay current in military doctrine and tactics—even if they spend most of their time editing briefs, fixing truck engines, or flying helicopters.

The same applies in civilian leadership. Leaders need to invest in their communication skills. They need to master basic skills, practice those skills, and continually enhance their capacity to lead verbally.

 *From* **Warfighting**

Every Marine has an individual responsibility to study the profession of arms. A leader without either interest in or knowledge of the history and theory of warfare—the intellectual content of the military profession—is a leader in appearance only. Self-directed study in the art and science of war is at least equal in importance to maintaining physical condition and should receive at least equal time.

Every executive has an individual responsibility to become effective in engaging others. A leader without either interest in or knowledge of the persuasive art is a leader in appearance only. Self-directed study in the art and science of stakeholder engagement is at least as important as other executive tasks, and should receive appropriate investment of time and effort.

Connecting at a Distance

In 1936 King George VI had to master connecting at a distance through the new and scary medium of radio. More than 70 years later the same applies, but with even more daunting technology.

In early 2008 one of my clients called me for an unusual consultation. He was then the president of one of the world's largest investment banks. I had first coached him on interpersonal communication skills some ten years earlier, when he was an investment banker. I continued to work with him as he rose in rank and responsibility, and by the time he was president I was meeting with him quarterly. But this time it was a bit different. His firm was in the running to win a very large deal to bring to the U.S. market the stock of a large government-owned Chinese company. He had just learned that the final round of meetings with the various competing firms would be later that night New York time, next morning Beijing time. But the meeting would not be in New York; it would be in Beijing. And he was expected to be there. His counterparts at other firms would be. But it was physically impossible for him to get there on time. That put his firm at a significant disadvantage.

Protocol required the senior-most executive at each firm to be at the meeting, and to lead the firm's presentation of its capabilities and its plan to bring the stock to market. The senior-most executives at the Chinese company, plus senior government officials from the ministry in which the company was housed, would be there. It wouldn't be possible to delay the meeting; there was no one else in his firm of sufficient rank who could get to the meeting in time.

So he had an audacious idea. He would attend via satellite hookup on a live television feed. And although his presentation would include all the requisite formalities and expressions of regret that he could not be there in person, he'd turn his absence into a positive; his disadvantage into an advantage. He'd use his video connection to demonstrate the truly global reach of his firm, the capacity to work effectively at a distance, the robustness of the firm's technology infrastructure.

But for this approach to succeed, his video presence would have to be of exceptional quality. Not on a computer hookup or video conference call—the video and sound quality would not be good enough. Rather, he'd attend the meeting remotely from the firm's television studio in lower Manhattan. He'd use the best equipment and present the firm's capabilities through a multimedia presentation. With a strong team of bankers in the room in Beijing, and a strong television production team in New York, his firm's presentation would be both high-touch and high-tech. And since a core element of what the firm had planned to highlight was its technological sophistication and its ability to work well across the globe, he would be able to demonstrate the capacity, not merely assert it.

But it also put extraordinary pressure on him. He'd have to overcome the violation of the cultural norm requiring his physical presence. The tone had to be just right. He couldn't be glib or flashy, but had to get a good balance of humility (for missing the meeting) and of strength. And his performance had to be flawless. We spent the day preparing. He mastered speaking his opening remarks and the firm's capabilities while looking into the camera and reading from a teleprompter, speaking as if spontaneously. He rehearsed fielding tough questions remotely. He rehearsed the interaction between himself, his team, and the video, and the different elements of the multimedia presentations. And he rehearsed the nonverbal elements—posture, facial expression, and especially what to do and how to look when others were speaking and he was listening.

It was a gutsy move. But it worked. His firm got the deal. It was one of the largest deals of the year, and an important inroad for the firm in building its business in China. He later told me that the only reason he even considered doing the session on TV was that he knew he already had a strong foundation on which to build the skills he would need for that meeting. I know that it's only because he had invested in his ongoing development as an engaged and engaging speaker. He took seriously the burden on him to inspire. And he did the hard work to get good at it.

Engaging Audiences

In the Introduction I noted that a leader is judged based on three fundamental public leadership attributes:

- The leader's bearing: how the leader carries himself or herself.
- The manner in which the leader engages with others.
- The words the leader uses to engage others.

Being effective in engaging audiences requires one additional element: an understanding of what audiences are capable of, and ways to break through the barriers and connect powerfully with an audience.

This chapter focuses on the leader's bearing and the manner in which the leader can engage others. The next chapter covers content: the choice of words and the management of meaning. The chapter following focuses on current insights from neuroscience and cognitive psychology on how audiences attend to speakers and how speakers can adapt to their audiences based on how attentive they are and can be.

From Warfighting

Basic individual skills are the essential foundation for combat effectiveness and must receive heavy emphasis.

> *Basic individual communication skills are the foundation for effective leadership engagement, and should receive heavy emphasis.*

Physicality: Let Me Hear Your Body Talk

An audience's first impression is visual. Charlene Barshefsky, U.S. Trade Representative in the Clinton Administration, needed to negotiate with world leaders from a position of strength. Being of diminutive stature, she needed to show physical presence. That meant perfectly tailored clothing and accessories. And it also meant carrying herself as someone worth taking seriously. She told *Fortune* magazine about the power of the visual: "The body speaks long before the mouth ever opens."[6]

Before the speaker even opens his or her mouth, the audience is making judgments. About whether even to pay attention; about whether to rely on what the speaker might say; about whether the speaker is likely to be credible or not. And once the speaker begins, the visual drives an audience's attention. Does the speaker look confident? At ease? Distracted? Scared? Angry? Mean?

These visual cues are nonverbal, but powerful. And they can define an audience's reaction independent of what the speaker might say.

When I attend a client's speech, whether to an investor group, an employee town hall meeting, or professional conference, I don't watch the client. I watch the audience. Are they looking at the speaker, nodding at the right places, leaning forward? Are they checking their e-mail, texting, or daydreaming? And when the speech is over, I make a beeline to the restroom or beverage table—anywhere people will speak candidly to each other. And then I listen to what they say. In these moments, members of the audience rarely ask each other, "What do you think about what he said?" Rather, they ask, "What did you think of him?" or "of her?" They speak in the vocabulary of personal judgments. They are assessing the speaker as a whole, not merely the content. They report their impressions, their feelings about what they saw and heard.

And the first thing they notice is the speaker's bearing. How the speaker holds himself or herself, whether standing or sitting. A speaker captures or loses the audience's attention in the first 15 seconds. Anything that suggests nervousness or discomfort causes an audience to look away. Once they look away, it's very hard to get them to pay attention. Anything that suggests comfort and confidence causes audiences to pay attention. And once they're paying attention, it's possible to keep their attention throughout the presentation.

Audiences are quick to detect nervousness, and to disengage from the speaker when they do. Speakers, for their part, need to understand that the first 15 seconds win or lose an audience's attention, trust, confidence, and support. But too often speakers use the first few minutes of their presentations to warm up to the audience, and in the process they lose the audience.

Among the easy-to-remedy speaker behaviors that cause audiences to disengage are these:

- Speaking while looking down, at notes, at the floor, or randomly around the room.
- Moving their hands randomly and without alignment with content. Any small, apparently random hand movements betray a nervous speaker. These include opening and closing the hands, rubbing them together, locking fingers of the two hands together, putting hands in the pockets, or touching one's face, hair, tie, jacket, the lectern, notes, pens, and the like.

- Holding, grasping, leaning against, or otherwise interacting with the lectern or table.
- Shuffling feet back and forth, rocking side to side or front to back, twisting in place while speaking.
- Licking lips randomly, locking one's gaze on some inanimate object rather than looking at the audience.
- Speaking in a monotone voice, whether softly or loudly, or in a singsong cadence that repeats, unrelated to the content of what is being said.

These and other nonverbal cues sabotage a speaker and immediately diminish the speaker's effectiveness. Wharton's Lisa Warshaw had these in mind when she referred to "the dozen minor things they do that weaken their presence."[7] But too often speakers are unaware of their own marginalizing behaviors. Coaches like me and my firm, and effective communication courses such as in the Wharton Communication Program, videotape leaders while presenting, and allow a speaker to discover his or her own nonverbal weaknesses, as a first step toward taking seriously the need to demonstrate presence.

The late comedian Andy Kaufman broke out of stand-up comedy and onto the national stage when he performed on the very first episode of NBC's *Saturday Night Live* in 1975. He came on stage portraying a meek, shy everyman. He placed a phonograph needle on an old-fashioned 45-RPM record and played the theme song to the cartoon Mighty Mouse. He stood nervously as the music played. Everything about his presence screamed discomfort. He exhibited an entire inventory of marginalizing behaviors. He slumped his shoulders. He curled his fingers open-and shut nervously. He shuffled his feet. He rocked back and forth. His eyes kept darting around the stage. He licked and pursed his lips. He seemed unsteady and unsure of himself.[8]

Then the music got to the chorus, and Kaufman was transformed. He stood upright, a confident smile on his face, feet planted firmly apart, one arm out above shoulder level, as he lip-synced the lyrics, "Here I come to save the day...." He was all presence, the very model of a confident speaker, completely in command of himself, his environment, and the audience. Then as the music continued, he reverted to the nervous everyman. Every time the record came to the chorus, "Here I come to save the day…," Kaufman changed back.[9] There was a Jekyll-and-Hyde quality to it. One moment paralyzed with fear; the next completely in command. The humor came from the sudden and unexpected transformation. The audience was initially uncomfortable watching a person so clearly out of his element; it began to empathize with his distress, to wonder whether the pressure of being on live TV had gotten to him. Their laughter was a release in the form of relief at seeing the confident performer that he was. Kaufman had played an elaborate practical joke on the audience, sucking them in and making them feel uncomfortable, then letting them off the hook. His timid character who occasionally becomes poised became part of his act— his ongoing character for the rest of his career, including a starring role on the TV series *Taxi*.

But there's a larger lesson from Kaufman's performance. It's that a cascade of small marginalizing behaviors have a compounding effect, and in that compounding they diminish a speaker. But simply eliminating the marginalizing behaviors allows a speaker to project strength, poise, composure, and calm. In our coaching with executives, we've seen an equivalent transformation from mousy to mighty. It isn't difficult. But it requires intentionality and an understanding of the behaviors that work and those to be avoided.

This book isn't intended to be a comprehensive guide to the mechanics of executive presentation. But effective leadership communication does require mastery of the key presentation skills. The balance of this chapter focuses on the basic critical skills to demonstrate presence and inspire trust and confidence; it's intended to point the way and get an executive started. The executive can then supplement what is here with personal coaching, group instruction, or readings from more tactical presentation how-to books.

Stand and Deliver

Effective speakers begin in a position of strength. The starting point is to get the posture right. And for most speakers, the key to getting the posture right is to start from a stable platform. If standing, that means planting the feet a bit farther apart front-to-back and side-to-side than is comfortable. There's a paradox in effective stage presence: To project confidence and comfort, sometimes it's necessary to stand or sit in a position that's initially uncomfortable.

Take standing posture. For many speakers, standing with the feet apart is uncomfortable, and seems unnatural. But the closer together the feet are, the higher toward the head and shoulders the speaker's center of gravity is, and therefore the more unsteady the speaker is. Standing with the feet together makes it easy to wobble back and forth like a metronome. Most speakers compensate by shuffling their feet, by grasping the lectern, by pacing randomly, or by shifting their weight from one leg to another. Each of these inadvertently creates the appearance of discomfort. Worse, with the center of gravity high, speakers are reluctant to gesture, because gesturing increases the wobble.

All of that can be prevented by planting the feet firmly apart. This lowers the center of gravity into the hips, eliminating the wobble completely. And with the wobble gone, the other counterproductive behaviors—shuffling the feet, grasping the lectern, pacing, shifting weight—also disappear. And the speaker can then gesture freely.

Initially my coaching clients are a bit resistant to speaking with feet planted apart. But seeing the effect of that posture on video tends to convince them. The burden of leadership is this: Posture and other elements of effective performance need to work not because they make the speaker feel good, but because of the effect of those elements on an audience. It's not about how the speaker feels; it's about inspiring trust and confidence in the audience. Whether it's posture, gesture, or facial expression, the key is to focus not on how it feels, but on the effect it creates.

When a speaker is presenting while seated, the stable platform is created by sitting close to the lip of the chair, with the speaker's back not touching the back of the chair. The feet can be planted on the floor, either one forward and one back for stability, or tucked under the lip of the chair. This allows the speaker to gesture fluidly. If sitting, the speaker may find that it helps to push the chair a few inches away from any table or desk. This allows a fluid gesture and prevents the speaker from leaning on the table or from playing with pens, papers, or other distractions while speaking.

Once the speaker is in a stable platform, either sitting or standing, the next step is to gesture while speaking. This is a particular challenge for many people when they first get coached. People gesture when speaking naturally. Some gesture broadly, some narrowly, but to some degree most people gesture. But when asked to present to a group, many speakers get self-conscious, and constrain their movements.

One of the biggest challenges the executives I coach face is comfort even with the idea of gesturing while presenting. In coaching sessions I often keep the video camera running after the executive has finished a passage from a speech. Very often the executive, now no longer in presentation mode, will passionately assert that he or she cannot gesture, but will be gesturing broadly while doing it. But that natural gesture is completely subconscious. The executive isn't even aware that he or she is doing it. I then play back the video of the executive in presentation mode refusing to gesture, and then in real life gesturing while arguing that he or she can't. After that the executive usually gives himself or herself permission to gesture.

Because the human body wants to gesture, executives who restrain their arm movements unintentionally gesture in other ways. Some emphasize key words by moving their eyebrows up and down. Some gesture by bobbing their heads. I had one client—a senior executive at a bank—who wouldn't gesture with his arms, but would flail his right foot for emphasis. All of those non-arm-movement forms of gestures are marginalizing. But, as with other performance elements, once the individuals see the video of themselves gesturing with eyebrows or head bobs, and then see the effect of proper gestures, they come around.

Audiences need the executive to gesture. Recent research into cognitive psychology and neuroscience points to a connection between seeing someone gesture and hearing that person speak. Audiences retain more when the speaker gestures. Because they are accustomed to seeing speakers in ordinary circumstances gesture while speaking, audiences are habituated to viewing the entire package—voice, gesture, and content—when they listen. And the gesture helps facilitate understanding. Audiences particularly pay attention when voice, gesture, and content are aligned. For example, an upward gesture while speaking about something growing; a downward gesture for something declining, and gesturing with hands moving apart to indicate something widening all help audiences more quickly understand and remember the speaker's points.

But there are other reasons to gesture. The first is biomechanical. Gesturing with the arms away from the rib cage creates a biomechanical effect on the body. The musculature of the abdomen contracts, harnessing more energy and allowing the speaker to better engage the audience. An effective gesture isn't the movement of a hand from the wrist to the fingertips; or the movement of the arms from the elbow to the fingertips. Rather, an effective gesture is the movement of the elbow away from the rib cage, followed by movement of the entire arm. Gesturing only from the wrist or only from the elbow inhibits the biomechanical benefit of the gesture.

The biggest effect of gesturing is nonvisual. So gestures are needed even when the audience can't see the speaker. I have found that investors on a conference call with management tend to listen more and better when the executives who are presenting gesture—even better when the executives gesture while standing. The same applies when bosses conduct meetings via speakerphone. In these cases the reason to gesture is the gesture's effect on the speaker's voice.

A broad and fluid range of gestures helps create a far more engaging voice range. Gestures allow the speaker to vary the voice's dynamic range, in three dimensions:

1. *Volume:* Loud and soft. Effective speakers vary the volume of their voice, moving from relatively loud to relatively soft throughout their presentation. Gestures make this easier. Gestures allow a speaker to control the volume, getting louder or softer based on how the arms move. The gesture also helps the speaker emphasize important words, helping the audience appreciate the key points of the speaker's content.

2. *Pitch:* High and low. Effective speakers also vary the pitch of their voice, sometimes going higher and sometimes lower. One way to vary the pitch is to smile, which has the effect of lubricating the voice. But gestures make it much easier to vary the pitch.

3. *Speed:* Fast and slow. Effective speakers vary the speed with which words pass their lips. Transitional language is typically spoken quickly; core message language is typically spoken more slowly. Pauses can be used for emphasis or to signal the end of one thought and the beginning of another. Gestures facilitate the variation of speed, and allow a speaker to be comfortable with silence in the pauses.

The gesture also serves as a mechanism for connecting with the audience directly. Effective speakers use gestures to involve the audience in what is being presented. They gesture in the direction of individuals in the audience. Or they use gestures of inclusion, such as sweeping both arms toward the audience and then back toward the speaker.

But the final reason to gesture is that the gesture helps the speaker remember content. New developments in neuroscience technology allow scientists to scan the human brain while the subject is engaging in ordinary activity. Increasing scientific consensus is emerging that the part of the human brain that controls gestures is connected to the part that controls word choice. When a speaker gestures broadly while speaking, he or she is simultaneously activating the word-choice part of the brain. So while gesturing the speaker chooses better words, stronger words, and fewer words.

A speaker who habitually gestures is able to speak extemporaneously far more effectively than the speaker who doesn't. Neuroscientists have an adage that "neurons that fire together wire together." The more a speaker gestures, the more robust the connections between the gesture and word choice become. So the speaker is better able to remember a memorized speech, or the content for which bullet point summaries are reminders. And the speaker is less likely to miscommunicate by using imprecise language. I advise my clients and students to rehearse their presentations aloud, standing and gesturing broadly as they would in front of a live audience. Invariably, this makes them better able to remember what to say and how to say it.

Other elements of presence include one's bearing before a presentation even begins. As soon as an audience is paying attention, the speaker must exhibit confidence. That includes walking to the front of the room or onto the stage, or while sitting in a meeting while others are speaking. A leader is "on" whenever he or she is being watched by an audience, even when not speaking.

Connecting with Eye Contact

Once a speaker is standing or sitting in a position of strength, and gesturing for both visual and nonvisual effect, the speaker needs to connect directly with the audience. And although an audience can be anywhere from one person to thousands, the goal is to make every member of the audience feel that he or she is connecting directly with the speaker.

Eye contact is a key part of that. The phrase "eye contact" is often misunderstood by speakers. Simply telling an executive to "make eye contact" isn't particularly helpful to the executive. Rather, "eye contact" is a metaphor for a complex series of interactions that cause each member of the audience to pay attention to the speaker.

Some speakers try to engage by sweeping their eyes across an audience. Or by looking in the general direction of one part of the audience, then another part. While better than not looking at the audience at all, these aren't effective ways to engage. Rather, effective eye contact means looking directly into the eyes of a single person, one person at a time.

Ideally, the sequence of steps goes like this:

1. Find a member of the audience, and look directly into that person's eyes.

2. Then give a brief smile. The smile triggers a mirror reaction: The audience member smiles back, and that member's attention is fully engaged. Very effective speakers supplement the small smile with a subtle head nod, which is often mirrored back to the speaker.

3. Then find another audience member to engage. The first member, having been fully engaged, will continue to pay attention, knowing that the speaker may come back for additional eye contact.

Effective speakers persistently make one-on-one contact with many members of the audience, regardless of the size of the audience. When they make contact with one audience member, other audience members sitting close to the one being engaged will also pay greater attention, thinking that they may soon be similarly engaged.

But what about when the speaker can't see the audience, because either the lights are low or the audience is very large? Then the technique is for the speaker to engage in the same behaviors as if making eye contact. He or she still needs to look at a single audience member, or in the direction of an audience member, and smile, nod, and then move to another. To the audience it will appear that the speaker is connecting with someone—probably someone sitting close by—and the audience will pay greater attention than if the speaker didn't try to connect.

The challenge for speakers who are reading or speaking from notes is to create the appearance of eye contact even as they read their script or follow their notes. Teleprompters allow a speaker to seem to be making audience contact even while reading from a script that appears on a one-way transparent screen. The speaker sees the words; the audience sees only the speaker.

But when the speaker is speaking from a script, it's much harder to make eye contact, because the speaker has to physically read words off a piece of paper and also try to make contact. This places a premium on mastering the content of the speech well ahead of time. Rather than memorizing just words, an effective speaker memorizes complete phrases and sentences. While speaking a memorized phrase, the speaker can look up from the text and make contact with an audience member before looking back at the text. Practicing aloud while gesturing also enhances memory, and makes it easier for the speaker to make contact during the speech.

And because the audience is won over in the earliest part of the speech, effective speakers often memorize the first 30 seconds or so, speaking confidently without having to look down at their scripts, making eye contact when it matters most, when audiences are most attentive.

There are also physical ways the speaker can make it easier to make contact. The first is to be sure the script is easy to read aloud.

That means using a large font (I have found Helvetica 18, double-spaced to work best for most clients). Some speakers format their scripts so that the lower third of the page is blank. This prevents them from having to look straight down as they get to the bottom of the page, which would cause them to break contact with the audience. Some further place their script as far up on the lectern as possible, ensuring that the angle of their head relative to the page still allows for the eyes to make contact with the audience. I sometimes carry a small notebook to use as an anchor to keep the pages up high on the lectern.

Effective speakers also keep their scripts easy to manage. No staples, paper clips, binders, or other devices that make it hard to move from page to page, or that would call attention to the speaker working from a text. Ideally, the speaker lays two pages next to each other, sliding pages from right to left while speaking. That ensures that the speaker can move fluidly from the bottom of one page to the top of the other without arbitrary pauses. For this to work well, the speaker needs to rehearse with the pages properly formatted and numbered—afterward the pages will be in reverse order.

Gesturing while reading the script also makes eye contact easier. The gesture varies the speed at which the words are spoken, and in the silences the speaker can look down and see what needs to be spoken next.

Many speakers find speaking from notes allows optimal eye contact. Notes—essentially reminders of what to say—allow the speaker to always speak while making contact with the audience. Effective speakers look at the notes during pauses, and speak only while making eye contact with an audience member.

Effective speakers also use pauses as an audience connection tool. During the pause, the speaker can make contact with one or more members of the audience. Some speakers use a water bottle or glass of water to enforce a long pause, for emphasis and to provide a longer opportunity to make eye contact. The pause can also be made for dramatic effect, to punctuate key points, to signal the change from one topic to another, or to solicit audience reaction, either verbal or nonverbal.

Stagecraft

Often leaders need to speak on a stage, usually standing behind a lectern. The lectern presents its own challenges. The first is that it's easy for the lectern to diminish the speaker's presence. Speakers who grasp the lectern, seemingly for dear life, inhibit their own effectiveness and audience engagement. It's also easy for speakers to lean against, interact with, or tap or pound the lectern, all to negative effect.

There are only three reasons to use a lectern: (1) when it is necessary to stand behind it in order to be seen or heard because the microphone is attached to it, a stationary video camera is pointing at it, or a spotlight has illuminated it; (2) to hold a script, notes, bottle or glass of water, or remote presentation mouse; or (3) because it presents a visual image that is part of the overall impression, such as a corporate logo or emblem of office—as when the President of the United States stands behind a lectern with the presidential seal.

Ideally, a speaker can speak without the lectern, or stand next to it. But whether at the lectern or beside it, or in the absence of a lectern, the standing posture is always the same: feet slightly farther apart than is comfortable, front to back and side to side. Often it is helpful for the speaker to stand just a bit further back from the lectern than is comfortable, to facilitate gesturing and to improve the angle of the head relative to the text on the pages that are resting on the lectern.

When there isn't a lectern, or when the speaker chooses not to use one, the speaker has a chance to more fully engage the audience. The absence of a physical barrier exposes the speaker to the full gaze of the audience. Some speakers become self-conscious and exhibit nervousness. Effective speakers exhibit poise by standing closer to the audience than the lectern would allow, using the correct standing posture, gesturing broadly in the audience's direction, and moving for effect. Random walking, back and forth without apparent reason, diminishes the speaker. But walking in synchrony with the content can create powerful audience engagement. Walking in the direction of one part of the audience, making a point, pausing, and then walking toward another part of the audience keeps an entire audience engaged. For a large audience, it's important for the speaker to work the entire stage, directing attention first to one part of the room, then to another, until the entire audience has been engaged.

Part of the burden of leadership is to be prepared for the setting in which the presentation takes place. Where possible, a speaker should arrive early and test all technology, including microphone sound levels, lighting, and audiovisual equipment. The speaker should rehearse key parts of the presentation onstage with all equipment functioning, to avoid surprises when the presentation begins. This diminishes anxiety or nervousness, and creates muscle memory for how to be engaging in the first moments of the presentation, when it matters most.

Using Visuals Effectively

Increasingly, leaders present using visuals, often in the form of slides created in PowerPoint or Keynote computer software. And while PowerPoint and its equivalents can amplify a speaker's points, too often the visuals become a crutch that diminishes both the audience's attention and the speaker's effectiveness. I have yet to meet someone in an audience who laments that the speaker didn't use enough PowerPoint. I often get the opposite: Death by PowerPoint, or the observation that PowerPoint corrupts absolutely.

Part of the problem is how corporate presentations are typically put together. In many corporations, typically junior staff are tasked with compiling information into slide form. Worried about missing something, they tend to create many slides, with a significant amount of information on each slide. By the time the presentation reaches the level of the executive who is to present, the executive takes the slides and makes incremental changes. As a result, visual support created at a low level is allowed to drive the content of the executive's agenda.

In many coaching engagements one "aha" moment for the executives is how dysfunctional this default method of developing presentations may be. The presentation should begin with what the executive wants the audience's reaction to be (this will be covered fully in the next chapter). Rather than starting at a low level with maximum complexity, preparation needs to begin at a high level with maximum clarity. Then the process should shift to ways to amplify the content visually, to make the meaning stick with the audience. Very often after I've coached an executive, he or she will ask me to brief the staff who prepare presentation materials, to enhance the preparation process.

Effective presentations with PowerPoint tend to use few slides. The slides should contain few words, powerful graphics that make a point well, and minimal special effects that might distract an audience. But too often the visuals are cluttered, hard to read, and a distraction. I have seen dozens, if not hundreds, of presentations in which each slide is covered with small-font words, numbers, charts, or some combination. With more than 100 data points on a single slide. They're unreadable. And they cause an audience to disengage.

The key question when using visuals is, who is in control of what? Are the visuals controlling the speaker, or the other way around? If the speaker merely reads what's on a slide, then the slides are seen to control the speaker. The speaker is merely the way to amplify what's on the screen. This diminishes the speaker. But effective speakers use slides to amplify their content. That places the burden of narrative exposition on the speaker. The slides are there for emphasis.

There are a few simple guidelines for developing effective visuals. The first is to limit the words. A simple way to do so is the Rule of 5 by 5: No more than five lines of text; no more than five words per line. Ideally, far fewer. The second is to use simple, intuitive graphs: a line moving up; a pie chart; a bar chart. The third is to use powerful photographs—of people, or products, or people using products.

But even the best visuals won't work if the speaker isn't effectively using them. Effective speakers align the use of visuals seamlessly into their presentations. There's no break in either substance or performance as the visuals appear. The speaker continues to look confidently at the audience while speaking the content that the visuals amplify. Ineffective speakers look at the slide while speaking, thereby breaking contact with the audience. Effective speakers always look toward the audience. Ideally, the speaker has some way to know what slide is up without looking back at the screen. I always connect my laptop to a projector extension cord that allows me to see the computer screen in front of me. I use the Presenter Tools function of PowerPoint to be able to see on my computer screen both what the audience sees on the projection screen and the slide that comes next. This allows me to maintain audience engagement even as I move from slide to slide.

Some speakers like to call attention to certain parts of a slide by using a laser pointer or even a physical pointer. In those cases it may be necessary for the speaker to turn and look at the presentation screen. But effective speakers place their laser dot on the slide, then hold it there while facing the audience and speaking to them. If the speaker wants to gesture toward a slide, the speaker should use the arm closest to the presentation screen. Using the hand farthest from the screen has the effect of turning the speaker's body toward the screen, and exposing part of the audience to the speaker's back.

Effective speakers also use language that doesn't call attention to the fact that they're using slides. Even mentioning the word "slide" or "graph" or "chart" has the effect of diminishing the speaker, who then seems to be elaborating on the visual. Saying, "This next slide outlines our strategy for next year...," calls attention to the slide, not to the strategy. An effective speaker says what the strategy is, beginning with, "Our strategy for next year is to [and then elaborates on what the strategy is])...." The slide then amplifies the speaker's content. Similarly, saying, "This chart shows our sales growth for the quarter," calls attention to the chart, not to the growth. An effective speaker using the same chart would say, "As you can see, our sales grew 5 percent during the last quarter...."

Recap: Best Practices from This Chapter

From Warfighting

Training programs must reflect practical, challenging, and progressive goals beginning with individual interpersonal communication skills and small-group dynamics.

One of the burdens of leadership is professional competence. As professionals charged with inspiring trust and confidence, leaders must be true experts in the persuasive art.

The purpose of all communication training is to develop the capacity to build trust, inspire loyalty, and lead effectively.

However, training should not stop when that trust and loyalty has been won; training must continue throughout a leader's tenure in office, to adapt to changing circumstances and needs.

Every executive has an individual responsibility to become effective in engaging others. A leader without either interest in or knowledge of the persuasive art is a leader in appearance only. Self-directed study in the art and science of stakeholder engagement is at least as important as other executive tasks, and should receive appropriate investment of time and effort.

Basic individual communication skills are the foundation for effective leadership engagement, and should receive heavy emphasis.

Lessons for Leaders and Communicators

Every Marine knows that part of his or her responsibility is to be a good shot and skilled in infantry tactics. Even if the Marine spends all day working as a lawyer, truck mechanic, or helicopter pilot. Part of the Marines' professionalism is their emphasis on continuous skill enhancement and readiness.

Executives have a similar responsibility: One of the burdens of leadership is to get good at engaging stakeholders well. They need to master basic skills, practice those skills, and continually enhance their capacity to lead verbally.

At a very basic level of tactical execution, being good at engaging well starts with understanding the physicality of audience engagement. The audience makes judgments based on nonverbal cues. A leader is judged based on, among other attributes, his or her bearing: how he or she carries himself or herself. First impressions matter, and the first impression is often visual.

The most effective leaders take seriously the physicality of their performance: Standing or sitting in a posture that creates a stable platform. Gesturing fluidly. Making eye contact and locking in the audience's attention. Using visuals to amplify the speaker's points, and not the other way around.

The fundamentals work. And from those physicality fundamentals a leader can build an effective presence to convey content well.

8

Content: Word Choice, Framing, and Meaning

I am an immigrant to the United States. I arrived as a very young child and spoke no English. Because my mother also spoke almost no English, we spoke our native language, Portuguese, at home. When I was six, just as I was beginning to get the hang of English, we returned to Brazil for a while. When we came back, I had forgotten all of it. Just in time to start school. And I struggled to master English over the next ten years. It was a rocky journey.

When I was about 10, my mother took me to see a movie that has stayed with me ever since. *Casablanca,* starring Humphrey Bogart and Ingrid Bergman, is, among other things, a movie about words. It has some of the most memorable lines in the history of cinema. A small sampling: "Round up the usual suspects." "'I am shocked, shocked to discover gambling on the premises!'... 'Your winnings, sir.'" "Here's looking at you, kid." "Louie, this could be the beginning of a beautiful friendship."[1]

I loved the movie (and still do). But I came away confused about one particular word, in one pivotal scene.

The plot of the 1942 film centers on Rick Blaine, who just before World War II lived in Paris and was romantically involved with Ilsa Lund, who was reticent about her life before she met Rick. As the Germans invaded Paris, Ilsa and Rick agreed to meet at the train station to escape to the south. Rick arrived only to get a note from Ilsa telling him that she couldn't go with him, and that he shouldn't ask why. He left, deeply traumatized.

In the course of the movie, the viewer learns that when Ilsa was involved with Rick she thought she was a widow. But just before she was to meet him at the train station, she learned that her husband was still alive. He was Victor Laszlo, a celebrated hero of the anti-Nazi resistance, who she thought had died in a concentration camp. But he had escaped, and was in Paris.

Some time later, Rick had settled in Casablanca, in German-occupied French West Africa (now Morocco). He had become an establishment figure, owner of Rick's Café Américain, the hot night-spot for refugees seeking to flee the war and get to America. He had come into possession of two prized letters of transit that would guarantee safe passage out of Casablanca.

That night Ilsa and Victor surprised Rick by showing up at his cafe. As he said later that night, "Of all the gin joints in all towns in all the world, she walks into mine."[2] After closing time, Ilsa snuck into Rick's office and appealed to him to give her the letters of transit. He refused. She persisted, and tried to appeal to memories of their happy times together.

Then Rick interrupted her and spoke the words I hadn't understood: "I wouldn't mention Paris if I were you. It's poor salesmanship."[3]

I was baffled. I had no idea what it meant. My mom couldn't explain it. So I asked my father, who was a language professor specializing in philology—a branch of linguistics that studies languages and their historic and literary roots. I thought that if anyone could figure it out, he could. Our exchange went something like this:

"Dad, what's Paris?"

"Paris, it's a city. In France."

"No, that can't be it."

"What do you mean? Paris, right?"

"Yeah, Paris. But I think it has something to do with selling things."

"Selling things?"

"Yeah. If you mention Paris, you can't sell things."

My father smiled, and said, "You've seen *Casablanca*." I nodded. He then explained what Rick had meant. Paris was indeed a city. But for Rick, Paris represented something more: the worst day of his life, when he lost the thing he held most dear, in a way that was deeply hurtful. Just thinking of Paris brought back feelings of abandonment, rejection, betrayal. When he told Ilsa that mentioning Paris was poor salesmanship, he was warning her that if she mentioned Paris, he not only would remember how he felt on the last day, but would actually relive her abandonment, rejection, and betrayal of him. And be unlikely to want to help her.

I was even more baffled.

"That's what Paris means?"

"Only to Rick."

I concluded that English is a very difficult language, when a single word can have such a powerful private meaning.

"How are we supposed to know what's going on when words mean different things to different people?"

My dad took this as a teachable moment. He began what became a years-long discussion with me about words. How they carry meanings much larger than literal dictionary definitions. That they trigger powerful emotions. He introduced me to poetry, in several languages, to demonstrate the emotions that words, phrases, and sounds provoke.

Metaphor and the Management of Meaning

Words are carriers of meaning well beyond the literal. Words trigger worldviews that determine what other meanings are possible. Metaphors—in which a word stands in for something much broader than its literal meaning—are particularly powerful carriers of content, of emotional resonance. For Rick, the mention of Paris would trigger a worldview that would make any further appeal by Ilsa fruitless. It would provoke such a powerful negative reaction that it would shut down any opportunity for further discussion.

Ineffective leaders get the metaphor wrong, and inadvertently trigger a counterproductive response: either indifference or worse. Think back to our introduction, and BP Chief Executive Officer Tony Hayward's metaphor, "I'd like my life back." But effective leaders use metaphor to shape the frame of reference in which their content is to be understood, in order to provoke powerful reactions in their followers. Think Steve Jobs: "1,000 songs in your pocket!"

To be effective, leaders need to understand the power of metaphor and know how to use metaphor well. We've known for millenniums that metaphors work, but we're only now beginning to understand why.

 From **Warfighting**

War is shaped by human nature and is subject to the complexities, inconsistencies, and peculiarities which characterize human behavior. Since war is an act of violence based on irreconcilable disagreement, it will invariably inflame and be shaped by human emotions.

> *Effective communication is shaped by human nature and is subject to the complexities, inconsistencies, and particularities which characterize human behavior. Since communication is intended to change the way people think and feel and what they understand, know, and do, it will invariably be shaped by human emotions.*

The cognitive linguist George Lakoff has made managing meaning his life's work. Lakoff, a professor of linguistics at the University of California in Berkeley, was little known outside academia until 2004. Lakoff refers to himself as a metaphor analyst, and focuses on how the human brain creates mental structures that determine meaning. Lakoff notes that we live our lives in metaphor but are generally unaware of the metaphors we live by.[4] (That phrase is a pun—"live our lives in metaphor" is itself a metaphor.)

In 1980, with University of Oregon professor Mark Johnson, he wrote *Metaphors We Live By*, arguing that metaphors are not merely about the way we speak, but about the way we think and act:

> Metaphor is typically viewed as characteristic of language alone, a matter of words rather than thought or action. For this reason, most people think they can get along perfectly well without metaphor. We have found, on the contrary, that metaphor is pervasive in everyday life, not just in language

but in thought and action. Our ordinary conceptual system, in terms of which we both think and act, is fundamentally metaphorical in nature.

The concepts that govern our thoughts are not just matters of intellect. They also govern our everyday functioning, down to the most mundane details. Our concepts structure what we perceive, how we get around in the world, and how we relate to other people. Our conceptual system thus plays a role in defining our everyday realities.[5]

In that book and several later ones, Lakoff explored the prevalence of metaphors and also how cognitive science is providing insights into the way the human brain processes information, with metaphor being one of the key elements of understanding. Human beings seem to be wired to understand metaphor. For example, when we hear on the news, "The White House today announced...," we don't think that a building is speaking. Rather, we all understand the metaphor: "White House" stands in for the Administration of the President of the United States. Similarly, we know that "Hollywood" refers not just to a town in California but to the entertainment industry; "Wall Street," to the financial markets, wherever they happen to be located. "The Pentagon" refers not just to a building, but to the U.S. military. "10 Downing Street" refers to the office of the British Prime Minister; "the Vatican," to the papacy.

As important for our purposes, Lakoff and Johnson challenge what they call the Myth of Objectivism, which they say has dominated Western culture for thousands of years. That is the sense that there are absolute and unconditional truths, and that if we only speak the facts to people, those truths will be revealed. That myth says:

> Meaning is objective and disembodied, independent of human understanding.... How a person understands a sentence, and what it means *to him*, is a function of the objective meaning of the sentence and what that person believes about the world, and about the context in which the sentence is uttered.[6]

Lakoff and Johnson take issue with that way of understanding meaning. And I agree. The objective meaning of "Paris" is of a city.

But to Rick Blaine it meant something different. And the context in which a sentence is uttered is not the same as the context in which it is received. Tony Hayward clearly intended his comment "I'd like my life back" to convey that he shared a sense of urgency to resolve the Gulf oil spill. But those who heard the words didn't have that context. They provided their own: "He wants his life back: He resents the intrusion into his day-to-day work that the oil spill has caused." Effective leaders focus on managing the context in which a sentence is received, not merely the context in which it is uttered.

In his 1987 book, *Women, Fire, and Dangerous Things: What Categories Reveal About the Mind,* Lakoff explores systematic structures that give rise to our understanding, and how seemingly unrelated metaphors seem to be part of a common frame of understanding. Take, for example, metaphors for emotional response. Take a single emotion, anger. Lakoff lists dozens of metaphors to express anger, including these:

- He *lost his cool*.
- He was *looking daggers* at me.
- I almost *burst a blood vessel*.
- He was *foaming at the mouth*.
- You're beginning to *get to me*.
- You make my *blood boil*.
- He's *wrestling* with his anger.
- Watch out! He's *on a short fuse*.
- He's just *letting off steam*.
- Don't *get a hernia*!
- Try to *keep a grip on yourself*.
- Don't *fly off the handle*.
- When I told him, he *blew up*.
- He *channeled* his anger into something constructive.
- He was *red with anger*.
- He was *blue in the face*.
- He *appeased* his anger.
- He was *doing a slow burn*.

- He *suppressed* his anger.
- She kept *bugging* me.
- When I told my mother, she *had a cow*.[7]

When we hear these expressions, we don't take them literally. We do not assume, for example, that someone's mother has given birth to a calf. We understand the underlying meaning for which the literal reference is the metaphor. But Lakoff argues something far more interesting and more significant for our understanding of metaphor. He argues that these expressions are not random. They are related to each other, even though the literal meanings of each expression don't necessarily relate to each other. But we understand all of them as being somehow connected.

> We know, for example, that someone who is foaming at the mouth has lost his cool. We know that someone whose blood is boiling has not had his anger appeased. We know that someone who has channeled his anger into something constructive has not had a cow.[8]

Lakoff argues that there is a coherent conceptual organization underlying the expressions. He then identifies ways that conceptual organization works, and the implications for understanding and for language. Speaking just one word or phrase triggers the entire conceptual organization.

In 1999, again in collaboration with University of Oregon professor Mark Johnson, Lakoff applied that conceptual framework to the history of Western civilization. In *Philosophy in the Flesh: The Embodied Mind and Its Challenge to Western Thought*, Lakoff and Johnson argue that human understanding takes place unconsciously as we hear what is being said. They note that cognitive scientists have shown experimentally that to understand even very simple statements the brain performs a number of very complex processes, without any awareness that such processes are taking place.

> Consider, for example, all that is going on below the level of conscious awareness when you are in a conversation. Here is only a small part of what you are doing, second by second:

Accessing memories relevant to what is being said

Comprehending a stream of sound as being language, dividing it into distinctive phonetic features and segments, identifying phonemes, and grouping them into morphemes

Assigning a structure to the sentence in accord with the vast number of grammatical constructions in your native language

Picking out words and giving them meanings appropriate to the context

Making semantic and pragmatic sense of the sentences as a whole

Framing what is said in terms relevant to the discussion

Performing inferences relevant to what is being discussed

Constructing mental images where relevant and inspecting them

Filling the gaps in the discourse

Noticing and interpreting your interlocutor's body language

Anticipating where the conversation is going

Planning what to say in response[9]

All of these things are happening in the background, without our being aware of them. It's almost like a computer operating system doing complex operations in the background as we do seemingly simple things on our computer keyboard. It's precisely those background operations that make our keystrokes possible. But we're oblivious to them.

Lakoff pursued his work writing 600-page tomes for primarily academic audiences for 25 years before breaking into the limelight in 2004. Then he became an active presence in the 2004 political campaign by distilling his work into a short and easy-to-read book intended to help the Democratic presidential nominee U.S. Senator John Kerry stop committing self-inflicted harm in his race against President George W. Bush.

I had dinner with Lakoff in 2005 when we spoke together on a panel at a conference. Lakoff, who is politically progressive, told me that he had become increasingly frustrated as the 2004 presidential campaign reached the post-primary phase in the summer. The likely nominee, Senator Kerry, was inadvertently playing into President Bush's communication agenda, and in the process failing to frame the issues in ways that helped him. Sometimes he framed them in ways that actually helped the President. Unable to get a meeting with the senator, Lakoff chose instead to write a quick book for the progressive community in the hope that it would be able to help Senator Kerry take back the communication agenda.

In early July a small progressive publishing house agreed to print Lakoff's book, but for it to be commercially successful it had to be on bookstore shelves before the Democratic National Convention later that month. So Lakoff churned out an instant book. It was small but it packed a wallop. And it introduced the language of framing to a general audience.

Don't Think of an Elephant! Know Your Values and Frame the Debate, was an instant hit with Democrats and progressives, and soon Lakoff was a media darling. The "elephant" in the title isn't intended to suggest the mascot of the Republican Party. Rather, it refers to an experiment Lakoff does with his students. I have been doing a similar experiment with my students, beginning years before I knew of Lakoff's work. I tell my students: "Whatever you do, don't think of a giant purple octopus with big red tentacles." Then I ask my students, "Who succeeded in *not* thinking of the octopus?" Invariably, no one succeeded. Lakoff does the same kind of exercise with his students: "Don't think of an elephant!" And of course they do.

Lakoff uses this observation to introduce the notion of frames. Lakoff says that frames are mental structures that are triggered by language. When we trigger a frame, we trigger an entire worldview:

> Every word, like *elephant,* evokes a frame, which can be an image or other kind of knowledge: Elephants are large, have floppy ears and a trunk, are associated with circuses, and so on. The word is defined relative to that frame. When we negate a frame, we evoke the frame. Richard Nixon found that out the hard way. While under pressure to resign during

the Watergate scandal, Nixon addressed the nation on TV. He stood before the nation and said, "I am not a crook." And everybody thought he was a crook.[10]

Negating a frame triggers the very frame you negate. It causes people to think the very thing you want them not to think. Telling them not to doesn't work. Leaders often fail to understand this, and are puzzled by the audience's reaction.

But effective framing is about more than avoiding triggering the negative frame. It also requires triggering a positive frame. And much framing involves metaphor.

Lakoff's frustration with Senator Kerry was that he was making a fundamental—and too common—blunder when arguing against someone: "Don't use their language. Their language picks out a frame—and it won't be the frame you want."[11]

In the 2004 political campaign, the big blunder had to do with tax relief, and Senator Kerry's inadvertently playing into President Bush's frame. Lakoff explained the framing underlying the phrase *tax relief:*

> Think of the framing for *relief.* For there to be relief there must be an affliction, an afflicted party, and a reliever who removes the affliction and is therefore a hero. And if people try to stop the hero, those people are villains for trying to prevent relief. When the word *tax* is added to *relief,* the result is a metaphor: Taxation is an affliction. And the person who tries to take it away is a hero, and anyone who tries to stop him is a bad guy.[12]

Senator Kerry and the Democrats played into the President's frame. Initially playing the role of bad guy trying to prevent relief, eventually Senator Kerry came up with his own *tax relief* plan. But once he was in the President's frame, he had essentially conceded that taxes were an affliction. At that point the only meaningful question for voters was, whose plan offered the greatest relief? And it wouldn't be Senator Kerry's. No matter what Senator Kerry would propose, his tax cuts would never be as large as President Bush's. So he would always fall short in the comparison of who would provide the greatest relief for the affliction that is taxes. Although he may then choose to argue the nuances of policy—about which taxpayers should pay more than others—the cause would still be lost. At that point he wouldn't be persuasive. If taxes are an affliction, then no one should be afflicted. Senator Kerry had lost as soon as he allowed himself to be drawn into using the tax relief frame. The President had set a trap for Senator Kerry, and he had walked into it.

Lakoff argued that progressives in general, and Senator Kerry in particular—if they should even talk about taxes in the first place—could have reframed the discussion away from taxes as an affliction. Lakoff suggests that the frame could be something like this:

> Taxation is what you pay to live in a civilized country—what you pay to have democracy and opportunity, and what you pay to use the infrastructure paid for by previous taxpayers.[13]

He says that the progressive frame could work with one or both of two metaphors: investment and dues. As investment:

> Our parents invested in the future, ours as well as theirs, through their taxes. They invested their tax money in the interstate highway system, the Internet, the scientific and medical establishments, our communications systems, our airline system, the space program. They invested in the future, and we are reaping the tax benefits, the benefits from the taxes they paid. Today we have assets—highways, schools and colleges, the Internet, airlines—that come from the wise investments they made.[14]

Or as dues, a frame particularly intended for those who might object to particular spending programs:

> Taxation is paying your dues, paying your membership fee in America. If you join a country club or a community center, you pay fees. Why? You did not build the swimming pool. You have to maintain it…. Otherwise it won't be maintained and will fall apart. People who avoid taxes, like corporations that move to Bermuda, are not paying their dues to their country. It is patriotic to be a taxpayer. It is traitorous to desert our country and not pay our dues. Perhaps Bill Gates Sr. said it best. In arguing to keep the inheritance tax, he pointed out

that he and Bill Jr. did not invent the Internet. They just used it—to make billions. There is no such thing as a self-made man. Every businessman has used the vast American infrastructure, which the taxpayers paid for, to make his money.[15]

To Lakoff's lament, Senator Kerry continued to play into President Bush's frames and lost the election. But Lakoff's book became a *New York Times* bestseller, and the language of framing became mainstream. From 2004 on, I have been asked by dozens of clients, universities, and professional conferences to speak about framing and managing meaning. Lakoff's book, and two subsequent expansions—2006's *Whose Freedom: The Battle over America's Most Important Idea* and 2008's *The Political Mind: Why You Can't Understand 21st-Century American Politics with an 18th-Century Brain*—have helped a new generation of leaders understand the power of framing. I have assigned all three books in various semesters of my NYU communication strategy course—the same course in which I assign *Warfighting.*

Among Lakoff's core principles that apply to leaders and their ability to win hearts and minds are these:

- Frames are mental structures that shape the way people see the world.
- When a frame is triggered, an entire worldview is triggered that determines the meaning of all that follows.
- Metaphors in particular trigger worldviews, and are powerful framing mechanisms.
- If facts are inconsistent with the frames in our brains, we ignore the facts. In Lakoff's language, when the facts don't fit the frame, the facts bounce off and the frames remain. (Facts bouncing off is itself a metaphor!)
- Speaking merely the facts causes audiences to provide their own frames or gives an opening for critics and others to provide the missing frame, usually to our disadvantage.
- To be persuasive, frames must precede facts.

But too often leaders fall into the trap of believing that facts are persuasive. This is part of the Myth of Objectivism. Facts aren't. Facts can be persuasive only to the degree that they fit some prior frame. I do lots of work with pharmaceutical executives, including people with lots of medical and scientific training. They typically want to speak only facts. They even say "the facts speak for themselves." But the facts don't speak. The facts are open to interpretation based on context, and we need to control the context. If we speak only facts, the audience either will not pay attention to those facts or will provide their own context—their own frames—to make sense of the facts.

I often ask my pharmaceutical clients something like this. Consider a particular drug. A study shows that 13 percent of patients have a certain kind of side effect. Is 13 percent good news or bad news? It depends. What is the difference in meaning among these statements?

- "Thirteen percent of patients experienced this side effect."
- "Only 13 percent of patients experienced this side effect."
- "Fully 13 percent of patients experienced this side effect."
- "As many as 13 percent of patients suffered from this side effect."
- "Even though 13 percent of patients experienced this side effect, the medicine was so effective in treating their disease that they still took their medicine."

The fact, 13 percent, is just a data point. It carries no particular meaning beyond the statistical. We need to make sense of it. If we don't, our audience will have to, and will provide its own frame. And it probably won't be a frame we like. Worse, it could very well be a frame that creates a false impression. Since those who say "the facts speak for themselves" usually associate facts with truth, framing helps them see that truth consists of facts embedded in a context that creates a true impression. Failing to provide that frame is in many ways a failure of leadership. It invites people to reach a false conclusion.

But even when leaders understand the importance of a frame, they often create the same kind of problem by defaulting to a kind of deductive, logical argument. They begin with facts, and present an accumulation of facts and then provide a conclusion, a framing statement, at the end. The risk is that along the way the audience will disengage, and not pay attention to the conclusion, or will provide their own frame of reference before the conclusion is reached. And once they've inserted their own frame, it will be much harder to get them to use our frame.

So effective leaders frame first and give facts second. Take the example of Citicorp, the parent of Citibank in the 1990s. In 1993, following the banking crisis that began in the late 1980s, Citibank was in trouble. Citicorp Chief Executive Officer John S. Reed launched a five-point turnaround plan, a key point of which was to increase the bank's capital base.

Then Citicorp set about implementing the plan. Early in 1993 it announced that it was suspending its dividend, the quarterly distribution of profit it made to investors in Citicorp stock. Normally the suspension of a dividend would be seen as a very negative event. If Citicorp had simply announced the fact that it was suspending its dividend, the investment community's reaction would likely be negative: "Struggling Citicorp is in such bad shape that it had to suspend its dividend!" I was present at the investor meeting at which the announcement was made. (Citi was a client at the time.) CEO John Reed began the meeting by reminding investors of the five-point plan for Citi's turnaround, and how one key element of it was to build its capital base. He said that Citi took that plan seriously. And one of the fastest ways to build its capital would be to retain its earnings by suspending the dividend. Such a strategy would discontinue distribution of profits to investors, for the short term, and apply those profits to its capital base in order to increase the bank's financial stability. So effective immediately, Citicorp was suspending its dividend. In that era before cellphones, I stood at a counter where the bank had provided dozens of phones for use by the investment analysts. I listened as analysts called their offices to alert investors of the news. What I heard was fascinating. Instead of interpreting the dividend suspension as distressing, analysts had a positive reaction. "Citicorp is serious about its turnaround. Its suspension of the dividend means it's willing to make tough choices to improve its capital base. Buy Citi." The frame—five-point turnaround plan, increase our capital base, retain earnings— determined the meaning of the fact—Citi is suspending its dividend. Citicorp managed the meaning of the fact by leading with the frame.

Lakoff notes that too often experts lead with facts when they need to do exactly the opposite.

In 2011 two Stanford University researchers demonstrated the importance of framing before providing facts. Paul Thibodeau and Lera Boroditsky published the results of a study of people's interpretation of data based on the frame that introduces the data. In "Metaphors We Think With: The Role of Metaphor in Reasoning," they described an experiment in which two groups of people were told about the crime problem in the fictional city of Addison. Both groups got exactly the same statistics, presented in exactly the same ways. But one group had crime described through the metaphor of a wild beast preying on the city; the other, as a virus infecting the city. Each group was then asked what the appropriate solution to the crime problem would be, and why. The first group was told:

> Crime is a wild beast preying on the city of Addison. The crime rate in the once peaceful city has steadily increased over the past three years. In fact, these days it seems that crime is lurking in every neighborhood. In 2004, 46,177 crimes were reported, compared to more than 55,000 reported in 2007. The rise in violent crime is particularly alarming. In 2004, there were 330 murders in the city; in 2007, there were over 500.[16]

The second group was told:

> Crime is a virus infecting the city of Addison. The crime rate in the once peaceful city has steadily increased over the past three years. In fact, these days it seems that crime is plaguing every neighborhood. In 2004, 46,177 crimes were reported, compared to more than 55,000 reported in 2007. The rise in violent crime is particularly alarming. In 2004, there were 330 murders in the city; in 2007, there were over 500.[17]

Each group was then asked to prescribe a solution to the crime problem in Addison. Of those who had crime framed through the wild beast metaphor, 74 percent proposed some form of law enforcement solution: Capture the criminals, punish the criminals, build more jails.

Only 56 percent of those who had crime described as a virus proposed a law enforcement solution. But those who got the virus frame were twice as likely to propose solutions involving reform: investigate root causes, invest in education, eliminate poverty.

The two frames—beast or virus—led to dramatically different policy solutions even though the facts were identical. But in an interesting twist, the reasons given were the same. Those who proposed law enforcement solutions and those who proposed reform solutions pointed to the same reason: the crime statistics.

In other words, people make judgments based on the frames in which the facts are embedded. But they justify those judgments based on the facts. It isn't that the facts don't matter. But the facts are invoked afterward. They're not determinative of a point of view.

Executives have a very difficult time with this. Many feel the need to focus just on facts. Or to lead with facts and allow the frames to follow. This is a mistake.

I have a client that needed to raise its prices to maintain financial stability. The client is an insurance company, and it was at risk of financial distress if it didn't receive a major increase in rates. It filed with its regulators a very aggressive rate plan, certain to provoke controversy. The initial draft of its public announcement, vetted by actuaries and underwriters, focused solely on the facts:

> On [date] [name of company] filed a rate request with [regulator], requesting a 42 percent increase in our overall rate level.

Because it led with facts, and the percentage amount was so high, audiences would need to provide their own frames—in all likelihood the inappropriateness of such a dramatic price increase. Thankfully, the company didn't send out that announcement. Its public affairs professionals, trained in framing, chose to lead with the need for the increase, framed in the ability to fulfill the company's promises to its customers:

> [Name of company] needs to stabilize its financial condition in order to protect its customers from the risk of catastrophic loss from natural disasters. While this is a painful situation, it is the only responsible choice.

That frame worked. While the rate increase request was still unpopular, the announcement provoked productive discussion among the public and regulators as to how consumers can be protected in the event of catastrophic events.

Reframing

Language not only frames, but can reframe. The libertarian culture writer Virginia Postrel gives a good example of reframing in a column she wrote in the *Atlantic* magazine in 2006. She explored an emerging new industry and how it had overcome some of the obstacles in its path. She wondered what it would take for that industry to become ubiquitous. The column was titled "The Next Starbucks? How Massage Went from the Strip Club to the Strip Mall."[18] Just the title is ripe with framing: "Next Starbucks" evokes something that was once hard to find—espresso coffee—but is now commonplace; at once everywhere but also expensive. "Strip Club" evokes seediness, sexualized activity, something vaguely inappropriate. "Strip Mall" evokes something totally banal: suburban sprawl, cookie-cutter retail establishments along a highway.

Postrel describes massage's trajectory: "Once a specialized therapy for injured athletes, an indulgence for the idle rich, or a cover for prostitution, massage has become a legitimate and seemingly ubiquitous enterprise."[19] She says, for example, that in 2005 some 47 million Americans had at least one massage. But to get there the massage sector had to overcome two significant hurdles.

> As a business, massage has two basic problems. The first is that prostitution is generally illegal. A brothel can't openly advertise its services: no "Madame Julia's House of Great Sex." Instead, Madame Julia pretends she runs a "massage parlor," which creates confusion, and sometimes legal obstacles, for people who want to buy and sell back rubs.[20]

In other words, the legitimate massage business is challenged by the illegitimate business that masquerades as a legitimate one.

The second problem is that most potential customers consider massage a luxury—an openly optional indulgence, if not a slightly shameful extravagance. So they're acutely sensitive to price. A massage business can't pass high labor costs along to consumers without suffering a rapid drop in sales.[21]

In some ways this is an even bigger challenge, because it theoretically applies to a much larger universe of potential customers. If massage is seen as an openly optional indulgence or extravagance, it would be very difficult to persuade customers to engage in the service.

The solution to both challenges, says Postrel, was to reframe the entire enterprise.

One way to attack these problems is to declare massage a medical service. Hence in 1983 the American Massage & Therapy Association dropped its ampersand to create a new profession: "massage therapy." Customers and legal authorities can be pretty sure—though not 100 percent certain—that a massage *therapist* isn't selling sex. A therapist not only will keep the client discreetly draped with a sheet but also will take a reassuringly clinical approach to kneading naked flesh.[22]

The reframing of massage into a medical service worked. The American Massage & Therapy Association took what had been two separate nouns, *massage* and *therapy,* and combined them into a single phrase, *massage therapy,* with *massage* as an adjective. Rather than two separate things, there was now one thing—therapy—with *massage* as the modifier for that thing. And people were already well acquainted with modifiers for therapy: physical therapy, occupational therapy, art therapy, aroma therapy.

The worldview triggered by the massage therapy frame is now of a clinical setting: of professionals who are trained and licensed; of facilities that are sanitary; of an experience that is routinized, predictable, and wholesome. And it makes return business more likely. Taking care of one's health is not seen as an indulgence, but as an appropriate, even as a responsible, thing to do.

Meeting People Where They Are

A recurring theme in this book is that if you want to move people, you need to meet them where they are. The same applies to framing. If you want to move people to think, feel, understand, or do something differently, the starting point has to be which frames would resonate with them in ways that help you. Understanding our audience means more than just understanding their demographics or their immediate concerns. It requires understanding the frames that matter to them. And speaking in ways that make an emotional connection with them.

In Chapter 3, "Words Aren't Enough," we saw how Microsoft's Bill Gates did this when he chose to speak about his house rather than about his software, in the process exciting his audience about the potential for a world with ubiquitous connectivity. We saw it also in Chapter 1, "Words Matter," in how Apple's Steve Jobs introduced a whole new category of consumer product with "iPod: 1,000 songs in your pocket." And in Chapter 4, "Speed, Focus, and the First Mover Advantage," we saw the Marines do it when they framed the Fallujah mosque incident as an investigation into an allegation of the unlawful use of force, and affirmed their commitment to the Law of Armed Conflict.

Part of meeting audiences where they are is demonstrating that we know where they are. In *The Art of Framing: Managing the Language of Leadership,* University of Cincinnati communications professor Gail T. Fairhurst and Robert Sarr, then the Chair of Santa Fe Southern Railways, emphasize the power of expressing understanding of the audience's point of view:

> If we communicate that we understand another's perspective, we show regard because we have taken time to consider an alternative view. If we show genuine regard, people tend to be more favorably disposed toward us.[23]

We saw precisely this lack of understanding another's perspective in Chapter 3: failure to understand or even acknowledge the concerns of Netflix's customers and Home Depot's investors.

Leaders who take audiences seriously also take framing seriously. They speak in ways that establish contexts that make audiences more likely to be movable. They trigger productive worldviews and move audiences to think and feel, know and do things differently.

Recap: Best Practices from This Chapter

 From Warfighting

Effective communication is shaped by human nature and is subject to the complexities, inconsistencies, and particularities which characterize human behavior. Since communication is intended to change the way people think and feel and what they understand, know, and do, it will invariably be shaped by human emotions.

Lessons for Leaders and Communicators

However much leaders may wish it were otherwise, facts don't speak for themselves. Objectivism is a myth. Human beings make judgments based not on facts, but on facts that make sense within a given context. That context is a frame: a worldview that gives meaning to the facts. Identical facts in different frames result in dramatically different audience response.

Leaders need to take framing seriously. Frames are mental structures triggered by language. Metaphors are particularly powerful framing devices because we humans live our lives in metaphor. George Lakoff teaches us that our understanding is based on complex conceptual organization in our brain that makes sense of metaphors. That complex organization operates in the background as humans engage with others, but we are oblivious to that operation, much as we are unaware of a computer's operating system that allows us to make simple keystrokes on our keyboard.

When a frame is triggered, an entire worldview is triggered, and the worldview determines the meaning of what comes next.

Leaders often make one of three framing mistakes:

1. They fail to frame at all, leaving the audience or critics to provide the frame, often to the leader's disadvantage.

2. They inadvertently trigger a negative frame, by either saying something counterproductive (as Ilsa was about to when interrupted by Rick's admonition, "I wouldn't mention Paris if I were you") or denying something, thereby inadvertently triggering the very frame they were trying to avoid ("I'm not a crook!").

3. They lead with the facts, and provide the frame only afterward. But by then the audience has either already provided the missing frame or ignored the facts altogether.

Framing has to come before the facts. We saw how identical data on the crime wave in the fictional city of Addison was interpreted in two dramatically different ways based on the metaphor used to introduce the statistics: a wild beast preying on the city, or a virus infecting the city. We also saw how although the frames determined the interpretation of the problem and proposed solutions (build jails; provide economic opportunity), the solutions were justified in each case by pointing to the data. This suggests that people make judgments based on the frames, but justify their views based on the facts.

In contested situations, it's usually a bad idea to accept the other side's frame, as Senator Kerry did to his ultimate demise in the 2004 presidential election. Rather, it's important to reframe. Reframing allows an alternative context and can neutralize resistance and even secure public support.

Finally, understanding and explicitly acknowledging the concerns of the audience can help make them more receptive to our frames in the first place.

9

Audiences: Attention, Retention, and How Hearts and Minds Work

About a dozen times in the past year I've stood in front of groups of executives or students and conducted a demonstration. One group was about 500 U.S. employees of a European bank. Another was about 20 people in the TV studio of a large U.S. insurance company, with another 200 watching remotely. Several groups were graduate students, some in NYU's executive MBA program and some in NYU's MS in PR/Corporate Communication program. And about half the groups were executives in different parts of a global pharmaceutical company, including one with several neuroscientists in attendance.

The demonstration comes about halfway through a three-hour workshop on persuasion and leadership communication skills, usually just after a break. I grasp a lemon between my thumb and middle finger, and hold it out to the audience. "What's this?" "It's a lemon." "Right. A lemon. Now, please pay attention." Then, with some flourish, I slice the lemon in half and hold the flesh side toward the audience. I then tuck the end of a towel into my collar, stab the lemon a few times with a fork, and hold the end of the towel away from me, to protect my suit. Then I aggressively and noisily shove the half lemon into my mouth, and chew the flesh vigorously while the juice runs down my cheeks and chin, through my beard, and onto the towel. The audience invariably shrieks, grunts, groans, or otherwise makes a fuss. Many look horrified. I then wipe my face, take a sip of water, grimace, and then smile. There's complete silence in the room. And a sense of shock.

After a dramatic pause, I ask the audience, "What was happening to you as I was chewing the lemon?" I always get the same range of answers:

- "My mouth puckered."
- "I tasted the lemon."
- "I couldn't stop my mouth from watering."
- "I felt the juice run down my throat."
- "I thought you were crazy. But I tasted the lemon."

I then challenge those responses. "What are you talking about? How on earth could *you* have tasted *my* lemon? How could *you* have felt the juice go down *your* throat, when you know full well it was going down *my* throat?" Invariably, they smile, grasping the puzzle.

I then put them out of their misery. "Here's how. I connected with you. You felt my lemon; you experienced the effect of my chewing on the lemon as if you were chewing on it. Even though you know that you weren't. Why?"

The answer is mirror neurons. Mirror neurons are structures in the brain that allow people to experience someone else's plight as if it's their own. In watching me eat the lemon, my clients and students experienced *empathy*—from two Greek words, literally meaning to *feel with* someone.

Leaders need to understand mirror neurons and the many ways the human brain makes connection with others possible. If leaders need to meet people where they are, they need to understand how to meet them. But human connection is not merely a function of proximity. It's a function also of biology.

 *From* **Warfighting**

Because war is a clash between opposing human wills,
the human dimension is central to war. It is the human dimension
which infuses war with its intangible moral factors.

> *Because communication is about human connection,*
> *the human dimension is central to communicating.*
> *It is the human dimension that makes communication possible.*
> *Leaders need to know how humans actually work.*

I Second That Emotion

Humans are wired to connect with each other. To feel with others.

In *The Empathic Civilization: The Race to Global Consciousness in a World in Crisis,* Jeremy Rifkin recounts the discovery of mirror neurons.[1] Mr. Rifkin is president of the Foundation on Economic Trends in Washington and a senior lecturer in the executive education program at the Wharton School of Business, University of Pennsylvania.

He tells how in 1992 in Parma, Italy, a team of neurophysiologists discovered an anomaly. They had implanted sensors into the brain of a macaque monkey to determine how its brain operated when the monkey did things, such as grab a peanut. But at one point a human entered the lab and reached for a peanut, and the scientists saw the same brain activity in the monkey as when the monkey reached for the peanut itself. They concluded that something must be wrong with their machine. But the more they looked into it, the more they realized that the machine was fine. Rather, the monkey's brain reacted the same way regardless of whether the monkey grabbed the peanut or watched a human grab the peanut.[2]

The team, led by Giacomo Rizzolatti, then tried this with humans, scanning humans' brains with functional magnetic resonance imaging. They found the same phenomenon. They had discovered mirror neurons. Says Rifkin:

> Mirror neurons allow humans—and other animals—to grasp the minds of others "as if" their thoughts and behavior were their own. The popular science press has begun to refer to mirror neurons as "empathy neurons." What is most striking, says Rizzolatti, is that the "[m]irror neurons allow us to grasp the minds of others not through conceptual reasoning but through directed stimulation. By feeling, not by thinking."[3]

I Feel Your Pain

We connect with others by feeling, not by thinking. This simple discovery has profound implications. In the 20 years since mirror neurons were discovered, there has been a revolution in biology, philosophy, linguistics, psychology, neurophysiology, and other fields to figure out how humans actually work. There's still a great deal to learn, and there has been some scientific push-back on the very idea of mirror neurons. But a consensus is emerging that historically we've given the human brain more credit for rationality than perhaps we should. All the new findings point to the primacy of emotion, even in our very developed societies.

This isn't easy to swallow. From the time of Aristotle to the present, Western civilization has assumed that persuasion involves rational processes: logic, facts, argument. Granted, Aristotle also spoke about the need for Pathos and Ethos to accompany Logos. But for much of Western history, Pathos and Ethos have been shunted aside for the primacy of Logos. The 17th-century French philosopher René Descartes famously named the essence of being human: "I think, therefore I am." Especially since the Enlightenment, reason and logic have been seen to be the cornerstones of civilization and progress. They are certainly seen as what matters in business, and what is taught in business and professional schools. But however important reason may be, emotion is now increasingly recognized as the key to moving hearts and minds. And hearts and minds (metaphor!) exist in the brain.

All too often leaders assume that facts matter; that logic should prevail; that if only we let the facts speak for themselves, people will understand and agree with us. We also know from observation that this doesn't necessarily work, but that leaders persist in pushing facts at people rather than connecting with them. They even continue to push facts after they realize that it isn't working. Paradoxically, leaders sometimes double down when they aren't connecting. They become even more determined to push data and facts rather than stopping and then trying a new approach. (Think of Netflix's persistent attempts to justify its business decision in terms of the company's operations, without any expression even of understanding that customers would be inconvenienced.) If leaders are to be effective, they need at least to appreciate, or better yet to understand, the role of emotion.

In the preceding chapter we noted what the Berkeley cognitive linguist George Lakoff called the Myth of Objectivism: that facts and data are persuasive. That's a conclusion based not merely on observation. There's a biological basis for Lakoff's insight.

George Washington University neurology professor Richard Restak argues, "We are not thinking machines. We are feeling machines who think."[4]

It isn't that reason and facts are unimportant. It isn't that we don't think. But rather that humans are unlikely to attend to the facts a speaker is presenting if there isn't the right emotional connection. We are feeling machines who *also* think. We've known for years that if an audience is angry and the speaker merely speaks facts without expressing any emotion, the audience tends to get angrier. We saw that in the Home Depot annual meeting, when investors expressed their frustration and anger but CEO Robert Nardelli simply responded with, "The board recommends that you reject this proposal." That turned investors' frustration and anger into a passionate determination to oust the CEO. But we also know that if people are angry and the speaker acknowledges the anger and shares some emotional connection with the audience, the anger can dissipate.

The rule I've always used in coaching clients in a crisis is that you can't meet emotion with logic. You have to meet it with emotion; once that emotional connection is made you can then move the audience to a conclusion with logic. Again, we are feeling machines, who think. But we need to feel first, and then to think.

If a stakeholder feels aggrieved, it's important to acknowledge that emotional starting point by expressing regret, sorrow, contrition, or at least empathy. If a leader doesn't start with some emotional connection, the rest seems hollow.

I'm often asked by clients why, in the aftermath of a tragic accident or incident, they need to say something like, "Our hearts go out to the family of those killed in the fire." They ask, "Doesn't that sound canned and insincere? Isn't it better just to get to the point and tell people what we're doing about it?" My response is, first, that it would be better if such a statement were not canned or insincere. But second, regardless of the sincerity, people in mourning need to hear an expression of sympathy before they will listen to anything else. And people who may not necessarily be in mourning but who empathize with those who are also need to hear an expression of sympathy. It may well be canned, but it is still necessary. Leaders who default to Logos in moments of emotional upheaval will likely fail to move stakeholders. But if they lead with Pathos, they are more likely to have the chance for Logos to prevail.

We Happy Few

In *The Empathic Civilization,* Jeremy Rifkin draws another conclusion from the emerging understanding of mirror neurons: Humans crave connection. He says:

> We've long known that human beings and other mammalian specials are "social animals." The discovery of mirror neurons, however, opens the door to exploring the biological mechanisms that make sociability possible.[5]

Rifkin challenges the historical Western assumption that human beings are by nature aggressive, materialistic, and self-interested. He argues from both a historical and a biological perspective that we're actually wired for sociability, for attachment, for companionship, and for affection. He says that our first drive is to actually belong. That sense of belonging is deeply wired in our brains.

Evolutionary biology suggests that humans developed a strong us/them, friend/foe instinct that was useful in dealing with immediate, life-threatening situations. A sense of belonging, whether to a family, clan, community, nation, team, or workforce, is a powerful driver of behavior, and can often trump self-interest. Think of a parent's selfless sacrifice for a child; a soldier's throwing himself on a grenade to protect his comrades; a worker's staying late to finish a project so as not to disappoint colleagues; or a fan, whose face is painted in a football team's colors, sitting in a freezing stadium to show solidarity with his team.

Identifying as part of a group is a powerful emotional connection. So powerful that George Lakoff, in *Don't Think of an Elephant!* says that in politics voters don't necessarily behave in ways that maximize their self-interest. Rather, people tend to vote in ways that confirm their self-identity:

> People do not necessarily vote in their self-interest. They vote their identity. They vote their values. They vote for who

they identify with. They may identify with their self-interest. That can happen. It is not that people never care about their self-interest. But they vote their identity. And if their identity fits their self-interest, they will vote for it. It is important to understand this point. It is a serious mistake to assume that people are simply always voting in their self-interest.[6]

Think of the emotional resonance in American politics in the following identities: Republican, Democrat, Libertarian, Progressive, Soccer Mom, Tea Party, the 99 Percent, Union Member, National Rifle Association Member. Identifying with one of these groups is a stronger predictor of how someone will vote than many other kinds of demographics.

The same applies beyond politics. Stakeholders don't necessarily make judgments and choices based on their own interests. Rather, they make judgments and choices based on who they want to be, how they want to be seen, and what they want to be a part of. This applies to teams in the workplace, to customers of luxury goods, and even to cliques in high school. The sense of belonging drives behavior.

When Apple launched its iPhone in the summer of 2007, thousands of people waited in lines on city streets through the night to get a chance to be the first to own the phone. They didn't need a new phone, and they certainly didn't need to spend the night outdoors waiting for one. But it became an identity play: "I'm so cool that I waited outside all night to get the iPhone." Millions of people crowd Times Square on New Year's Eve, sometimes in subzero temperature, for a chance to be in the crowd when the ball drops. They could get a better view, certainly in more comfort, watching it at home. But they want to be part of the experience.

Leaders who appeal to self-interest alone will often fail to move their audiences. But leaders who appeal to identity—to being part of a team, a cause, an event, a mission—can move people to put aside their self-interest.

Perhaps the best example is found in Shakespeare's *Henry V.* That play recounts the true story of the decisive moment in a war that put England on the map as a power to be reckoned with, the Battle of Agincourt in 1415. The English troops, far from home and beyond their supply lines, are being pursued by the French. The English are outnumbered, exhausted, sick, and in a desperate situation. The battle will commence shortly and the English prospects are very poor. King Henry V rallies the troops by appealing to their honor and their connection to each other—a band of brothers:

> That he which hath no stomach to this fight,
> Let him depart…
> We would not die in that man's company
> That fears his fellowship to die with us.
> This day is call'd the feast of Crispian.
> He that outlives this day, and comes safe home,
> Will stand a tip-toe when this day is nam'd,
> And rouse him at the name of Crispian.
> He that shall live this day, and see old age,
> Will yearly on the vigil feast his neighbours,
> And say "To-morrow is Saint Crispian."
> Then will he strip his sleeve and show his scars,
> And say "These wounds I had on Crispian's day."
> Old men forget; yet all shall be forgot,
> But he'll remember, with advantages,
> What feats he did that day…
> From this day to the ending of the world,
> But we in it shall be remembered-
> We few, we happy few, we band of brothers;
> For he to-day that sheds his blood with me
> Shall be my brother; be he ne'er so vile.[7]

The speech is all Ethos and Pathos. Ethos in appealing to identity, a sense of belonging, of shared destiny: He today that sheds his blood with me shall be my brother. And Pathos in predicting a sense of pride and honor: He will stand on tiptoe and remember with advantages the feats he did that day. Henry rallied his troops and secured a stunning upset victory. And the metaphor of a band of brothers has stayed with us, even becoming the title of an HBO miniseries about American troops in World War II.

While most leaders won't necessarily have the same rhetorical flourishes as the Bard, they can intentionally focus on the emotional connection of identity: We're in this together.

Baby, I Was Born This Way

The default to emotion is part of the human condition.

To better appreciate the role of emotion and what it allows an audience to do, we need to take a brief detour into evolutionary biology. The human brain can be understood as three separate brains working in tandem, if not completely integrated with each other. Because humans are still evolving, the three brains don't work as well together as they might.

The oldest part of our brain, which we share with many other life-forms, emerged about 300 million years ago. Often called the "primitive brain" or "reptilian brain," this structure sits at the base of our modern brain, and it controls the core autonomic functions of the body: breathing, digestion, excretion, and so on. It's the basic operating system of an animal, keeping us alive simply by keeping things working in the body.

About 200 million years ago mammals developed a second structure, called the limbic brain. This is where emotions originate, where memories are stored, and where unconscious moral judgments are made.

Only about 65 million years ago did primates and other mammals such as dolphins develop what we now think of as the distinctly thinking brain: the prefrontal cortex where reasoning takes place. Humans have the largest prefrontal cortex relative to the rest of the brain of any species. It takes up about two-thirds of the human brain's mass. It is this part of the brain that we think of as distinctly human: It is this part that governs language and abstract thinking, where understanding arises. It is where logic and facts are processed, where planning takes place, where decisions are considered and made.

In humans there's a pretty constant interplay between the prefrontal cortex and the older structures of the brain. Historically, we've seen this as a tug of war between reason and emotion. Plato said that we can understand the human struggle between reason and emotion by thinking of a chariot pulled by two horses: one well trained and obedient, and the other wild and untamed. The charioteer has to constantly balance the two horses, who are working at cross purposes to each other. Neuroscience now shows us that Plato was onto something. It explains how that tug of war works.

The primitive brain and the limbic brain collectively make up the limbic system, which governs emotion. The limbic system is where emotions arise, where we associate things as either pleasurable or repugnant, where fear, anger, joy, anxiety, and other emotions are triggered. The limbic system also controls the endocrine system, where hormones and other chemicals are released into the bloodstream. The limbic system is where our fight-or-flight impulses arise, where any perceived threat immediately triggers the release of chemicals into our bloodstream that creates a heightened sense of arousal and facilitates our ability to respond quickly. Evolutionarily, that response often took the form of confronting the threat or fleeing from it. Even though most threats these days are abstract rather than physical, we're still engineered to have powerful physical responses to any threatening stimulus. Also to any pleasurable stimulus.

Within the limbic system there is a structure called the amygdala, which leaders need to understand. The amygdala is the center for triggering emotions such as fear, anger, sexual arousal, and joy. When faced with a stimulus, the amygdala turns our emotions on. It does so instantaneously, without our having to think about it. We find ourselves responding to a threat even before we're consciously aware of it. Think of jumping back when we see a sudden movement in front of us, or being startled by the sound of a loud bang. We also respond instantaneously to positive stimulus without thinking about it: Note how we tend to smile back when someone smiles at us; how we are immediately distracted when something we consider beautiful enters our line of sight.

The amygdala is the key to understanding an audience's emotional response, and to connecting with an audience.

In the interplay between the amygdala and the prefrontal cortex, the rational part often tries to control, contain, or even turn off the emotional part. But it's not a fair fight. New York University neuroscience professor Joseph Ledoux told the PBS documentary program *This Emotional Life* how the wiring of the brain affects our ability to manage our emotions:

> The prefrontal cortex has no connectivity with the amygdala. The amygdala has superhighways to talk to the cortex, but the prefrontal cortex has only back roads and side streets to get to the amygdala.[8]

In other words, emotions can easily overcome reason. The connection from the emotion-triggering part of the brain to the rational part is direct and powerful. When the amygdala talks, the prefrontal cortex listens and follows instructions. The amygdala can shut down reasoning, at least for a while. Because the amygdala acts instantaneously and pumps stress hormones into our bloodstream, it can take a while for the chemicals in our blood to dissipate and for reasoning to catch up. We may see something that looks menacing—a snake!—and jump back. It may take a few moments for our prefrontal cortex to catch up to the amygdala and conclude that there was no snake, just a stick that looked like a snake. But all the while we'll feel the change in our bodies: If we had been sleepy, we're now wide awake; if we had been hungry, we no longer feel the hunger. The amygdala makes us focus on the immediate threat and ignore everything else. And after the threat dissipates, it takes a while for the chemicals that heightened our state of arousal to clear our bodies. It takes time for us literally to calm down.

Daniel Goleman, author of *Emotional Intelligence*, explains how the amygdala works:

> The amygdala is the brain's sentinel. It has a privileged position in perception. Everything we see in every moment goes mostly to the sensory cortex but a small part of it goes to the amygdala...which scans it to see "is this a threat?" That's a constant question in evolution: "Is this a threat?" Or more generally, the amygdala has presumably been the structure that answers the one critical question for survival, "Do I eat it or does it eat me?"... The amygdala is a hair trigger. In other words it would rather be safe than sorry. It gets a very fuzzy picture of what's going on. But if it thinks it has a match it has the ability to trigger...a rush of stress hormones. It changes the entire way the brain prioritizes information.[9]

But it's much harder for reason to control emotion. There are no direct connections between the prefrontal cortex and the amygdala. Rather, signals from the rational part of the brain can reach the emotional part only indirectly and inefficiently. The prefrontal cortex may talk, but the amygdala may not hear what it is saying. It is possible to train the brain to control emotion—we see this with firefighters, fighter pilots, the military, and others who need to overcome fear. The brain soft-wires connections among neurons through repetition, making it easier for particular threats to be managed. But it's still much easier for emotions to overcome reason than the other way around. And the more upset people are, the more primitive they become: the more the amygdala takes over and makes reasoning almost impossible.

Leaders need to appreciate the role of the amygdala, both to avoid succumbing to the amygdala's attempt to shut down thinking in critical moments, and to appreciate what audiences are even capable of.

Keep Calm and Carry On

Tony Hayward was tired, frustrated, and feeling besieged. And he said something counterproductive: "I'd like my life back." President Obama felt empathy for a friend who had been mistreated by the police. So he said something that derailed his attempt to control the healthcare debate: "The Cambridge police acted stupidly." And the HP board, according to a board member, was so tired, beleaguered, and weary of infighting that it hired a CEO without even meeting him or the two other candidates that the four-person nominating committee had brought forward.

An observer could rightly ask, in each of those situations, what were they thinking? The short answer is, they weren't. They were momentarily unable to think clearly because the amygdala had seized control.

Neuroscientists speak of an amygdala hijacking, in which the body's survival mechanisms take over and shut down thinking. *Emotional Intelligence* author Daniel Goleman explains:

> [When the amygdala perceives that] something is urgent, it creates what is called an amygdala hijack, the signs of which are three: you have a very strong emotional response, it's very sudden and intense, and you do something or say something, or send an email, that when the dust settles you really regret. That is the sign of an amygdala hijack and it happens to really intelligent people because we get really dumb when the

amygdala takes us over. Because we are being run by our fears and our anger, by emotional repertoires that were learned unconsciously in childhood. We become very childlike.[10]

Just as firefighters and fighter pilots can condition themselves to be less vulnerable to an amygdala hijacking—to keep calm and carry on even in the face of serious threats—leaders need to recognize in themselves the signs that their amygdala may be taking control, and to resist the temptation to let the amygdala govern. In the *Casablanca* anecdote that opened Chapter 8, "Content: Word Choice, Framing, and Meaning," we saw just this self-awareness when Rick warned Ilsa not to mention Paris: He knew that just hearing her speak the word would cause his amygdala to take over.

The Amygdala and Audience Engagement

The amygdala is also key to other elements of audience engagement. For example, it plays an important role in *salience,* what grabs and keeps our attention. In other words, attention is an emotion-driven phenomenon. If we want to get and hold an audience's attention, we need to trigger the amygdala to our advantage. Only when we have an audience's attention can we then move them to rational argument.

I have become somewhat notorious in the programs I teach in at NYU for the way I start each class. I teach all-day sessions on Saturdays, and as the 9 AM start time approaches, most students are still milling about, getting settled, and chatting with each other. At precisely 9 AM I touch a button on my remote mouse and play a sudden blast of very loud rock music. Most of the time it's the chorus of "Let's Get It Started" by the Black Eyed Peas, but to keep the element of surprise I sometimes vary the selection. After a 10-second burst of very loud music, I have every student's undivided attention. I then lock in the connection: I smile, welcome them, thank them for investing a full Saturday in developing their careers. Only then do I begin the class. I have hijacked their amygdalas. Note also that in the anecdote with which I opened this chapter I had the audience's complete attention once I had shocked them with my lemon-chewing demonstration. There was complete silence and full attention by the time I began to explain mirror neurons. We need audiences to feel first, and then to think.

Note also that in Chapter 7, "Performance: The Physicality of Audience Engagement," I described eye contact as consisting of both looking into an audience member's eyes and smiling. It's the smile that makes the connection, causing the audience member to unconsciously smile back and pay attention. The amygdala in action.

The amygdala also plays an important role in how audiences pay attention once we have their attention. Whenever people are under stress, there's a likelihood of their having only a limited or selective attention. When someone is afraid, angry, anxious, insulted, tired, and so on, he or she is likely to engage in cognitive tunneling, focusing completely on the thing that is the threat and ignoring everything else.

Emotional Intelligence author Daniel Goleman describes why:

> The problem is that the amygdala functions today the way it always has. And we don't operate in a world now that has actual physical threats. We operate in a complex symbolic reality where what we face are complex symbolic threats: He's not treating me fairly; she's dissing me. Whatever it may be. These threats today trigger the [release of stress hormones]. So when we are caught in the grip of a distressing emotion it means that attention narrows, and fixates, and we get into a state that is suboptimal for most of life.[11]

This selective attention is the case even when the threat is simply the need to focus on a challenging task. Several years ago two psychologists at Harvard University conducted an experiment. Daniel Simons and Christopher Chabris showed a video of six people, three in white T-shirts, and three in black T-shirts, passing basketballs to each other in front of a bank of elevators in what appears to be a business office. They instructed their subjects to watch the 90-second video and keep a silent count of how often the basketball is passed from someone in a white T-shirt to someone else in a white T-shirt. In the video, while the players are passing the ball, someone in a gorilla suit walks into the scrum, looks at the camera and thumps its chest, and then walks away. When the film ended, the psychologists asked their subjects how many times the ball had been passed among white-shirted people. But of course, that wasn't the point of the exercise. They then asked, "But did you see the gorilla?" More than half of the people who watched the video missed the gorilla.[12]

I have shown the video to graduate students and clients (in the same session in which I suck the lemon), and far more than half the people in the room said they didn't see the gorilla. Several argued strenuously that there wasn't a gorilla. They were then somewhat shaken up when I played the tape again, and they indeed saw the gorilla. Some told me that they had seen the gorilla walk on, but had assumed that it was a trick to get them to miscount the basketball passes, so they ignored it. Most of these didn't see the gorilla pound its chest and were very surprised to see that it did.

In *The Invisible Gorilla: How Our Intuitions Deceive Us*, Simons and Chabris explain that people think they see the world as it is, but they miss a lot.[13]

This is particularly the case with what is commonly called multitasking: the process of apparently doing several things at once. Increasing scientific study shows that what we think of as multitasking is in fact micro-attention tasking. We aren't simultaneously doing several things. Rather, we are doing one thing at a time, briefly. And while doing the one thing, we aren't doing the other thing. This is why texting while driving or other forms of distracted driving are such a problem. When texting (as when counting the basketball passes), we don't see what's on the road ahead (as we don't see the gorilla). But in corporate environments, with the prevalence of smartphones, iPads, and distracting technologies, it's common for audiences to be multitasking while a leader is engaging them. And as a result, members of the audience may miss important elements of what the leader is saying.

Audiences' actual capacity to pay attention is something many leaders miss. Especially when audiences are under stress, either task-focused or multitasking or emotionally upset in some way, it is much harder to get and keep their attention.

When people are under stress, they also have difficulty hearing, listening, and remembering. For example, when doctors talk to patients about their medical conditions, patients typically remember only 50 percent of what they're told; depending on the circumstances, 40 to 80 percent may be forgotten immediately, according to Robert H. Margolis, a University of Minnesota professor.[14] More important, when patients do recall information, they remember about half of it incorrectly. So, according to Dr. Margolis, half of what patients hear about their medical condition is forgotten immediately, and half of what is remembered is wrong.

So cognitive tunneling makes people focus on a threat and ignore other things. Selective attention in general allows them to miss what might otherwise be directly in front of them but that isn't part of the threat or task. And because they're under stress, they have trouble hearing, listening, or remembering.

There are several other amygdala-related challenges. The first is what is known as the Primacy Effect: People tend to remember the first thing they hear, but not what follows immediately thereafter. Hence, the need for frames to precede facts. The second is known as the Recency Effect: People tend to remember the last thing they hear. The third is the Rule of Threes. As general principle, people under stress can hold no more than three ideas, thoughts, or topics in their minds simultaneously. They can remember no more than three things. And they generally respond well to things spoken in groups of threes. (Note also that in the history of rhetoric for thousands of years we've known that audiences tend to pay more attention and remember more when content is grouped in threes. Now we know why. This is often referred to as the Rule of Threes.)

Adapting to the Amygdala: Five Strategies for Audience Engagement

There are a number of ways to overcome these challenges. When leaders are speaking to audiences that are under stress—even if the audience is merely tired or distracted—the leader can take the amygdala into account in determining how the content is structured and how the audience is engaged. Here are five ways to engage effectively:

1. Establish connection before saying anything substantive. And remember that the connection is physical. Techniques to connect include asking for the audience's attention, if only with a powerful and warm greeting, followed by silence and eye contact. The key is to make sure the audience isn't doing something else so that they pay attention. (Think of the leader as the gorilla, and the audience's distraction as counting basketballs. You need to get the audience to stop counting and to pay attention to the gorilla.)

2. Take the Primacy Effect seriously. Say the most important thing first once you have their attention. The most important thing should be a powerful framing statement that will control the meaning of all that follows. Remember that frames have to precede facts.

3. Take the Recency Effect seriously. Close with a recapitulation of the powerful framing statement that opened the presentation.

4. Make it easy to remember. Keep in mind how hard it is for people to listen, hear, and remember. One way is to repeat key points. I often hear from clients, "But I've already said this. I don't need to say it again." Or, "I don't want to say it again." Or, "If I have to say this again, I'll throw up. I'm tired of repeating myself." But leaders need to constantly repeat the key themes, within any given presentation, and in general as a matter of organizational strategy. It doesn't matter if they're bored with saying it. The audience needs to hear it, again and again. And again. As a general principle, people need to hear things three times if they are to even pay attention to it. And because any given audience member at any time may be distracted or inattentive, he or she is unlikely to hear or attend to everything that is said. So leaders need to repeat key points far more than three times to be sure that everyone has heard it at least three times. One of the burdens of leadership is to have a very high tolerance for repetition.

5. Follow the Rule of Threes: Have three main points. But no more than three main points; no more than three topics; no more than three examples per topic. Group thoughts in threes;

words in threes; actions in threes. (See how I just used the Rule of Threes in that sentence?) Think of Abraham Lincoln in the Gettysburg Address: "We cannot dedicate, we cannot consecrate, we cannot hallow this ground."

General Electric's chief executive officer spoke about the power of the Rule of Threes and the need to have a high tolerance for repetition soon after he succeeded Jack Welch at GE's helm. Asked by *Fast Company* magazine the top leadership lesson he had learned from Mr. Welch, Jeff Immelt said, "Every leader needs to clearly explain the top three things the organization is doing. If you can't, you're not leading well."[15]

The Primacy of the Visual: The Eyes Have It

Several years ago the leadership team of one of my clients was presenting to an investment conference in New York. After the formal presentation, the team was fielding questions, and one investor asked for an update on the company's quality initiative. The CEO handed off the question to the president of the manufacturing division, the part of the company that actually made the things that the company sold: "Quality is part of manufacturing, and I'll let Jim, who heads manufacturing, take your question."

Jim stood up and confidently said the following: "Our quality initiative is well underway. And quality continues to improve every single quarter." Then he rattled off a bunch of statistics.

The framing was right, and it was true: Quality was improving. There was just one problem. As he said it, he held his hand out in front of his body, at shoulder level. As he spoke, the hand moved down diagonally in front of his body. It was the gesture of something in decline. But his words were of something improving. No one on the stage noticed the anomaly. But the audience did.

After the investment conference, analysts posted negative references to the company, expressing concerns about the quality of the company's products. When the investor relations department called the analysts to understand their views, they said their concerns arose from the division president's remarks.

I was asked to meet with the division president and I reviewed the videotape of his comments with him. As he watched it, he saw no problem. I asked him what the downward diagonal sweep of his hand meant. He said, "It means quality is improving." I said, "No, it doesn't." He challenged me: "Of course it does." I asked him, "What do you mean when you say 'quality'?" He replied, "You know, quality. The number of defects per thousand units of production."

Then we both burst out laughing, as we recognized the miscommunication. He had fallen prey to the Curse of Knowledge, where a technical expert cannot conceive that someone without his technical expertise doesn't know what he knows. It's all too common in specialized fields such as medicine, law, finance, and manufacturing. To Jim, an engineer by training, quality was a frame about things that didn't work well. The goal of the quality initiative was to reduce the number of defects, to minimize customer complaints, to reduce the number of replacements under warranty. And the other executives who were at the conference, who were similarly cursed with that knowledge, didn't notice anything unusual about what he said and how he said it. But for investors there was a completely different frame: Quality was something positive. The goal of a quality initiative was to do something better, to make something more effective, to build customer loyalty. In other words, for things to go up.

But Jim's gaffe also pointed to something about the human brain. When there's inconsistency between what the ears hear and what the eyes see, the eyes tend to prevail. When investors saw the downward swoop of his gesture as he spoke about quality, the visual overtook the verbal, and investors were left with a false but powerful impression: Quality was declining. The framing came not from the word "improving" but from the combination of the word "quality" and the downward gesture. That triggered the worldview. The statistics didn't matter. The audience had already reached an impression. The facts bounced off.

We see the same kind of disconnect when leaders express pride in the company achieving a milestone, but do so without any facial expression. Or when they say they're pleased to announce something without a trace of a smile on their faces.

In 1976 two professors at the University of Surrey in Great Britain published in the journal *Nature* the result of their study into multimodal perception—what happens when two sensory systems are working at the same time. Harry McGurk and John MacDonald concluded that although most verbal communication occurs in settings where the listener can see the speaker, speech perception is still normally regarded as a purely auditory process. They demonstrated the "previously unrecognized influence of vision upon speech perception."[16]

The McGurk Effect, outlined in that paper, is based on showing people a video in which a speaker repeats a certain sound, such as *ba-ba-ba,* again and again. But in some parts of the video, the speaker is seen to mouth the sound *ba-ba-ba;* in others, the speaker is seen to mouth the sound *fa-fa-fa* or *ga-ga-ga* or *da-da-da.* But the sound never changes. Ask the viewer what the speaker is saying, and the viewer will say, alternately, *ba-ba-ba* or *fa-fa-fa* or *ga-ga-ga* or *da-da-da,* depending on what the mouth seems to be doing. But ask the viewer to listen to the same tape, with eyes closed, and the viewer will hear only *ba-ba-ba.* When I do this with students and clients, they don't believe what's happening. Even closing their eyes and hearing only *ba-ba-ba* isn't convincing. I need to play the tape multiple times, as they close their eyes on the second or third *fa.* Eventually they come to terms with the fact that they had mistakenly believed they had heard something that they didn't actually hear. It is always disconcerting.

Lawrence Rosenblum, a professor of psychology at the University of California Riverside, and author of *See What I'm Saying: The Extraordinary Power of Our Five Senses,* explained the McGurk Effect on the BBC's *Horizon* television program:

> In the illusion what we see overrides what we hear. So the mouth movements we see when we look at a face can actually influence what we believe we're hearing. If we close our eyes, we actually hear the sound as it is. If we open our eyes, we actually see how the mouth movements can influence what we're hearing. The effect works no matter how much you know about the effect.[17]

In the 1933 Marx Brothers movie *Duck Soup*, the Groucho character famously asks, "Who are you going to believe, me or your own eyes?"[18] Embedded in that joke is the comedian's understanding that people actually believe their own eyes rather than what they may hear. When what audiences hear conflicts with what audiences see, the eyes have it. (In fact, the Marx Brothers' quote itself is an example of the phenomenon it describes. Although widely attributed to Groucho Marx, the quote was actually spoken by Chico, but while he was impersonating Groucho. The eyes have it even in puns about the primacy of the visual.)

The McGurk effect—the visual overriding the verbal—has significant consequences to effective leadership communication. Leaders need to worry not only about what they say and how they say it, but also about how they look when they say it.

Air Thin

Words matter. So do visuals. The combination can be unbeatable.

This book began with Steve Jobs introducing the iPod in 2001. Mr. Jobs captured people's imagination with his introduction to the very idea of an iPod: 1,000 songs in your pocket.

We close with Steve Jobs again, in January 2008. He was about to launch the newest Apple computer, the MacBook Air. He teased the Macworld Conference audience: "There's something in the air." Then he framed what was to follow:

> As you know, Apple makes the best notebooks on the planet: the MacBook and the MacBook Pro. These are the standards in the industry by which competitive products are judged. Well, today we're introducing a third kind of notebook. It's called the MacBook Air. Now, what is the MacBook Air? In a sentence, it's the world's thinnest notebook.[19]

He then showed examples of competitors' slim notebooks. He showed a visual of the side profile of the best-selling competitor's notebook and of the MacBook Air, and noted how the thickest part of the MacBook Air was still thinner than the thinnest part of the competitor's computer. He then talked about how, unlike the competitor, the MacBook Air would have a full-size screen and keyboard, and full memory capacity:

> So, it's so thin that it even fits inside one of these envelopes that we've all seen floating around the office. And so let me show it to you now.[20]

As he spoke, the screen behind him showed a yellow 9" x 12" interoffice envelope. Jobs walked to a lectern and pulled out just such an envelope. He held up the envelope. It was flat. It looked empty. He dramatically unscrolled the red string that held the envelope closed. Then he slid from the envelope a new MacBook Air. There was hushed silence in the audience, accompanied by the occasional "wooo." He held it flat to show how thin it is. Then he opened it to show the full-size display and keyboard.

Then he said, "But the real magic is in the electronics." Behind him appeared a photograph of the guts inside the computer. "This is a complete Mac on a board. You think, okay, what's so special about that?"[21]

Then a plain number 2 pencil appeared next to the circuitry. The two were the same size. "It's really tiny. And to fit a whole Mac on this thing was an amazing feat of engineering."[22]

Those two images—the new computer coming out of a flat interoffice envelope, and the guts of a full-power computer no longer than a regular pencil—told the entire story. Jobs's presentation was masterful: Complete command of the physicality of his engagement with audiences—the right words, conveyed in the right order, with the right images—provoked an emotional connection.

Steve Jobs showed us how to use communication as a leadership tool.

The burden of leadership is to create a package: a presence that combines posture, gesture, bearing, with the sounds that are made as the leader speaks, with content that works, and powerful visual imagery, all the while connecting with audiences. It isn't easy. But it is a critical element of building trust, inspiring confidence, and leading effectively.

Recap: Best Practices from This Chapter

 *From* Warfighting

Because communication is about human connection,
the human dimension is central to communicating.
It is the human dimension that makes communication possible.
Leaders need to know how humans actually work.

Lessons for Leaders and Communicators

Human connection is not merely a function of proximity. It's also a function of biology. Taking audiences seriously requires leaders to understand what audiences are capable of, how humans actually work. And that requires understanding the human brain, where hearts and minds reside.

Humans are wired to connect with each other. Mirror neurons allow people to actually experience sensory perception from afar. When we watch a skier twist a knee, we feel our own knees hurt. When we watch someone chewing on a lemon, our mouths water and we taste the lemon. Or think we do. Humans are empathic. We *feel with* other people. Mirror neurons are a powerful connection mechanism, and effective leaders connect with audiences not merely intellectually and emotionally, but also physically.

Mirror neurons also provide a biological explanation for why humans are social creatures. Identity drives behavior, because our first drive is to belong. So leaders need to connect by showing that they and their followers have something in common.

Leaders too often assume that facts matter, that logic prevails, and that if only they let the facts speak for themselves stakeholders will understand and agree. But humans aren't wired that way. They are emotional creatures before they're rational creatures. There is a constant interplay between our limbic system and our prefrontal cortex, between emotion and reason.

The default to emotion is part of the human condition. The amygdala governs the fight-or-flight impulse, the triggering of powerful emotions, and the release of chemicals that put humans in a heightened state of arousal. There's a superhighway from the amygdala to the prefrontal cortex, which governs reasoning, logic, facts, planning, and decision making. The amygdala can shut down reasoning. But there are only side roads and back channels from the prefrontal cortex to the amygdala. So it's much harder for the prefrontal cortex to get emotions under control. While it's possible to soft-wire more efficient connections through repetition, it's easier for emotion to control reason than the other way around.

Humans are not thinking machines. We're feeling machines who also think. We feel first, and then we think. As a result, leaders need to meet emotion with emotion before they can move audiences with reason.

The amygdala also plays important roles in what an audience can pay attention to and how. When people feel threatened, cognitive tunneling takes place, making it difficult to focus on anything beyond the threat. And as people become more and more upset, they become more and more primitive: They use the older, more emotional parts of their brains.

Even when people aren't immediately threatened, selective attention causes people under stress to ignore everything outside the scope of their immediate point of focus. People tasked with counting something don't notice a gorilla walking in front of them, just as drivers who are texting don't notice an obstacle in the road.

When people are under stress, they have difficulty hearing, listening, and remembering. Primacy means they remember what they hear first. Recency means they remember what they hear last. And the Rule of Threes means they can't remember more than three things. This places a premium on keeping things simple and repeating key points.

These are the five strategies for adapting to the amygdala when engaging audiences:

1. Establish connection before saying anything substantive.

2. Take the Primacy Effect seriously: Frames have to precede facts.

3. Take the Recency Effect seriously: Repeat the frame at the end.

4. Make it easy to remember: Repeat. And repeat again. And again.

5. Follow the Rule of Threes.

Verbal engagement is not merely an auditory process, but also a visual one. When there's an inconsistency between what the eyes see and what the ears hear, the eyes tend to prevail. So leaders need to align what they say with how the body portrays it.

10

Putting It All Together: Becoming a Habitually Strategic Communicator

Communication Is a Leadership Discipline

Whatever else leadership may be, it is experienced publicly. While it may emanate from within, it is a public phenomenon.

A burden of leadership is to be good at communicating. As Marine Lieutenant Colonel Rob Riggle said in the Foreword, "If you can't communicate effectively, you will not lead."

But there's a paradox: Unlike most other skills a leader needs to master, communication seems to be something leaders already know; they've been communicating their whole lives. Just as a fish is unaware of the water it swims in, leaders often are unaware of their own communication abilities. Or lack thereof.

Communication has power, but like any powerful tool it needs to be used effectively or it can cause self-inflicted harm. In this book we've seen how leaders can suffer career-defining blunders if they don't take communication as seriously as they take most other elements of their jobs. And how they can dramatically enhance their competitive position if they communicate well.

Warfighting quotes the German military strategist Hans von Seeckt: "Intellect without will is worthless; will without intellect is dangerous."[1] Leaders need both. They need will in order to organize their communication toward a goal; they need intellect in order to understand what works and why.

Harnessing the power of communication is a fundamental leadership discipline. Effective leaders see communication as a critical professional aptitude and work hard at getting it right.

And getting it right requires becoming strategic as a first resort: thinking through the desired change in the audience and the ways to make that happen.

Effective communicators take change seriously: They ground their work in moving people to be different. To think differently; to feel differently; to know or do things differently.

Effective communicators also take audiences seriously. They work hard to ensure that all engagements move people toward their goal. That means caring about what audiences think and feel now, and what it will take to get them to think and feel something else. And listening carefully to the reaction, and adapting where needed.

Effective communicators also take words seriously. They know that words trigger worldviews and provoke reactions. They plan their engagements so that the right words are used to trigger the right reaction.

Effective communicators also know that the best communication can be counterproductive if it isn't aligned with action.

And effective communicators take seriously the need to package all that an audience experiences—the verbal, the visual, the abstract, and the physical—into one powerful experience.

This book is grounded in nine fundamental leadership communication principles that together contribute to becoming a habitually strategic communicator:

1. See communication as the continuation of business by other means:
   - It is intentional.
   - It is interactive.
   - It is intended to provoke a reaction.
2. To move people, meet them where they are.
3. Walk the talk.
4. Control the communication agenda.

5. Remember that even small events, changes, or blunders can have big consequences.

6. Plan ahead and align tactics with strategy.

7. Invest in continuous improvement in communication skills.

8. Harness the power of language and of framing.

9. Understand how the human brain works.

 *From* **Warfighting**

[Marines] must be individuals both of action and of intellect, skilled at "getting things done" while at the same time conversant in the military art.

Leaders must be individuals both of action and of intellect, skilled at "getting things done" while at the same time conversant in communication skills, in winning hearts and minds.

Here is a more expansive account of each, tracking the chapters of the book.

Nine Principles of Effective Leadership Communication

1. See Communication as the Continuation of Business by Other Means

Intention

The purpose of communication is not to communicate, but to accomplish some tangible business goal. The only reason to communicate is to change something—to influence the way audiences think and feel, and what they know and do, in order to enhance our competitive position.

Communication is merely one of the ways to fulfill a business or organizational goal. But it is one of many means. By itself it is rarely sufficient to accomplish most organizational goals. Rather, communication is what the military calls a force multiplier: It helps you do more, better, faster than you otherwise would be able to do. Effective communication can help accomplish any particular purpose better, and faster, and with fewer resources. But however effective, it must be paired with action that is consistent with what is said.

Words matter. Words shape worldviews. Words provoke action and reaction, which in turn provoke more words. Getting the words right is critically important. Getting the action right is also critically important. And aligning the words and actions is even more important.

All effective communication is done on purpose. It is intentional. It starts with an understanding of an audience and then moves to influence that audience.

An audience is a living, breathing entity. It is a collection of human beings. Collectively, an audience tends to care about certain things in certain ways, and tends not to think at all about the concerns of those trying to influence it. And at any given time any member of any audience is distracted, inattentive, unconcerned with others' concerns, and focused only on his or her immediate interests.

Interactivity

Effective leadership communication is always interactive. Interactivity involves people, either directly or at a distance.

Communication cannot take place in one direction. Sending is not the same as receiving. And receiving doesn't ensure understanding. Effective communication is two-way or multidirectional, and always involves a feedback loop.

Effective communicators know that they need to adapt. They need to adapt if they recognize that they're not being understood. They need to adapt based on how their audience reacts to the initial engagement, based on what critics or adversaries say; on changes in the environment in which communication is taking place; as facts become outdated or as new developments require attention.

Adapting to change is not a sign of weakness or of indecision. Rather it is a discipline.

If we see effective leadership communication as a process of continuous mutual adaptation, of give and take, of move and counter-move, with a goal always in mind, we can maintain control of the communication agenda, even as things change. We avoid the illusion that communication has taken place.

Reaction

Influencing an audience requires active engagements that cause the audience to take notice, and to do so in ways we want them to. But this requires knowing what the audience feels, thinks, is capable of, and cares about. And it requires caring about those things too.

A habitually strategic communicator never begins with "what do we want to say" but rather with a sequence of prior questions. The habitually strategic communicator always begins by asking questions in a certain sequence:

1. What do we have? What is the challenge or opportunity we are hoping to address?

2. What do we want? What's our goal? Communication is merely the continuation of business by other means. We shouldn't communicate unless we know what we're trying to accomplish.

3. Who matters? What stakeholders matter to us? What do we know about them? What further information do we need to get about them? What are the barriers to their receptivity to us, and how do we overcome those barriers?

4. What do we need them to think, feel, know, or do in order to accomplish our goal?

5. What do they need to see us do, hear us say, or hear others say about us to think, feel, know, and do what we want them to?

6. How do we make that happen?

2. To Move People, Meet Them Where They Are

We need to meet people where they are: physically, emotionally, intellectually, spiritually, and ideologically. The bigger the gulf between "us and them," the less likely it is that effective communication will take place.

Communication isn't about telling our story. That's undisciplined, self-indulgent, and often illusory. The power of communication is getting audiences to listen—and to care.

Taking stakeholders seriously requires respecting the point of view of those whom we would engage. It requires curiosity about what matters to them, about what it takes to win them over and to keep their trust and confidence. Effective leaders connect with audiences by understanding what matters to them, and by speaking in ways that resonate with them.

Leaders are particularly prone to seeing the world from the perspective of their own organization, and to fail to consider—or to dismiss as irrelevant—the concerns of stakeholders. This is an occupational hazard that needs to be acknowledged and managed.

Audiences typically don't care about a company's operations. They don't have sympathy for the business challenges or logistical issues a company may face. They care only about the impact on them. Audiences don't know—and don't want or need to know—about a company's internal operations in order to be customers. To get an audience to care, a company and its leaders need to begin with the audience's concerns and then link those concerns to what the company is doing.

For leaders who live and breathe the company's operations, this common-sense observation is hard to grasp. Audiences have their own ideas, their own concerns, their own frames of reference. And if we want to maintain their trust and confidence, we need to start by taking those ideas, concerns, and frames of references seriously.

Taking stakeholders seriously is not easy. But failure to do so is a critical failure of leadership. For any given stakeholder group, a leader should seek to understand three basic things, by asking three basic categories of questions:

1. **What do we know about the group?**

   An inventory of current knowledge

2. **How does the group work?**

   Grounding to predict behavior

3. **How does the group relate to us?**

   The link between audiences and outcomes

Taking stakeholders seriously also means connecting with them. Very often, that connection requires using all three of Aristotle's attributes—Logos, Ethos, Pathos—simultaneously:

1. *Logos*: Reasoning, logical argument, empirical evidence, rational explanation, and facts.

2. *Ethos*: An element of personal character, identity, or personal attributes; the characteristic spirit and prevalent tone or sentiment of a person, people, or community.

3. *Pathos*: Emotion, passion, and especially the triggering of an emotional reaction from and connection with the audience.

Winning minds requires Logos—facts, reasoning, argument, and data. But winning minds also requires Ethos—some element of personal character or experience that connects the speaker to the audience. And it requires Pathos—initially as passion on the part of the speaker, but fundamentally the triggering of an emotional reaction with the audience. Done well, the Pathos can be positive: enthusiasm, support, trust, confidence. Done poorly, the Pathos can be negative: anger, mistrust, a feeling of betrayal, leading ultimately to disengagement of the audience from the leader. But we need to win hearts first, and minds second.

Companies often dismiss the significance of Ethos and Pathos. They stay stuck in Logos, to their and their stakeholders' ultimate disappointment.

3. Walk the Talk

Leaders are judged on the fulfillment of expectations. When leaders make promises, either implicit or explicit, they are establishing criteria by which they ask to be judged. Once an expectation is set, the leader must either fulfill the expectation or reset it, or risk disappointment that shatters trust.

Resetting an expectation may cause some short-term pain. But it's preferable to wholesale disappointment.

However tempting, leaders must resist saying what merely sounds good in the moment. And especially when things go wrong, leaders learn the hard way that they can't talk their way out of a business problem. They certainly can't talk their way out of a problem they behaved their way into. And once they've committed a say-do gap, it's hard even to talk their way out of a problem they talked their way into.

4. Control the Communication Agenda

One burden of leadership is to seize the initiative when it can do the most good. Leaders know that they need to be in control of the communication agenda: both the topics they talk about and the words they use. This requires speed, focus, and the first mover advantage.

Speed isn't just acting quickly. Rather, speed is best understood as tempo: the consistent ability to be effective in a timely way. It's about acting effectively and engaging stakeholders promptly.

The consistent ability to act and engage stakeholders quickly and effectively creates a competitive advantage in the best of times. But it is in the worst of times that it matters most: It can prevent a negative event from becoming a tragedy, or worse. It is precisely in high-stakes situations that stakeholders, critics, and adversaries look for leadership in the form of effective engagement.

As important as the consistent ability to operate quickly is focus: the ability to concentrate attention on the right thing, and to align multiple communications by multiple parties.

Shaping the communication agenda requires considering more than what we may be minimally required to say, but rather identifying what we optimally should say in order to maintain trust, confidence, and loyalty.

The first mover advantage is a form of maneuver that prevents critics and adversaries from framing the situation. Leaders need to define the crisis, their motives, and their actions first, consistently, and persistently. When stakeholders expect their leaders to step up, the leaders need to.

Especially in contested situations, there is a constant interplay between being in control of the communication agenda and having to respond to others who are trying to control it. Because the battle for hearts and minds is often a competitive one, it's critical for leaders to be able to capture, retain, and exploit the initiative.

The most effective way to make decisions about when to communicate is to operationalize the first mover advantage by asking four related questions, all of which have to do with stakeholder awareness and expectations:

1. **Will those who matter to us expect us to do or say something now?** If so, we need to act and communicate now.

2. **Are others talking about us now, shaping the perception about us, among those who matter to us? Do we have reason to believe they will be soon?** If so, we need to communicate quickly and fully before others define the crisis, our motives, or our actions.

3. **Will silence be seen as indifference or as an affirmation of guilt?** If so, we need to not be silent, but rather to engage fully to prevent the perception of indifference.

4. **If we wait, will we lose the ability to control the outcome?** If so, we should not wait.

If the answer to all four questions is no, then the leader should watch and wait, prepare to engage stakeholders, and then engage whenever the answer to any of them turns from no to yes. But as soon as the answer to any of the four questions is yes, the leader needs to overcome fear, inertia, embarrassment, or anxiety, and engage stakeholders effectively and quickly.

Once the decision is made to engage stakeholders, the rule of thumb for communicating bad news is as follows:

- Tell it all: Say all that is necessary to establish stakeholder understanding, buy-in, or neutrality.
- Tell it fast: Bundle the bad news into a single news cycle, and avoid dripping out new details over time, which creates a new news cycle and causes stakeholders to question the leadership skills of those communicating.
- Tell 'em what you're doing about it.
- Tell 'em when it's over.
- Get back to work.

5. Remember That Even Small Events, Changes, or Blunders Can Have Big Consequences

Leaders know that not all actions are equivalent and that there isn't necessarily a one-to-one stimulus-response relationship. The same applies in communication: Not all words are created equal. Different words have different impacts. And because communication is a process of mutual adaptation, of move and countermove, the leader needs to consider the response his or her words are likely to provoke. And to resist the temptation to say anything that triggers a response different from the desired response. Saying the wrong thing—or the right thing at the wrong time—can derail an otherwise carefully planned event and hand the initiative to one's opponents.

The first mover advantage is a further example of disproportionality. A delay of just a few minutes can allow an adversary, a critic, a competitor, the media, social media, or others to seize the initiative and move an audience to think, feel, or do the opposite of what we might want it to.

Disproportionality applies not only to what one says but to when one says it. The longer it takes to fulfill appropriate stakeholder expectations, the harder it becomes. Incremental delays in fielding an appropriate response have a greater than incremental effect on the outcome. An apology on Day 1 may be sufficient to prevent loss of trust by stakeholders; an apology on Day 10 after uninterrupted expressions of outrage probably won't be sufficient.

Ideally, a leader can exercise the first mover advantage. But sometimes that isn't possible. But even when others begin to define a situation before a leader can, there's still an opportunity to protect one's reputation and regain control of the agenda. It just gets harder and harder to control the agenda as time passes.

The longer it takes to control the communication agenda, the harder it becomes. That's because more and more people are reaching conclusions about the situation, making judgments, and believing and acting on what they hear. What would have been sufficient in the early phases of a situation becoming public would be woefully inadequate hours or days or weeks later.

The general principle in applying the Golden Hour to controlling the communication agenda is the rule of 45 minutes, six hours, three days, two weeks. That's the sequence of disproportionate effects that arise in particular intervals in the cycle of visibility—what used to be called the "news cycle" but with the ubiquity of social media is now far more widespread. This principle suggests that it's possible to defend one's self against negative visibility, but that the longer it takes to organize a sufficiently persuasive response, the harder it becomes.

That's why speed is so important—speed defined not as impulse but as the predisposition to make sound decisions quickly and to communicate them effectively. (Refer back to Figure 5.1 showing the Golden Hour of Crisis Response.)

6. Plan Ahead and Align Tactics with Strategy

Planning

Projecting thoughts forward is the key to planning. And as we project our thoughts forward, we need also to project our stakeholders' thoughts and likely reaction forward.

Planning isn't just determining a sequence of actions and writing a statement based on what you want to say or are minimally required to say. It's about a chessboard, not a calendar. It's about thinking several moves ahead: If we do X, what will they do, and what will we then need to do next? If we do Y, what will they do, and so on. So planning requires understanding the absolutely predictable and appropriate expectations of stakeholders, anticipating and then meeting those expectations.

As in the rule from carpentry—measure twice, cut once—we need to be so well prepared at the moment of execution that we get the communication right the first time.

Communication planning can also serve as the canary in the coal mine—as a leading indicator that something is amiss in the business planning process. The need to explain something often calls attention to some inconsistency in decision makers' thought processes.

Strategy

Strategy is the process of ordered thinking: of thinking in a particular order. Effective leaders never confuse means with ends, goals and strategies with tactics. The key is to have clarity about the situation as it presents itself, the goal one is trying to accomplish, and the means by which one will accomplish it.

Communication cannot be crafted in a vacuum. All communication tactics (the specific engagements with stakeholders) need to be directly supportive of communication goals (the outcomes we want to achieve). Communication goals, in turn, need to support business goals. Any communication goals or tactics conceived or executed in the absence of clearly defined business goals are likely to be ineffective.

The business goals describe changes or outcomes in the business environment or in a company's competitive position: build market share, attain fair stock market valuation, enhance employee productivity, secure regulatory approval of a new product, and the like. The communication goals describe changes in stakeholder attitudes, feelings, understanding, knowledge, or behavior. Each needs to be clearly articulated, with communication goals subordinate to, and supportive of, the business goals.

Planning at the strategic level begins with desired outcomes. What do we need our stakeholders to think, feel, know, and do if we are to change the business environment or our competitive position? The more clarity we have about each of these questions, the more likely we are to be able to plan effectively.

The operational level is where the actual planning of stakeholder engagement takes place. Once we know (from the strategic level) what we want the change in our stakeholders to be, we can then determine the best manner, time, message, and messenger to engage stakeholders. The operational level is where we make choices. Of what to say, of when to say it, and of how to say it. It is at the operational level that we anticipate stakeholder reaction by inventorying their current level of awareness, their concerns, fears, and hopes, and their likelihood to care about our content. It is at this level that we can project alternative ways of engaging, alternative content, and alternative messengers to anticipate reactions and choose the more likely effective path.

It is precisely at the operational level that many leaders and leadership teams fall short. By failing to anticipate and adapt, they end up speaking in ways that may make them feel better but that aren't necessarily going to move stakeholders the way we need them to.

The tactical level is where communication actually takes place. Tactics are the things we actually say to people, the contact we actually make. The tactical level is where we have the press release, the speech, the employee e-mail, the press conference.

Most leaders default to the tactical as a first resort. But the tactical must be in the service of the operational, which in turn is in the service of the strategic. Rather than default to the tactical, effective leaders get to the tactical by considering the other levels first.

Unity of effort is alignment of all communication tactics and messages. Unity of effort in the service of clearly defined goals, with an operational framework that makes smart choices about what to say, when, how, and to whom, is the key to effective leadership communication.

7. Invest in Continuous Improvement in Communication Skills

One of the burdens of leadership is to get good at engaging stakeholders well.

In many cases the skills that get leaders to the top of their organizations are not sufficient to do the work at that level. The higher one goes in a company, not-for-profit, or government agency, the more success is measured in winning hearts and minds rather than in the mastery of some technical skill—from medicine, law, finance, education, engineering, and the like. It isn't that their core disciplines don't matter—they do. But they're not enough.

Rather, leaders need to be good at interpersonal verbal engagement—one-on-one and large group, in person and at a distance. There is a high correlation between leaders seeing part of their work as continually developing their communication skills and their overall success.

Leaders need to invest in their communication skills. They need to master basic skills, to practice those skills, and to continually enhance their capacity to lead verbally.

At a very basic level of tactical execution, being good at engaging well starts with understanding the physicality of audience engagement. The audience makes judgments based on nonverbal cues.

A leader is judged based on, among other attributes, his or her bearing: how he or she carries himself or herself. First impressions matter, and the first impression is often visual.

The most effective leaders take seriously the physicality of their performance: Standing or sitting in a posture that creates a stable platform. Gesturing fluidly. Making eye contact and locking in the audience's attention. Using visuals to amplify the speaker's points, and not the other way around.

The fundamentals work. And from those physicality fundamentals a leader can build an effective presence to convey content well.

8. Harness the Power of Language and of Framing

Words are carriers of meaning well beyond the literal. Words trigger worldviews that determine what other meanings are possible. Metaphors—where a word stands in for something much broader than its literal meaning—are particularly powerful carriers of content, of emotional resonance.

Ineffective leaders get the metaphor wrong, and inadvertently trigger a counterproductive response: either indifference or worse. But effective leaders use metaphor to shape the frame of reference in which their content is to be understood, in order to provoke powerful reactions in their followers.

We've known for millenniums that metaphors work, but we're only now beginning to understand why.

Frames are mental structures that are triggered by language. When we trigger a frame, we trigger an entire worldview. Negating a frame triggers the very frame you negate. It causes people to think the very thing you want them not to think. Telling them not to doesn't work. Leaders often fail to understand this, and are puzzled by the audience's reaction.

But effective framing is about more than avoiding triggering the negative frame. It also requires triggering a positive frame. And much framing involves metaphor.

But too often leaders fall into the trap of believing that facts are persuasive. This is part of the Myth of Objectivism. Facts aren't. Facts can be persuasive only to the degree that they fit some prior frame.

The facts are open to interpretation based on context, and we need to control the context. If we speak only facts, the audience either will not pay attention to those facts or will provide their own context—their own frames—to make sense of the facts.

Leaders often make one of three framing mistakes:

1. They fail to frame at all, leaving the audience or critics to provide the frame, often to the leader's disadvantage.

2. They inadvertently trigger a negative frame, by either saying something counterproductive ("I wouldn't mention Paris if I were you") or denying something, thereby inadvertently triggering the very frame they were trying to avoid ("I'm not a crook!").

3. They lead with the facts, and provide the frame only afterward. But by then the audience has either already provided the missing frame or ignored the facts altogether. Framing has to come before the facts. Finally, understanding and explicitly acknowledging the concerns of the audience can help make them more receptive to our frames in the first place.

9. Understand How the Human Brain Works

Human connection is not merely a function of proximity. It's a function also of biology. Taking audiences seriously requires leaders to understand what audiences are capable of, how humans actually work. And that requires understanding the human brain, where hearts and minds reside.

Humans are not thinking machines. We're feeling machines who also think. We feel first, and then we think. As a result, leaders need to meet emotion with emotion before they can move audiences with reason.

Humans are wired to connect with each other. Mirror neurons allow people to actually experience sensory perception from afar. Humans are empathic. We *feel with* other people. Mirror neurons are a powerful connection mechanism, and effective leaders connect with audiences not merely intellectually and emotionally, but also physically.

Mirror neurons also provide a biological explanation for why humans are social creatures. Identity drives behavior, because our first drive is to belong. So leaders need to connect by showing that they and their followers have something in common.

Leaders too often assume that facts matter, that logic prevails, and that if only they let the facts speak for themselves stakeholders will understand and agree. But humans aren't wired that way. They are emotional creatures before they're rational creatures. There is a constant interplay between our Limbic System and our prefrontal cortex, between emotion and reason.

The default to emotion is part of the human condition. The amygdala governs the fight-or-flight impulse, the triggering of powerful emotions, and the release of chemicals that put humans in a heightened state of arousal. There's a superhighway from the amygdala to the prefrontal cortex, which governs reasoning, logic, facts, planning, and decision making. The amygdala can shut down reasoning. But there are only side roads and back channels from the prefrontal cortex to the amygdala. So it's much harder for the prefrontal cortex to get emotions under control. While it's possible to soft-wire more efficient connections through repetition, it's easier for emotion to control reason than the other way around.

The amygdala also plays important roles in what an audience can pay attention to and how. When people feel threatened, cognitive tunneling takes place, making it difficult to focus on anything beyond the threat. And as people become more and more upset, they become more and more primitive: They use the older, more emotional parts of their brains.

Even when people aren't immediately threatened, selective attention causes people under stress to ignore everything outside the scope of their immediate point of focus. When people are under stress, they have difficulty hearing, listening, and remembering. Primacy means they remember what they hear first. Recency means they remember what they hear last. And the Rule of Threes means they can't remember more than three things. This places a premium on keeping things simple and repeating key points.

There are five strategies for adapting to the amygdala when engaging audiences:

1. Establish connection before saying anything substantive.
2. Take the Primacy Effect seriously: Frames have to precede facts.
3. Take the Recency Effect seriously: Repeat the frame at the end.
4. Make it easy to remember: Repeat. And repeat again. And again.
5. Follow the Rule of Threes.

Verbal engagement is not merely an auditory process, but also a visual one. When there's an inconsistency between what the eyes see and what the ears hear, the eyes tend to prevail. So leaders need to align what they say with how the body portrays it.

Closing Considerations

In A.D. 386 a certain 32-year-old North African named Aurelius Augustinus was appointed Rhetor of Milan, which was then the provisional capital of the Roman Empire (while the emperor concerned himself with troubles on the Northern border). Aurelius's job was to explain and advocate the emperor's policies to all relevant stakeholders. In other words, he was the Roman equivalent of the President's press secretary. And he was very good at his craft.

But after some time in government service, the young man found religion, left Milan, and became a priest and later a bishop in the Catholic Church. What he encountered in the Church distressed him. It was insular, it was fragmented, and it didn't do a very good job establishing a compelling identity, recruiting new adherents, and reinforcing a common culture. There was no unity of effort. And the preaching left much to be desired. As he began to gain influence within the Church, he set out to change it. And he succeeded.

We know him today as St. Augustine. Although best known for his *Confessions* and *City of God,* his most influential work from our perspective is a book he worked on intermittently for decades, and published in A.D. 426. In *On Christian Teaching* Augustine outlined a plan for mobilizing the masses.

He prescribed a campaign of what today we would call brand identity, based on powerful and universally recognizable visual imagery. The book included guidelines for inspiring preaching, derived from the Roman orator Cicero. Augustine urged clergy to use Ciceronian persuasion techniques, rhetorical flourishes, and dramatic storytelling to engage audiences. He emphasized the need for preachers to help people feel a connection to the Church, to establish a common culture. It worked.

His prescription for preachers applies to leadership communication today. Quoting Cicero's *Orator,* Augustine instructs:

> It has been said by a man of eloquence, and quite rightly, that the eloquent should speak in such a way as to instruct, delight, and move their listeners. He then added: "instructing is a matter of necessity, delighting a matter of charm, and moving them a matter of conquest."[2]

Not a bad frame of reference for modern leaders whose job includes winning hearts and minds. It's a matter of conquest.

A

Warfighting Principles for Leadership Communication

From Warfighting

In Chapter 1, "Words Matter"

War is fundamentally an interactive social process.

> *Effective communication is fundamentally*
> *an interactive social process.*

Clausewitz called it a *Zweikampf* (literally, a "two-struggle")
and suggested the image of a pair of wrestlers locked in a hold,
each exerting force and counterforce to try to throw the other.

War is thus a process of continuous mutual
adaptation, of give and take, of move and countermove.

> *Effective communication is thus a process of continuous mutual*
> *adaptation, of give and take, of move and countermove.*

Since war is a fluid phenomenon, its conduct requires flexibility of
thought. Success depends in large part on the ability to adapt—to
proactively shape changing events to our advantage as well as to
react quickly to constantly changing conditions.

> *Since communication is a fluid phenomenon, its conduct requires*
> *flexibility of thought. Success depends in large part on the ability*
> *to adapt—to proactively shape changing events to our advantage*
> *as well as to react quickly to constantly changing conditions.*

It is critical to keep in mind that the enemy is not an inanimate object to be acted upon but an independent and animate force with its own objectives and plans.

> *It is critical to keep in mind that the audience is not an inanimate object to be acted upon but a collection of living, breathing human beings with their own goals, concerns, needs, priorities, attention spans, and levels of desire even to be in relationship with us.*

 *From* **Warfighting**

In Chapter 2, "Taking Audiences Seriously"

It is essential that we understand the enemy on his own terms. We should not assume that every enemy thinks as we do, fights as we do, or has the same values or objectives.

> *It is essential that we understand the audience on its own terms. We should not assume that every audience thinks as we do, decides as we do, or has the same values, goals, or concerns as we do.*

We must try to see ourselves through our enemy's eyes in order to anticipate what he will try to do so that we can counteract him.

> *We must try to see ourselves through our audience's eyes in order to anticipate what the audience will do so that we may adapt our engagement to secure the desired outcome.*

Maneuver warfare attacks the enemy "system." We should try to "get inside" the enemy's thought processes and see the enemy as he sees himself so that we can set him up for defeat.

> *Effective communication focuses on the audience's worldview. We should try to "get inside" the audience's thought processes and see the audience as it sees itself.*

From Warfighting

In Chapter 3, "Words Aren't Enough"

It is important to recognize that many political problems cannot be solved by military means. Some can, but rarely as anticipated. War tends to take its own course as it unfolds.

> *It is important to recognize that many business problems cannot be solved by communication means. Some can, but rarely as anticipated. Communication tends to take its own course as it unfolds.*

We should base our decisions on *awareness* rather than on mechanical *habit*. Rather, we must act on a keen appreciation for the essential factors that make each situation unique instead of from a conditioned response.

We must make our decisions in light of the enemy's anticipated reactions and counteractions.

> *We must make our decisions in light of the audience's anticipated reactions and counteractions.*

We should recognize that war is not an inanimate instrument, but an animate force which may have unintended consequences that may change the political situation.

> *We should recognize that communication is not an inanimate instrument, but an animate force which may have unintended consequences that may change the business situation.*

From Warfighting

In Chapter 4, "Speed, Focus, and the First Mover Advantage"

Speed is rapidity of action. It applies to both time and space.
Speed over time is tempo—the consistent ability to operate quickly.
Speed over distance, or space, is the ability to move rapidly.
Both forms are genuine sources of combat power.
In other words, *speed is a weapon.*

> *Speed is rapidity of action. It applies to both time and space.*
> *Speed over time is tempo—the consistent ability to operate quickly.*
> *Speed over distance, or space, is the ability to move rapidly.*
> *Both forms are genuine sources of competitive advantage.*
> *In other words, speed is a weapon that provides*
> *competitive advantage.*

The offense contributes *striking power.*
We normally associate offense with initiative:
The most obvious way to seize and maintain the initiative is
to strike first and keep striking.

> *The offense contributes the first mover advantage.*
> *We normally associate offense with initiative:*
> *The most obvious way to seize and maintain the initiative is*
> *to communicate first and keep communicating.*

Also inherent [in maneuver warfare] is the need to *focus* our efforts
in order to maximize effects. We must focus efforts not only at
the decisive location but also at the decisive moment. We achieve
focus through cooperation toward the accomplishment of a
common purpose. This applies to all elements of the force,
and involves the coordination of ground combat, aviation,
and combat support services. The combination of speed
and focus adds "punch" or "shock" effect to our actions. It
follows that we should strike with the greatest
possible combination of speed and focus.

Also inherent in effective communication is the need to focus our engagements in order to maximize effect. We achieve focus through consistency of message and tone, delivered in a timely way, across multiple spokespeople and multiple communication channels. The combination of speed and focus provides maximum impact. It follows that we should engage stakeholders with the greatest possible combination of speed and focus.

From Warfighting

In Chapter 5, "Initiative, Maneuver, and Disproportionality"

Minor actions and random incidents can have disproportionately large—even decisive—effects.

In communication, incremental changes or minor events can have a greater-than-incremental impact on outcomes.

All actions in war, regardless of the level, are based upon either taking the *initiative* or reacting in *response* to the opponent. By taking the initiative, we dictate the terms of conflict and force the enemy to meet us on our own terms. The initiative allows us to pursue some positive aim even if only to preempt an enemy initiative. It is through the initiative that we seek to impose our will on the enemy.

All communications are based upon either taking the initiative or reacting in response to the audience, adversaries, or the environment. By taking the initiative, we dictate the terms of discussion and the communication agenda. It is through the initiative that we seek to influence our audience.

The Marine Corps concept for winning is a warfighting doctrine based on rapid, flexible, and opportunistic maneuver. The essence of maneuver is taking action to generate and exploit some kind of advantage over the enemy as a means for accomplishing our objectives as effectively as possible.

> *Our concept of effective communication is*
> *based on rapid, flexible, and opportunistic maneuver.*
> *The essence of maneuver is taking action to generate*
> *and exploit some competitive advantage to influence audiences*
> *so as to accomplish our objectives as effectively as possible.*

The flux of war is a product of the continuous interaction
between initiative and response. Actions in war
more or less reflect the constant imperative to seize
and maintain the initiative. The initiative is clearly
the preferred form of action because only through
the initiative can we ultimately impose our will on the enemy.

> *Communication is a product of continuous interaction between*
> *initiative and response. Effective communication is more or*
> *less the constant imperative to seize and maintain the initiative.*
> *The initiative is clearly the preferred form of action because only*
> *through the initiative can we ultimately impose our will to*
> *influence our audience.*

The defense, on the other hand, contributes *resisting power*,
the ability to preserve and protect ourselves. The defense generally
has a negative aim: that of resisting the enemy's will.

> *The defense, on the other hand, contributes* resisting power,
> *the ability to preserve and protect ourselves. The defense generally*
> *has a negative aim: to avoid losing the*
> *trust and confidence of stakeholders.*

From **Warfighting**

In Chapter 6, "Goals, Strategies, and Tactics: Preparing and Planning"

To influence the action to our advantage, we must project our
thoughts forward in time and space. We frequently do this
through planning.

To influence our stakeholders to our advantage,
we must project our thoughts forward in space and time.
We frequently do this through planning.

[Planning] does not mean that we establish a
detailed timetable of events. We have already concluded
that war is inherently disorderly, and we cannot expect to dictate
its terms with any sort of precision. Rather, we attempt to shape
the general conditions of war.... Through shaping,
commanders gain the initiative, preserve momentum,
and control the tempo of operations.

Planning does not mean that we establish a
detailed timetable of events. Rather, we attempt to shape
the general conditions under which our communication
will work.... Through shaping, leaders gain the initiative,
preserve momentum, and control the communication agenda.

We should try to shape events in a way that allows
us several options so that by the time the moment for
decisive operations arrives, we have not restricted
ourselves to only one course of action.

Planning plays as important a role in the preparation
for war as it does in the conduct of war.

Planning plays as important a role in
the preparation for communication as it does
in the implementation of communication.

Strategy involves establishing goals, assigning forces, providing
assets, and imposing conditions on the use of force in the theaters of
war. Strategy derived from political and policy objectives must
be clearly understood to be the sole authoritative basis for all
operations.

Strategy involves establishing goals, assigning resources,
and imposing conditions on the scope of communication.
Strategy derived from business or organizational objectives
must be clearly understood to be the sole authoritative basis
for all communication.

Activities in war take place at several interrelated levels which form a hierarchy. These levels are the strategic, operational, and tactical.

Activities in communication take place at several interrelated levels which form a hierarchy. These levels are the strategic, operational, and tactical.

The highest level is the *strategic* level. Activities at the strategic level focus directly on policy objectives. We distinguish between national strategy, which coordinates and focuses all elements of national power to attain the policy objectives, and military strategy, which is the application of military force to secure the policy objectives. Military strategy thus is subordinate to national strategy. Military strategy can be thought of as the art of winning wars and securing peace.

The highest level is the strategic *level. Activities at the strategic level focus directly on achieving objectives. We distinguish between business or organizational strategy, which coordinates and focuses all elements of a company's or organization's resources to attain its objectives, and communication strategy, which is the application of stakeholder engagement to secure the business or organizational objectives. Communication strategy thus is subordinate to business or organizational strategy. Communication strategy can be thought of as the art of winning in the marketplace and securing trust and confidence.*

[The strategic level] focuses directly on achieving policy objectives: Winning wars.

The strategic level focuses directly on achieving business objectives: Winning the marketplace.

[The operational level is] the link between strategy and tactics. The science of winning campaigns. Deciding when, where, and under what conditions to engage an enemy.

The operational level is the link between the strategic level and tactics. The science of winning campaigns. Deciding when, where, and under what conditions to engage an audience.

[The tactical level] focuses on winning engagements.

The tactical level focuses on engaging audiences.

The first requirement is to establish what we want to accomplish, when, and how. Without a clearly defined concept of intent, the necessary unity of effort is inconceivable.

The first requirement is to establish what we want to accomplish, when, and how. Without a clearly defined concept of intent, the necessary unity of effort is inconceivable.

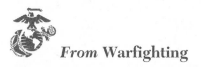 *From* **Warfighting**

In Chapter 7, "Performance: The Physicality of Audience Engagement"

Training programs must reflect practical, challenging, and progressive goals beginning with individual and small-unit skills.

Training programs must reflect practical, challenging, and progressive goals beginning with individual interpersonal communication skills and small-group dynamics.

Marine Corps doctrine demands professional competence among its leaders. As military professionals charged with the defense of the nation, Marine leaders must be true experts in the conduct of war.

One of the burdens of leadership is professional competence. As professionals charged with inspiring trust and confidence, leaders must be true experts in the persuasive art.

The purpose of all training is to develop forces that can win in combat. Training is the key to combat effectiveness and therefore is the main effort of a peacetime military. However, training should not stop with the commencement of war; training must continue during war to adapt to the lessons of combat.

The purpose of all communication training is to develop the capacity to build trust, inspire loyalty, and lead effectively. However, training should not stop when that trust and loyalty has been won; training must continue throughout a leader's tenure in office, to adapt to changing circumstances and needs.

Every Marine has an individual responsibility to study the profession of arms. A leader without either interest in or knowledge of the history and theory of warfare—the intellectual content of the military profession—is a leader in appearance only. Self-directed study in the art and science of war is at least equal in importance to maintaining physical condition and should receive at least equal time.

Every executive has an individual responsibility to become effective in engaging others. A leader without either interest in or knowledge of the persuasive art is a leader in appearance only. Self-directed study in the art and science of stakeholder engagement is at least as important as other executive tasks, and should receive appropriate investment of time and effort.

Basic individual skills are the essential foundation for combat effectiveness and must receive heavy emphasis.

Basic individual communication skills are the foundation for effective leadership engagement, and should receive heavy emphasis.

From Warfighting

In Chapter 8, "Content: Word Choice, Framing, and Meaning"

War is shaped by human nature and is subject to the complexities, inconsistencies, and peculiarities which characterize human behavior. Since war is an act of violence based on irreconcilable disagreement, it will invariably inflame and be shaped by human emotions.

Effective communication is shaped by human nature and is subject to the complexities, inconsistencies, and particularities which characterize human behavior. Since communication is intended to change the way people think and feel and what they understand, know, and do, it will invariably be shaped by human emotions.

 **From Warfighting**

In Chapter 9, "Audiences: Attention, Retention, and How Hearts and Minds Work"

Because war is a clash between opposing human wills, the human dimension is central to war. It is the human dimension which infuses war with its intangible moral factors.

> *Because communication is about human connection, the human dimension is central to communicating. It is the human dimension that makes communication possible. Leaders need to know how humans actually work.*

 **From Warfighting**

In Chapter 10, "Putting It All Together: Becoming a Habitually Strategic Communicator"

[Marines] must be individuals both of action and of intellect, skilled at "getting things done" while at the same time conversant in the military art.

> *Leaders must be individuals both of action and of intellect, skilled at "getting things done" while at the same time conversant in communication skills, in winning hearts and minds.*

Endnotes

Introduction

1. Jessica Durando, "BP's Tony Hayward: 'I'd like my life back,'" *USA Today,* June 1, 2010, http://content.usatoday.com/communities/greenhouse/post/2010/06/bp-tony-hayward-apology/1.

2. Clifford Krauss, "Oil Spill's Blow to BP's Image May Eclipse Costs," *The New York Times,* April 29, 2010, www.nytimes.com/2010/04/30/business/30bp.html?hp.

3. George Lakoff and Mark Johnson, *Metaphors We Live By,* Chicago: The University of Chicago Press, 1980: 1.

4. Carl Von Clausewitz, Michael Howard, and Peter Paret, *On War,* Princeton, NJ: Princeton UP, 1976: 149.

5. Von Clausewitz, *On War:* 87.

Chapter 1

1. Steve Jobs, Apple Music Event, Cupertino, California, October 23, 2001, Speech.

2. Apple Inc., *Apple Reinvents the Phone with iPhone, Apple.com,* Apple Inc., January 9, 2007, www.apple.com/pr/library/2007/01/09Apple-Reinvents-the-Phone-with-iPhone.html.

3. United States Marine Corps, *Warfighting,* United States Government, 1997: Foreword.

4. Bud Abbott and Lou Costello, "Who's on First," transcribed by *The Baseball Almanac,* www.baseball-almanac.com/humor4.shtml.

5. Tiha Von Ghyczy, Bolko Von Oetinger, Christopher Bassford, and Carl Von Clausewitz, *Clausewitz on Strategy: Inspiration and Insight from a Master Strategist,* New York: Wiley, 2001: 55.

6. "Mike Tyson," *BrainyQuote.com,* Xplore Inc., 2011, www.brainyquote.com/quotes/quotes/m/miketyson382439.html.

7. Von Ghyczy, Von Oetinger, Bassford, and Von Clausewitz, *Clausewitz on Strategy:* 55.

8. John Bentley, "McCain Says 'Fundamentals' Of U.S. Economy Are Strong," *CBS News,* CBS Interactive Inc., September 15, 2008, www.cbsnews.com/8301-502443_162-4450366-502443.html.

9. Bentley, "McCain."

10. Bentley, "McCain."

11. Edwin Chen and Julianna Goldman, "McCain Suspends Campaign; Obama Presses for Debate (Update 2)," *Bloomberg News,* Bloomberg LLC, September 24, 2008, www.bloomberg.com/apps/news?pid=newsarchive.

12. Chen and Goldman, "McCain."

13. Chen and Goldman, "McCain."

14. "David Letterman Reacts to John McCain Suspending Campaign," *YouTube.com,* September 24, 2008, www.youtube.com/watch?v=XjkCrfylq-E.

15. "David Letterman Reacts to John McCain Suspending Campaign."

16. "David Letterman Reacts to John McCain Suspending Campaign."

17. "David Letterman Reacts to John McCain Suspending Campaign."

18. "David Letterman Reacts to John McCain Suspending Campaign."

19. Mark Zuckerberg, "Thoughts on Beacon," *The Facebook Blog,* Facebook, December 5, 2007, http://blog.facebook.com/blog.php?blog_id=company&blogger=4.

20. Mark Zuckerberg, "Our Commitment to the Facebook Community," *The Facebook Blog,* Facebook, November 29, 2011, http://blog.facebook.com/blog.php?post=10150378701937131.

21. Amy Zalman, *Countering Violent Extremism: Beyond Words,* Policy Paper (EastWest Institute 2008), i.

22. Zalman, i.

23. Zalman, 2.

24. Zalman, 10.

25. Zalman, 2.

26. United States Department of State, *Words That Work and Words That Don't: A Guide for Counter Terrorism Communication,* Internal Advisement, United States Department of State, March 14, 2008, www.investigativeproject.org/documents/misc/127.pdf.

27. Michael G. Mullen, "Strategic Communications: Getting Back to Basics," *Joint Force Quarterly,* 55 (2009), 4.

28. Mullen, "Strategic," 4.

29. Zalman, 20-21.

30. Mullen, "Strategic," 4.

31. Mullen, "Strategic," 4.

32. Mullen, "Strategic," 4.

Chapter 2

1. Barry Mike, "The Making of a Minor Communication Disaster (1): It's Not What You Say, It's Who You Are," Web log post, *Strategic Leadership Communication,* April 20, 2011, http://strategicleadershipcommunication. com/2011/04/20/the-making-of-a-minor-communication-disaster-1-it%E2%80%99s-not-what-you-say-it%E2%80%99s-who-you-are/.

2. Mike, "The Making (1)."

3. Mike, "The Making (1)."

4. Barry Mike, "The Making of a Minor Communication Disaster (2): It's Not What You Say, It's Who You Are," Web log post, *Strategic Leadership Communication,* April 20, 2011, http://strategicleadershipcommunication. com/2011/04/20/the-making-of-a-minor-communication-disaster-2-it%E2%80%99s-not-what-you-say-it%E2%80%99s-who-you-are/.

5. Mike, "The Making (2)."

6. Mike, "The Making (2)."

7. Mike, "The Making (2)."

8. Mike, "The Making (2)."

9. Barry Mike, "The Making of a Minor Communication Disaster (3): It's Not What You Say, It's What You Symbolize," Web log post, *Strategic Leadership Communication,* April 20, 2011, http://strategicleadershipcommunication. com/2011/04/20/the-making-of-a-minor-communication-disaster-3-it%E2%80%99s-not-what-you-say-it%E2%80%99s-what-you-symbolize/.

10. Jessie Becker, "Netflix Introduces New Plans and Announces Price Changes," Web log post, *The Netflix Blog,* Netflix Inc., July 12, 2011, http://blog.netflix. com/2011/07/netflix-introduces-new-plans-and.html.

11. Becker, "Netflix."

12. Becker, "Netflix."

13. Becker, "Netflix."

14. Becker, "Netflix."

15. Becker, "Netflix."

16. Aimée Reinhart Avery, "Re: Netflix Introduces New Plans and Announces Price Changes," Web log comment, *The Netflix Blog*, Netflix Inc., July 13, 2011, http://blog.netflix.com/2011/07/netflix-introduces-new-plans-and.html.

17. Craig Harkins, "Re: Netflix Introduces New Plans and Announces Price Changes," Web log comment, *The Netflix Blog*, Netflix Inc., July 13, 2011, http://blog.netflix.com/2011/07/netflix-introduces-new-plans-and.html.

18. Greg Heitzmann, "Re: Netflix Introduces New Plans and Announces Price Changes," Web log comment, *The Netflix Blog*, Netflix Inc., July 13, 2011, http://blog.netflix.com/2011/07/netflix-introduces-new-plans-and.html.

19. James E. Lukaszewski, *Influencing Public Attitudes: Direct Communication Strategies That Reduce the Media's Influence on Public Decision-Making*, Leesburg, VA: IAP, 1992.

20. Reed Hastings, "An Explanation and Some Reflections," Web log post, *The Netflix Blog*, Netflix Inc., September 18, 2011, http://blog.netflix.com/2011/09/explanation-and-some-reflections.html.

21. Hastings, "An Explanation."

22. Hastings, "An Explanation."

23. Hastings, "An Explanation."

24. Hastings, "An Explanation."

25. Patrick Seitz, "Netflix Tries Damage Control; Qwikster Doesn't Help," *Investor's Business Daily*, Investor's Business Daily, Inc., September 19, 2011, http://news.investors.com/Article/585222/201109191639/Netflix-Apologizes-To-Customers-Then-Angers-Them.htm.

26. David Pogue, "Parsing Netflix's 'Apology,'" *The New York Times*, September 22, 2011, http://pogue.blogs.nytimes.com/2011/09/22/parsing-netflixs-apology/.

27. Pogue, "Parsing."

28. Pogue, "Parsing."

29. Pogue, "Parsing."

30. Reed Hastings, "DVDs Will Be Staying at Netflix.com," Web log post, *The Netflix Blog*, Netflix Inc., October 10, 2011, http://blog.netflix.com/2011/10/dvds-will-be-staying-at-netflixcom.html.

31. Hastings, "DVDs."

32. Hastings, "DVDs."

33. Lori Burelle, "Re: DVDs Will Be Staying at Netflix.com," Web log comment, *The Netflix Blog,* Netflix Inc., October 10, 2011, http://blog.netflix.com/2011/10/dvds-will-be-staying-at-netflixcom.html.

34. Alison Green, "Re: DVDs Will Be Staying at Netflix.com," Web log comment, *The Netflix Blog,* Netflix Inc., October 10, 2011, http://blog.netflix.com/2011/10/dvds-will-be-staying-at-netflixcom.html.

35. Geoffrey Sperl, "Re: DVDs Will Be Staying at Netflix.com," Web log comment, *The Netflix Blog,* Netflix Inc., October 10, 2011, http://blog.netflix.com/2011/10/dvds-will-be-staying-at-netflixcom.html.

36. Balaji Krishnapuram, "Re: DVDs Will Be Staying at Netflix.com," Web log comment, *The Netflix Blog,* Netflix Inc., October 10, 2011, http://blog.netflix.com/2011/10/dvds-will-be-staying-at-netflixcom.html.

37. Holman Jenkins, "Business World," *The Wall Street Journal,* August 19, 1998: A19. Print.

38. Patricia Sellers, "Something to Prove Bob Nardelli Was Stunned When Jack Welch Told Him He'd Never Run GE. 'I Want an Autopsy!' He Demanded," *CNNMoney,* Cable News Network, July 24, 2002, http://money.cnn.com/magazines/fortune/fortune_archive/2002/06/24/325190/index.htm.

39. Del Jones and Matt Krantz, "Home Depot Boots CEO Nardelli," *USA TODAY,* January 3, 2007, www.usatoday.com/printedition/money/20070104/1b_homedepotcov04.art.htm.

40. Sellers, "Something."

41. Julie Creswell, "With Links to Board, Chief Saw His Pay Soar," *The New York Times,* May 24, 2006, www.nytimes.com/2006/05/24/business/24board.html?pagewanted=all.

42. Claes Fornell, *Fourth Quarter 2005,* Rep., The American Consumer Satisfaction Index, February 21, 2006, www.theacsi.org/index.php?option=com_content&view=article&id=81:acsi-quarterly-commentaries-q4-2005&catid=18&Itemid=149.

43. Marc Hogan, "Big Box Battle: Home Depot vs. Lowe's," *Businessweek,* August 22, 2006, www.businessweek.com/investor/content/aug2006/pi20060821_417402.htm.

44. Creswell, "With Links."

45. Creswell, "With Links."

46. Joe Nocera, "The Board Wore Chicken Suits," *The New York Times,* May 27, 2006, www.nytimes.com/2006/05/27/business/27nocera.html?pagewanted=all.

47. Nocera, "The Board."

48. Nocera, "The Board."

49. Nocera, "The Board."

50. Nocera, "The Board."

51. Nocera, "The Board."

52. The Associated Press, "Home Depot Shareholders Still Seething," *MSNBC. com,* June 9, 2006, www.msnbc.msn.com/id/13231109/ns/business-us_ business/t/home-depot-shareholders-still-seething/.

53. Jeremy W. Peters, "Home Depot Alters Rules for Electing Its Directors," *The New York Times,* June 2, 2006, www.nytimes.com/2006/06/02/business/02depot. html.

54. Joann S. Lublin, Ann Zimmerman, and Chad Terhune, "Behind Nardelli's Abrupt Exit," *The Wall Street Journal,* January 4, 2007, www2.gsu. edu/%7Ewwwseh/Behind%20Nardelli%27s%20Abrupt%20Exit.pdf.

55. Julie Creswell and Michael Barbaro, "Home Depot Ousts Highly Paid Chief," *The New York Times,* January 4, 2007, www.nytimes.com/2007/01/04/ business/04home.html?pagewanted=all.

56. Del Jones and Matt Krantz, "Home Depot Boots CEO Nardelli," *USA TODAY,* January 3, 2007, www.usatoday.com/printedition/money/20070104/1b_ homedepotcov04.art.htm.

57. Chuck Lucier, Steven Wheeler, and Rolf Habbel, "The Era of the Inclusive Leader," *Strategy + Business,* Summer 2007, Booz & Company Inc., May 29, 2007, www.strategy-business.com/article/07205?pg=all&tid=27782251.

Chapter 3

1. "14 Days—A Timeline | The Storm | FRONTLINE | PBS," *PBS: Public Broadcasting Service,* November 22, 2005, www.pbs.org/wgbh/pages/frontline/ storm/etc/cron.html.

2. Federal Emergency Management Agency, *National Situation Report,* Rep., Department of Homeland Security, August 28, 2005, http://www.truth-out.org/ sites/default/files/2005Aug28_FEMA_Natl_sitrep.pdf.

3. "14 Days—A Timeline | The Storm | FRONTLINE | PBS."

4. The White House, Office of the Press Secretary, *President Discusses Hurricane Katrina, Congratulates Iraqis on Draft Constitution, The White House,* August 28, 2005, http://georgewbush-whitehouse.archives.gov/news/ releases/2005/08/20050828-1.html.

5. Lisa Stark, "FEMA Was Unprepared for Katrina Relief Effort, Insiders Say," *ABC News,* September 8, 2005, http://abcnews.go.com/WNT/ HurricaneKatrina/story?id=1108268.

6. Von Clausewitz, *On War:* 87.

7. United States, Cong., Senate, Committee of Homeland Security and Governmental Affairs, *Hurricane Katrina: A Nation Still Unprepared,* 109th Cong., 2nd sess., S. Rept. 109-332, Washington, D.C., United States Senate, 2006: 311.

8. "14 Days—A Timeline | The Storm | FRONTLINE | PBS."

9. Eric Lipton, Christopher Drew, Scott Shane, and David Rohde, "Breakdowns Marked Path from Hurricane to Anarchy," *The New York Times,* September 11, 2005, www.nytimes.com/2005/09/11/national/nationalspecial/11response. html?pagewanted=print.

10. *The Storm.* Prod. Martin Smith. *PBS.* Public Broadcasting Service, 22 Nov. 2005. Web. http://video.pbs.org/video/1555897742/#.

11. "14 Days—A Timeline | The Storm | FRONTLINE | PBS."

12. *The Storm.*

13. The White House, Office of the Press Secretary, *President Outlines Hurricane Katrina Relief Efforts, The White House,* August 31, 2005, http://georgewbush-whitehouse.archives.gov/news/releases/2005/08/20050831-3.html.

14. *The Storm.*

15. The White House, *President Outlines Hurricane Katrina Relief Efforts.*

16. "Leadership Vacuum Stymied Aid Offers," *CNN.com,* Cable News Network, September 16, 2005, http://edition.cnn.com/2005/US/09/15/katrina.response/.

17. U.S. Department of Homeland Security, Office of the Press Secretary, Press Conference with Officials from Homeland Security, the Environmental Protection Agency, and the Departments of Health and Human Services, Energy, Transportation, and Defense, U.S. Department of Homeland Security, August 31, 2005, www.dhs.gov/xnews/releases/press_release_0724.shtm.

18. Dan Froomkin, "A Dearth of Answers," *The Washington Post,* September 1, 2005, www.washingtonpost.com/wp-dyn/content/blog/2005/09/01/ BL2005090100915_pf.html.

19. "Mayor C. Ray Nagin's Interview," *The New York Times,* September 2, 2005, www.nytimes.com/2005/09/02/national/nationalspecial/02TEXT-NAGIN. html?pagewanted=print.

20. *The Storm.*

21. "The Daily Show with Jon Stewart-9/7/05." *The Daily Show with Jon Stewart.* Comedy Central. New York, New York, 7 Sept. 2005. Web. http://www. thedailyshow.com/watch/wed-september-7-2005/headlines---meet-the-f--kers.

22. *The Storm.*

23. "The Daily Show with Jon Stewart-9/7/05."

24. The White House, Office of the Press Secretary, *President Arrives in Alabama, Briefed on Hurricane Katrina, The White House,* September 2, 2005, http:// georgewbush-whitehouse.archives.gov/news/releases/2005/09/20050902-2.html.

25. Matthew Cooper, "Dipping His Toe into Disaster," *Time Magazine,* September 6, 2005, www.time.com/time/magazine/article/0,9171,1101329,00.html.

26. Anjali Kamat, "Kanye West: 'Bush Doesn't Care About Black People,'" *Democracy Now,* September 5, 2005, www.democracynow.org/2005/9/5/ kanye_west_bush_doesnt_care_about.

27. The White House, Office of the Press Secretary, *President Addresses Nation, Discusses Hurricane Katrina Relief Efforts, The White House,* September 3, 2005, http://georgewbush-whitehouse.archives.gov/news/ releases/2005/09/20050903.html.

28. "The Daily Show with Jon Stewart-9/7/05."

29. "Transcript for September 4—Meet the Press—Msnbc.com," *Msnbc.com,* September 4, 2005, www.msnbc.msn.com/id/9179790/ns/meet_the_press/t/ transcript-september/.

30. *The Storm.*

31. "Barbara Bush Calls Evacuees Better Off," *The New York Times,* September 7, 2005, www.nytimes.com/2005/09/07/national/nationalspecial/07barbara.html.

32. "The Daily Show with Jon Stewart-9/7/05."

33. "Michael Chertoff's Announcement," *The New York Times,* September 9, 2005, www.nytimes.com/2005/09/09/national/nationalspecial/09text-chertoff. html?pagewanted=all.

34. "TIME Magazine Cover: System Failure—Sep. 19, 2005," *Time Magazine,* September 19, 2005, www.time.com/time/covers/0,16641,20050919,00.html.

35. "Leadership Please," Cartoon, *Time Magazine,* September 19, 2005. Print.

36. Mullen, "Strategic," 4.

37. Frank J. Navran, "If 'Trust Leads to Loyalty' What Leads to Trust?" *Ethics Resource Center,* 1996, www.ethics.org/resources/articles-organizational-ethics.a.

38. Navran, "If 'Trust Leads to Loyalty' What Leads to Trust?"

39. "FEMA Deputy Administrator Harvey Johnson Holds a News Briefing on the California Wildfires—Political Transcript Wire," *HighBeam Research,* October 23, 2007, www.highbeam.com/doc/1P3-1370505771.html/print.

Chapter 4

1. Mark Tatge, "Can Bell Ring in New McDonald's?" *Forbes,* April 19, 2004, www.forbes.com/2004/04/19/cz_mt_0419mcd2.html.

2. Tatge, "Can Bell Ring in New McDonald's?"

3. Carol Hymowitz and Joann S. Lublin, "McDonald's CEO Tragedy Holds Lessons for Directors," *The Wall Street Journal,* April 20, 2004, http://online. wsj.com/article/0,,SB108241709119287202,00.html.

4. Hymowitz and Lublin, "McDonald's."

5. Hymowitz and Lublin, "McDonald's."

6. Hymowitz and Lublin, "McDonald's."

7. Melanie Warner and Patrick McGeehan, "Change at Helm, but a Steady Course at McDonald's," *The New York Times,* November 24, 2004, www. nytimes.com/2004/11/24/business/24burger.html.

8. Tom Bowman, "Videotape Reveals War's Impact," *The Baltimore Sun,* November 17, 2004, http://articles.baltimoresun.com/2004-11-17/ news/0411170230_1_marine-unit-mosque-wounded.

9. "Military Investigates Shooting of Wounded Insurgent," *CNN World,* Cable News Network, November 16, 2004, http://articles.cnn.com/2004-11-15/world/ marine.probe_1_marine-shot-insurgents-navy-s-criminal-investigative-service?_ s=PM:WORLD.

10. William Saletan, "Rape Rooms: A Chronology: What Bush Said as the Iraqi Prison Scandal Unfolded," *Slate Magazine,* The Slate Group, LLC, May 5, 2004, www.slate.com/articles/news_and_politics/ballot_box/2004/05/rape_ rooms_a_chronology.single.html.

11. Barbara Starr, "Details of Army's Abuse Investigation Surface," *CNN.com,* Cable News Network, January 21, 2004, www.cnn.com/2004/US/01/20/sprj. nirq.abuse/index.html.

12. "The President's News Conference with President Vicente Fox of Mexico in Monterrey, Mexico," *The American Presidency Project,* University of California, Santa Barbara, January 12, 2004, www.presidency.ucsb.edu/ws/index. php?pid=63792#axzz1c0eQJGXk.

13. The White House, Office of the Press Secretary, *President Bush Discusses Importance of Democracy in Middle East, The White House,* February 4, 2004, http://georgewbush-whitehouse.archives.gov/news/ releases/2004/02/20040204-4.html.

14. Antonio M. Taguba, *Investigation of the 800th Military Police Brigade,* Rep. no. AR-15-6, U.S. Department of Defense, 2004. Print.

15. Taguba, *Investigation of the 800th Military Police Brigade.*

16. Taguba, *Investigation of the 800th Military Police Brigade.*

17. Saletan, "Rape Rooms."

18. Saletan, "Rape Rooms."

19. The White House, Office of the Press Secretary, *President Discusses Tax Relief in Iowa, The White House,* April 15, 2004, http://georgewbush-whitehouse. archives.gov/news/releases/2004/04/20040415-7.html.

20. "Kimmitt-Bayley Brief Transcript," *Coalition Provisional Authority,* April 28, 2004, www.iraqcoalition.org/transcripts/20040428_Apr28_KimmittBayley.html.

21. "Army Probes POW Abuse," *60 Minutes II,* CBS News, April 28, 2004, *CBS News,* CBS Interactive Inc., June 14, 2006, www.cbsnews.com/video/watch/?id =614704n&tag=contentBody;storyMediaBox.

22. "Rumsfeld Says Extent of Post-War Problems Misjudged—Msnbc Tv— Hardball with Chris Matthews—Msnbc.com," *Msnbc.com,* April 29, 2004, www.msnbc.msn.com/id/4865948/ns/msnbc_tv-hardball_with_chris_ matthews/t/rumsfeld-post-war-problems-occupation-underestimated/.

23. The White House, Office of the Press Secretary, *President Bush Welcomes Canadian Prime Minister Martin to White House, The White House,* April 30, 2004, http://georgewbush-whitehouse.archives.gov/news/releases/2004/04/ print/20040430-2.html.

24. The White House, *President Bush Welcomes Canadian Prime Minister Martin to White House.*

25. "Rice Offers Apology on Arab TV," *The Washington Post,* May 4, 2004, www. washingtonpost.com/wp-dyn/articles/A1415-2004May4.html.

26. U.S. Department of Defense, Office of the Assistant Secretary of Defense (Public Affairs), *Defense Department Operational Update Briefing, U.S. Department of Defense,* May 4, 2004, www.defense.gov/utility/printitem. aspx?print=http://www.defense.gov/transcripts/transcript. aspx?transcriptid=2973.

27. "Transcript: President Bush's Interview with Al Hurra TV," *The Washington Post,* May 5, 2004, www.washingtonpost.com/ac2/wp-dyn/A3854- 2004May5?language=printer.

28. "Transcript of President Bush's Interview on Al Arabiya Television," *The New York Times,* May 5, 2004, www.nytimes.com/2004/05/05/ international/06BUSH-FULLTXT.html?ei=5070.

29. The White House, Office of the Press Secretary, *Press Briefing by Scott McClellan, The White House,* May 5, 2004, http://georgewbush-whitehouse. archives.gov/news/releases/2004/05/20040505-3.html.

30. The White House, Office of the Press Secretary, *Press Briefing by Scott McClellan.*

31. "Transcript: Bush and Abdullah in Washington," *The Washington Post,* May 6, 2004, www.washingtonpost.com/ac2/wp-dyn?pagename=article.

32. Thomas L. Friedman, "Restoring Our Honor," *The New York Times,* May 6, 2004, www.nytimes.com/2004/05/06/opinion/restoring-our-honor.html.

33. "Rumsfeld Testifies Before House Armed Services Committee," *The Washington Post,* May 7, 2004, www.washingtonpost.com/ac2/wp-dyn/A9251-2004May7?language=printer.

34. "David Letterman Admits to Sexual Affairs with Female Staffers," *YouTube. com,* October 2, 2009, www.youtube.com/watch?v=YOrNoP4dyXY.

35. "David Letterman Admits to Sexual Affairs with Female Staffers."

36. "David Letterman Admits to Sexual Affairs with Female Staffers."

37. "David Letterman Admits to Sexual Affairs with Female Staffers."

38. "David Letterman Admits to Sexual Affairs with Female Staffers."

39. "David Letterman Admits to Sexual Affairs with Female Staffers."

40. "David Letterman Admits to Sexual Affairs with Female Staffers."

41. "David Letterman Admits to Sexual Affairs with Female Staffers."

Chapter 5

1. "President Obama's Primetime Press Conference on Health Reform," *The White House,* July 22, 2009, www.whitehouse.gov/video/President-Obamas-Primetime-Press-Conference-on-Health-Reform.

2. "President Obama's Primetime Press Conference on Health Reform."

3. "President Obama's Primetime Press Conference on Health Reform."

4. "President Obama's Primetime Press Conference on Health Reform."

5. "Pres. Obama Remarks on Cambridge, MA Police Controversy," *YouTube.com,* July 24, 2009, www.youtube.com/watch?v=N7-LD-GzYKc.

6. "Obama Addresses Congress," *YouTube.com,* September 9, 2009, www.youtube.com/watch?v=l3Xx4zYb3UM.

7. "Obama Addresses Congress."

8. "Obama Addresses Congress."

9. "Obama Addresses Congress."

10. "Obama: Heckling the President—60 Minutes—CBS News," *CBS News,* CBS Interactive Inc., September 13, 2009, www.cbsnews.com/video/watch/?id=5307333n.

11. "'I'm Too Pretty to Do Homework' T-shirt Yanked," *CBS News,* CBS Interactive Inc., September 1, 2011, www.cbsnews.com/stories/2011/09/01/earlyshow/living/parenting/main20100427.

Chapter 6

1. Hewlett-Packard Development Company, L.P, "HP CEO Mark Hurd Resigns; CFO Cathie Lesjak Appointed Interim CEO; HP Announces Preliminary Results and Raises Full-year Outlook," *HP.com,* Hewlett-Packard Development Company, L.P., August 6, 2010, www.hp.com/hpinfo/newsroom/press/2010/100806a.html.

2. Hewlett-Packard Development Company, L.P, "HP CEO Mark Hurd Resigns; CFO Cathie Lesjak Appointed Interim CEO; HP Announces Preliminary Results and Raises Full-year Outlook."

3. Hewlett-Packard Development Company, L.P, "HP CEO Mark Hurd Resigns; CFO Cathie Lesjak Appointed Interim CEO; HP Announces Preliminary Results and Raises Full-year Outlook."

4. "Hewlett-Packard Shares Tumble After CEO Shake-up," Associated Press, reprinted in *Bloomberg Businessweek,* www.businessweek.com/ap/financialnews/D9HG0V180.htm.

5. CNET News Staff, "HP's Letter to Employees on Hurd Resignation," *CNET News,* CBS Interactive Inc., August 6, 2010, http://news.cnet.com/8301-1001_3-20012971-92.html.

6. Steven Musil, "Woman in Hurd Probe: Surprised, Saddened," *CNET,* August 8, 2010, http://news.cnet.com/8301-1001_3-20012996-92.html.

7. Mary Thompson, "HP CEO Hurd's Severance Pay Could Hit $40 Million: Experts," *CNBC,* August 9, 2010, http://www.cnbc.com/id/38624369/HP_CEO_Hurd_s_Severance_Pay_Could_Hit_40_Million_Experts.

8. Henry Blodget, "Wait a Minute—Why Does Mark Hurd Get $50 Million Severance When He Lied on His Expense Report? *Business Insider,* August 6, 2010, http://articles.businessinsider.com/2010-08-06/tech/30038960_1_expense-reports-hp-shareholders-hp-ceo-mark-hurd.

9. Ashlee Vance, "Oracle Chief Faults HP for Forcing Hurd Out," *The New York Times,* August 9, 2010, www.nytimes.com/2010/08/10/technology/10hewlett.html?ref=business.

10. Chad Berndtson, "HP Partners Wrestle with Hurd 'Shock,' Wonder What Comes Next," *CRN,* August 6, 2010, www.crn.com/news/channel-programs/226600191/hp-partners-wrestle-with-hurd-shock-wonder-what-comes-next.htm;jsessionid=FtarGJaY5JvbJs7ecekUEw°°.ecappj01?pgno=1.

11. Chloe Albanesius, "HP Shareholders Sue Board, Hurd for 'Gross Mismanagement,'" *PCMag.com*, www.pcmag.com/article2/0,2817,2367786,00. asp.

12. James B. Stewart, "H-P Shake-Up Leaves Too Many Questions," *Smart Money*, Dow Jones & Company, Inc., August 10, 2010, www.smartmoney.com/invest/ stocks/h-p-shakeup-leaves-too-many-questions/.

13. Ashlee Vance and Matt Ritchel, "Hewlett Took a P.R. Firm's Advice in the Hurd Case," *The New York Times*, August 9, 2010, www.nytimes. com/2010/08/10/technology/10hp.html.

14. Vance and Ritchel, "Hewlett Took a P.R. Firm's Advice in the Hurd Case."

15. Stewart, "H-P Shake-Up Leaves Too Many Questions."

16. Ina Fried, "HP's Dunn Says Others Supervised Probe," *CNET News*, September 27, 2006, http://news.cnet.com/HPs-Dunn-says-others-supervised- probe/2100-1014_3-6120365.html?tag=lia;rcol.

17. Sean Gregory, "Corporate Scandals: Why HP Had to Oust Mark Hurd," *Time Magazine*, August 10, 2010, www.time.com/time/business/ article/0,8599,2009617,00.html.

18. "Letter from Gloria Allred to Mark Hurd," *The New York Times*, June 24, 2010, http://graphics8.nytimes.com/packages/pdf/business/hurd_letter.pdf.

19. Adam Lashinsky and Doris Burke, "What Really Happened Between HP Ex-CEO Mark Hurd and Jodie Fisher?" *Fortune Magazine*, Cable News Network, November 4, 2010, http://tech.fortune.cnn.com/2010/11/04/ what-really-happened-between-hp-ex-ceo-mark-hurd-and-jodie-fisher.

20. Hewlett-Packard Development Company, L.P, "HP CEO Mark Hurd Resigns; CFO Cathie Lesjak Appointed Interim CEO; HP Announces Preliminary Results and Raises Full-year Outlook."

21. Hewlett-Packard Company v. Mark Hurd et al., lawsuit filed in Superior Court of California, County of Santa Clara, September 7, 2010.

22. Felix Salmon, "Why Is HP Suing Hurd?" *Seeking Alpha*, September 7, 2010, http://seekingalpha.com/article/224217-why-is-hp-suing-hurd.

23. Oracle, "Oracle Responds to HP Lawsuit," *Oracle*, September 7, 2010, www. oracle.com/us/corporate/press/170699.

24. Erica Ogg, "HP Settles with Former CEO Hurd," *CNET News*, September 20, 2010, http://news.cnet.com/8301-31021_3-20016963-260.html.

25. James B. Stewart, "Voting to Hire a Chief Without Meeting Him," *The New York Times*, September 21, 2011, www.nytimes.com/2011/09/22/business/ voting-to-hire-a-chief-without-meeting-him.html?pagewanted=all.

26. Stewart, "Voting to Hire a Chief Without Meeting Him."

27. Hewlett-Packard Development Company, L.P., "Léo Apotheker Named CEO and President of HP," *HP.com,* Hewlett-Packard Development Company, L.P., September 30, 2010, http://www.hp.com/hpinfo/newsroom/press/2010/100930c. html.

28. Adam Lashinsky, "HP's Curious Choice," *Fortune,* Cable News Network, September 30, 2010, http://tech.fortune.cnn.com/2010/09/30/hps-curious-choice/?iid=EL.

29. Robert A. Guth, Ben Worthen, and Justin Scheck, "Accuser Said Hurd Leaked an H-P Deal, CEO Lost Out as Board Lost Faith," *The Wall Street Journal,* November 6, 2010, http://online.wsj.com/article/SB10001424052748703805704 575594343622319312.html?mod=WSJ_hp_LEFTTopStories.

30. Henry Blodget, "HP's Board Finally Wises Up and Tells the Whole Story of Why It Sacked Mark Hurd," *Business Insider,* November 7, 2010, www. businessinsider.com/hps-board-finally-wises-up-and-tells-the-whole-story-about-why-it-sacked-mark-hurd-2010-11.

31. Blodget, "HP's Board Finally Wises Up and Tells the Whole Story of Why It Sacked Mark Hurd."

32. Jay Yarrow, "Finally, We Learn the Real Reason Mark Hurd Got Fired," *Business Insider,* November 7, 2010, www.businessinsider.com/mark-hurd-fired-letter-2010-11.

33. Maureen O'Gara, "Hurd Reportedly Leaked EDS Deal," *SysCon,* November 8, 2010, http://hp.sys-con.com/node/1601709.

34. Julianne Pepitone, "4 HP Directors Step Down After Hurd Scandal," *CNNMoney,* Cable News Network, January 20, 2011, http://money.cnn. com/2011/01/20/technology/HP_board_of_directors/index.htm.

35. Nick Winfield, "Meg Whitman Is Named Hewlett-Packard Chief," *The New York Times,* September 22, 2011, www.nytimes.com/2011/09/23/technology/whitman-expected-to-be-named-at-hp.html?pagewanted=all.

36. Poornima Gupta, "Analysis HP: Dial M for Mayhem," *Reuters,* August 21, 2010, www.reuters.com/article/2011/08/21/idUSN1E77K05S20110821.

37. Hewlett-Packard Development Company, L.P., "HP Names Meg Whitman President and Chief Executive Officer," *HP.com,* Hewlett-Packard Development Company, L.P., September 22, 2011, www.hp.com/hpinfo/newsroom/press/2011/110922xb.html.

38. Hewlett-Packard Development Company, L.P., "HP to Keep PC Division," *HP.com,* Hewlett-Packard Development Company, L.P., October 27, 2011, http://www.hp.com/hpinfo/newsroom/press/2011/111027xa.html.

39. Stewart, "Voting to Hire a Chief Without Meeting Him."

Chapter 7

1. Telephone interview, December 14, 2011.

2. Telephone interview, December 14, 2011.

3. Telephone interview, December 14, 2011.

4. Telephone interview, December 14, 2011.

5. *The King's Speech,* Dir. Tom Hooper, Perf. Colin Firth, Geoffrey Rush, and Helena Bonham Carter, UK Film Council and The Weinstein Company, 2010, DVD.

6. Raleigh Mayer, *Protecting Your Professional Brand,* New York: Raleigh Mayer Consulting, 2008.

7. Personal interview with the author, December 14, 2011.

8. "Andy Kaufman: Mighty Mouse Original (Here I Come to Save the Day)," *YouTube.com,* October 13, 2011, www.youtube.com/watch?v=kGx94VPb8V8.

9. "Andy Kaufman: Mighty Mouse Original (Here I Come to Save the Day)."

Chapter 8

1. *Casablanca.* Dir. Michael Curtiz, Perf. Humphrey Bogart, Ingrid Bergman, Paul Henreid, Claude Rains, Conrad Veidt, Sydney Greenstreet, Peter Lorre, S. Z. Sakall, Dooley Wilson, John Qualen, Leonid Kinskey, Curt Bois, Helmut Dantine, Marcel Dalio, Ludwig Stossel, Frank Puglia, and Dan Seymour, Warner Bros. Pictures, Inc., 1942, Film.

2. *Casablanca.*

3. *Casablanca.*

4. George Lakoff and Mark Johnson, *Metaphors We Live By:* 1.

5. Lakoff and Johnson, *Metaphors We Live By:* 1.

6. Lakoff and Johnson, *Metaphors We Live By:* 196.

7. George Lakoff, *Women, Fire, and Dangerous Things: What Categories Reveal About the Mind,* Chicago: University of Chicago Press, 1987: 380-381.

8. Lakoff, *Women, Fire, and Dangerous Things:* 381.

9. George Lakoff and Mark Johnson, *Philosophy in the Flesh: The Embodied Mind and Its Challenge to Western Thought,* Basic Books, 1999: 10-11.

10. George Lakoff, *Don't Think of an Elephant! Know Your Values and Frame the Debate,* Chelsea Green Publishing, 2004: 3.

11. Lakoff, *Don't Think of an Elephant!:* 3.

12. Lakoff, *Don't Think of an Elephant!:* 3-4.

13. Lakoff, *Don't Think of an Elephant!*: 24.

14. Lakoff, *Don't Think of an Elephant!*: 24.

15. Lakoff, *Don't Think of an Elephant!*: 25-26.

16. Paul H. Thibodeau and Lera Boroditsky, 2011, "Metaphors We Think With: The Role of Metaphor in Reasoning," PLoS ONE 6(2): e16782, doi:10.1371/journal.pone.0016782: 6-7.

17. Thibodeau and Boroditsky, "Metaphors We Think With: The Role of Metaphor in Reasoning."

18. Virginia Postrel, "The Next Starbucks? How Massage Went from the Strip Club to the Strip Mall," *The Atlantic,* July/August 2006, http://dynamist.com/articles-speeches/atlantic/massage.html.

19. Postrel, "The Next Starbucks?"

20. Postrel, "The Next Starbucks?"

21. Postrel, "The Next Starbucks?"

22. Postrel, "The Next Starbucks?"

23. Gail T. Fairhurst and Robert A. Sarr, *The Art of Framing: Managing the Language of Leadership,* Jossey-Bass, 1996: 87.

Chapter 9

1. Jeremy Rifkin, *The Empathic Civilization: The Race to Global Consciousness in a World in Crisis,* Penguin, 2009: 83.

2. Rifkin, *The Empathic Civilization:* 83.

3. Rifkin, *The Empathic Civilization:* 83.

4. "New Science Changes the Persuasion Game," Web log post, *The 7 Triggers to Yes,* ProEd Corporation, November 15, 2010, http://the7triggers.com/blog/page/2/.

5. Rifkin, *The Empathic Civilization:* 83.

6. Lakoff, *Don't Think of an Elephant!*: 19.

7. William Shakespeare and Claire McEachern, *The Life of King Henry the Fifth,* New York: NY: Penguin, 1999: 83-84.

8. Chana Gazit and Daniel Gilbert, "Facing Our Fears." *The Emotional Life,* Dir. Chana Gazit, Public Broadcasting Service, January 6, 2010, Hulu, www.hulu.com/watch/227956/this-emotional-life-facing-our-fears.

9. Daniel Goleman, lecture, "Emotional Intelligence or Behavioral Control? (part 1)," *YouTube.com,* March 18, 2010, www.youtube.com/watch?v=LTItzKrNX68.

10. "Emotional Intelligence or Behavioral Control? (part 1)."

11. "Emotional Intelligence or Behavioral Control? (part 1)."

12. "The Invisible Gorilla by Chris Chabris & Daniel Simons," *YouTube.com,* April 18, 2011, www.youtube.com/watch?v=D_m_9N_3u7o.

13. "The Invisible Gorilla by Chris Chabris & Daniel Simons."

14. Robert H. Margolis, *Hearing Journal,* Volume 57, Issue 6, June 2004: 10.

15. "GE's Jeff Immelt on the 10 Keys to Great Leadership," Fast Company, April 2004: 96.

16. Harry McGurk and John MacDonald, "Hearing Lips and Seeing Voices," *Nature,* December 1976: 264, 746-748.

17. Lawrence Rosenblum, interviewed on BBC Horizon television program, October 24, 2010.

18. "Macworld San Francisco 2008—The MacBook Air Intro (Pt. 1)," *YouTube. com,* January 15, 2008, www.youtube.com/watch?v=OIV6peKMj9M.

19. "Memorable Quotes for *Duck Soup,*" *IMDB.com,* www.imdb.com/title/tt0023969/quotes.

20. "Macworld San Francisco 2008—The MacBook Air Intro (Pt. 1)."

21. "Macworld San Francisco 2008—The MacBook Air Intro (Pt. 1)."

22. "Macworld San Francisco 2008—The MacBook Air Intro (Pt. 1)."

Chapter 10

1. *Warfighting,* 51.

2. Augustine, *On Christian Teaching,* Trans. R. P. H. Green, Oxford, England: Oxford UP, 1997: 117.

Index

Q-R

S